THE LITERARY RELATIONS
OF ENGLAND AND GERMANY
IN THE SEVENTEENTH CENTURY

T0370642

THE LITERARY RELATIONS
OF ENGLAND AND GERMANY

IN THE SEVENTEENTH CENTURY

by

GILBERT WATERHOUSE, M.A.

Formerly Scholar of St John's College, Cambridge
First Tiarks University German Scholar
English Lecturer in the University of Leipzig

Cambridge:

at the University Press

1914

CAMBRIDGE
UNIVERSITY PRESS

University Printing House, Cambridge CB2 8BS, United Kingdom

Cambridge University Press is part of the University of Cambridge.

It furthers the University's mission by disseminating knowledge in the pursuit of education, learning and research at the highest international levels of excellence.

www.cambridge.org
Information on this title: www.cambridge.org/9781107486577

© Cambridge University Press 1914

First published 1914
First paperback edition 2015

A catalogue record for this publication is available from the British Library

ISBN 978-1-107-48657-7 Paperback

PREFACE

THE present volume is the result of researches prosecuted during my tenure of the Tiarks German Scholarship. My choice of the subject was inspired by Professor Herford's *Studies in the Literary Relations of England and Germany in the Sixteenth Century*, but when I submitted it to the electors I confess I had little idea of the extent of my task. My main intention was to supplement Professor Herford's chapters where necessary, but I also expected to find sufficient material in connection with the influence of the English drama in Germany and of German hymns in England to occupy my attention for the full period of my tenure. It seemed highly improbable that much evidence of intercourse in any other branch of literature would be forthcoming.

My researches had not been long in progress before I discovered that the work of Erich Schmidt, Brie, Rühl and Bergmeier had placed the old themes beyond need of further supplement[1]. On the other hand, every day brought such additions to my dramatic bibliography that I was soon obliged to omit from my plan all discussion of the dramatic relations of England and Germany, with the exception of those dramas which deal with English or German history. The subject will easily fill another volume. As for hymns, the most important

[1] See Erich Schmidt: "Das Verhältnis der deutschen Volksschauspiele zu Marlowe's Tragical History of Dr Faustus." In *Sitzungsber. der pr. Acad. der Wiss.* 1900.

W. D. Brie: *Eulenspiegel in England.* (*Palaestra*, xxviii.) 1903.

F. Brie: *Die englischen Ausgaben des Eulenspiegel und ihre Stellung in der Geschichte des Volksbuches.* Breslau. (Diss.) 1903.

Ernst Rühl: *Grobianus in England.* Berlin. Mayer und Müller. 1904.

Fritz Bergmeier: *Dedekinds Grobianus in England.* Greifswald. (Diss.) 1904.

production of the century for Germany, I was unable to discover any trace of their appearance in England before 1720[1]. The contents of this volume, therefore, differ considerably from my original conception.

Nor can I always lay claim to originality. This is indeed the first systematic attempt to collect all the evidence of literary intercourse between England and Germany in the seventeenth century, but several isolated points have been very thoroughly treated by other scholars and I have not hesitated to make the fullest use of their discoveries. I refer more particularly to the work of Urban on Owen, Fischer and Bohm on Weckherlin, Kipka on Mary Stuart, Eichler on Dryden and Wernicke, and Becker and Schmid on Barclay[2]. Dr Schmid is at present engaged on a supplementary volume entitled *Barclays Einfluss auf die Literatur* and very kindly offered to place his manuscript at my disposal. If literature of a similar calibre had existed for all the seventeenth century authors discussed by me, this volume would have been little more than a compilation. As it is, I am thoroughly conscious of its shortcomings and shall welcome suggestions and corrections.

A complete list of the books and articles which afforded me assistance, however slight, will be found in the numbered bibliography in Appendix A, to which reference is made throughout the text. Appendices B and C contain further lists of books which I either consulted to no purpose or was unable to obtain.

The greater part of the work was done in the Royal Prussian Library at Berlin and I take this opportunity of tendering my warmest thanks to the Director, Professor Harnack, who granted me exceptional privileges, and to the Departmental Librarian, Dr Ippel, for their great courtesy and valuable assistance. For the same reason I wish to thank Dr Franke,

[1] J. C. Jacobi: *A Collection of Divine Hymns.* London. 1720. Enlarged and republished (in collaboration with J. Haberkorn) as *Psalmodia Germanica* in 1722. Further editions 1725, 1732 and 1765. See also the Moravian Hymn-Books of 1742, 1754 and 1789, and Julian: *Dictionary of Hymnology.* 1892. Bibl. 250.

[2] See Bibl. 82, 83, 136, 137, 148, 159 and 263.

Professor Pietschmann, and Dr Lohmeier, Directors respectively of the University Libraries of Berlin and Göttingen and the Landesbibliothek at Cassel. Nor must I omit Professors Brandl and R. M. Meyer, of Berlin, and the Rev. H. F. Stewart, of St John's College, Cambridge, all of whom took the liveliest interest in my work and readily gave me information and advice. The same applies to Dr B. Neuendorff and Dr Traugott Böhme, both of Berlin. I am also obliged to the press readers for valuable assistance rendered during the correction of the proofs. Last but not least, I wish to thank, as many Cambridge students have done before me, my former teacher, Professor Karl Breul, for advice and assistance on every possible occasion and in every possible form.

If these studies have thrown light into a dark corner of literary history and prepared the way for a thorough investigation of the literary relations of England and Germany in the eighteenth century, they will have realised the expectation of the author.

G. W.

Leipzig.
January, 1914.

CONTENTS

CHAP.   PAGE

     INTRODUCTION xi

I.   EARLY TRAVELLERS 1

II.   EARLIER LYRICAL POETRY 9

III.   SIDNEY'S "ARCADIA" IN GERMANY 18

IV.   THE LATIN NOVEL 38

V.   THE EPIGRAM 59

VI.   HISTORY IN LITERATURE 69

VII.   ENGLISH PHILOSOPHERS IN GERMANY 85

VIII.   THE THEOLOGIANS 95

IX.   LATER TRAVELLERS 113

X.   THE AWAKENING OF GERMANY AND THE GROWTH OF
    ENGLISH INFLUENCE 117

XI.   LATER LYRICS 128

XII.   LATER SATIRE 132

XIII.   MILTON IN GERMANY 136

XIV.   CONCLUSION 143

     APPENDIX A 145

     APPENDIX B 176

     APPENDIX C 178

     INDEX 180

ERRATA

p. 16, l. 12, *for* 1640 *read* 1634.

p. 26, l. 23, *read* Justum Lipsium.

p. 49, l. 10, *for* Urban III *read* Urban VIII.

p. 72, l. 18, *for* Carve Thomas *read* Thomas Carve (Carew).

p. 87, l. 39—p. 88, l. 1. *Die Farben (oder Kennzeichen) des Guten und Bösen* is almost certainly a translation of Bacon's *The Colours of Good and Evil.* Correct accordingly p. 88, n. 1 and p. 102, n.

INTRODUCTION

THE chief feature of the literary relations of England and Germany in the sixteenth century is the predominance of German influence over English. Miles Coverdale translated Luther's hymns, religious controversy gave rise to polemical dialogues which were translated or adapted for English use, and the same reception was accorded the Latin dramas of the German humanists. Yet the influence of Protestantism proved abortive in the end. Coverdale's *Goostly Songs and Spiritual Psalmes*, Roy's and Barlow's dialogue, *Rede me and be not wrothe*, were proscribed by Henry VIII, and a performance of Kirchmayer's papal drama, *Pammachius*, in the Hall of Christ's College in 1545 incurred the wrath of Gardiner. To quote Herford[1], "in lyric, in dialogue, in drama, the imaginative language which the genius of German Protestantism had shaped out for itself was caught up with fitful and momentary energy, and then as rapidly forgotten." The fate of the popular secular motives was different. The Ship of Fools, Faustus, Eulenspiegel and Grobianus became firmly established in English literature and survived until long after the close of the century.

In the eighteenth century the positions are reversed. From the very beginning a strong current of English influence sets in and quickly becomes an irresistible flood. After a supremacy

---

[1] Charles H. Herford: *Studies in the literary relations of England and Germany in the Sixteenth Century*. 1886. Bibl. 59.

N.B. All foot-notes which refer to books included in the numbered Bibliography (Appendix A) are indicated in the text by a small figure. For other notes the asterisk and other usual signs are employed.

A few titles which are mentioned only once throughout the text are given in full at the bottom of the page and do not re-appear in Appendix A.

of over half a century the influence of France is undermined
and German literature receives new life and vigour. Milton,
Thomson, Prior, Richardson, Young, Ossian, Percy, Shakespeare
and others all appear sooner or later in a German dress, all play
a part in the creation of a literature which may bear comparison
with that of any country and of any age[1]. It is the beginning
of that cult of England and things English which, at first
embracing literature alone, rapidly spread to industry, commerce
and politics and is even now only beginning to decline.

If, then, at the commencement of the eighteenth century,
we find England repaying with interest the debt contracted in
the sixteenth, we may well ask ourselves what had happened
in the meantime. With the exception of a few monographs,
e.g. H. Fischer on Weckherlin, P. A. Becker and K. F. Schmid
on Barclay (see Preface), there is little literature on the subject.
The period has little attraction, as far as Germany is concerned,
and receives scant attention in most histories of literature,—
and with good reason, for the majority of the works of the
age are absolutely worthless. They do possess a certain
evolutionary interest but have no intrinsic value. The object,
therefore, of the present volume is not to claim that German
literature of the seventeenth century is, after all, worth reading
for its own sake, but simply to trace the literary relations of
England and Germany from the sixteenth century to the
eighteenth, to follow the decline of German influence on
England, to watch the two countries as they drift apart, to
note that intercourse, although spasmodic, is never completely
interrupted, and that finally, towards the end of the century,
a connection is re-established which has continued to increase
in strength down to our own time.

It is hardly necessary to state that many names of importance for the history of German literature will play a very
minor part in these pages. Thus Opitz is for us little more
than the translator of Sidney and Barclay, Fleming contributes
one epigram, while Gerhardt does not appear at all. On the
other hand many long-forgotten authors receive a prominence

[1] See Max Koch: *Über die Beziehungen der englischen Litteratur zur deutschen im XVIII Jahrhundert.* 1883. Bibl. 277.

to which they would not have the slightest claim in any ordinary history of literature. My object throughout has been to discover what English authors were read in Germany and *vice versâ*. Consequently I must ask my readers patiently to endure the fulsome prefaces of many insufferable busy-bodies for the sake of the sober reflections of a Morhof[1] or the romantic narrative of a Captain Henrie Bell[2].

The beginning of the century is for Germany a period of absolute stagnation. The popular, we might almost say plebeian, interest in literature has waned, religious controversy and petty intrigues occupy the attention of bishops and princes, the language of scholars is Latin and the leisured classes read Boccaccio and Ronsard[3]. In a word, German is at its lowest ebb. Half the words in use are borrowed from Latin or French and supplied with German endings*. Vernacular literature is practically non-existent. Poetry consists of sickly eulogies of patrons, dull paraphrases of the Psalms or insipid eclogues and pastorals in imitation of the Italians. To quote Lemcke[4]: "The poetry of the age lacks vigour, rummages in text-books and fails to find matter. It is pedantic, counts syllables and imitates foreign fashions. Whatever it touches is turned, not to gold, as it should be, but to wood. Tame, inartistic, formless, colourless, it lives a weary life. And yet it is the age of Shakespeare and the great, impetuous English dramatists. It is the age of Rubens, the age of Kepler,— just to indicate the strength of the Germanic races in art and science. And yet the Germans of this epoch were not deaf to the merits of poetry. On the contrary, they torment and torture themselves in the quest. It is a veritable search for the Holy Grail. They try the most various ways, inquire,

---

[1] Bibl. 255. [2] Bibl. 193.

[3] According to Karl Borinski: *Die Poetik der Renaissance*, 1886 (Bibl. 50), Italian was actually the Court language of South Germany, e.g. in Hessen and at Vienna, French was spoken at Stuttgart, English at Heidelberg.

* Koberstein (Bibl. 35) quotes Moscherosch: *Gesichte Philanders von Sittewalt*, 1642 (Zugabe zum ersten Teil): "Wenn man eines neusüchtigen Deutschlings Herz öffnen und sehen sollte, würde man augenscheinlich befinden, dass fünf Achtel desselben französisch, ein Achtel spanisch, eins italienisch und kaum eins deutsch daran gefunden werden."

[4] Carl Lemcke: *Geschichte der deutschen Dichtung neuerer Zeit*, p. 5, 1871. Bibl. 47.

seek and struggle with good will, enormous pains and right lamentable success."

As the years roll on, the influence of Italy gives place to that of France, so that, roughly speaking, the first quarter of the century may be said to be the period chiefly of Italian influence and the last quarter almost solely that of French, while both are equally operative in the middle of the century. The influence of Dutch literature, more particularly that of the Renaissance drama, spreads more or less over the first sixty years, and we must also note a strong Spanish influence about 1650. Last and least comes the influence of England.

Here I must repeat that the object of this volume is not to prove that the literary relations of England and Germany in the seventeenth century are more important than has hitherto been supposed, assuming the matter to have received some consideration, but to give a precise explanation of the nature of those relations. Many reasons, not the least being the flourishing state of literature in France and Holland, caused Germany to be in a sense cut off from intercourse with England. This being so, emphasis must be laid on the fact that the part played by Italy and France in the history of German literature during this period is immeasurably greater than that of England.

It must not be supposed that the corrupt state of the German language at the beginning of the century was altogether unregretted and disregarded. No evil state of things can continue interminably and a few patriotic spirits soon felt that the neglect of the national tongue was a disgrace not to be endured. The splendour of Italian literature kindled here and there the fire of emulation and active efforts were made to cultivate the German tongue and place it on a level with its rivals. These took the form of Sprachgesellschaften or "Language Societies," the first and most important of which was founded in 1617 by Prince Ludwig of Anhalt-Cöthen at the suggestion of Caspar von Teutleben, who proposed as a model the Florentine Accademia della Crusca (1582). The principal object of the society was to be the cultivation of the German language, and three rules were drawn up, as follows:

Firstly,

All members of the Fruchtbringende Gesellschaft, irrespective of rank or religion, must be honourable, intelligent and wise, virtuous and courteous, useful and entertaining, affable, and moderate in all things; when they meet they must be amiable, cheerful, and friendly, and just as it is strictly forbidden at the meetings for one member to take in bad part an offensive word from another, so must they on the other hand be firmly pledged to refrain from all unseemly remarks and vulgar jests.

Secondly,

The first duty of the members must be, above all things, to preserve and cultivate most carefully, in speech, writing, and poetry, our beloved mother-tongue in its true form and proper meaning, without admixture of foreign patch-words; also as far as possible, especially within the Society, to insure that this principle be in no way infringed but rather obediently complied with...

Thirdly,

As an appropriate sign of gratitude for the honour of membership, all members are requested to wear, on a parrot-green ribbon, a gold medal, with the palm-tree and motto of the Fruchtbringende Gesellschaft on one side; on the other the member's own emblem with his name and motto; so that they may the more easily recognise one another at the meetings and that the highly laudable object of the latter may thereby be made known[1].

The first President of the Society was Ludwig of Anhalt. He was succeeded in 1651 by Duke Wilhelm of Saxe-Weimar, under whom the society prospered exceedingly. By 1662, according to Neumark[2], it numbered seven hundred and fifty members, including Karl Gustav, Count of the Rhenish

---

[1] These rules are quoted by Otto Schulz: *Die Sprachgesellschaften des siebzehnten Jahrhunderts.* 1824. Bibl. 44.

[2] *Der Neu-Sprossende Teutsche Palmenbaum,* 1668. Bibl. 42. Herdegen (Bibl. 43) says the book did not actually appear until 1673 owing to delay in printing the copperplates.

Palatinate, afterwards King of Sweden, 3 Electors, 149 Dukes*, 4 Margraves, 10 Landgraves, 8 Counts Palatine, 19 Princes and 35 Barons (Freiherren). After Wilhelm's death the same year the fortunes of the society waned and it gradually died out.

Other societies were rapidly founded in imitation of the Fruchtbringende Gesellschaft. In 1633 the Aufrichtige Tannengesellschaft was established in Strassburg by Jesaias Rompler von Löwenhalt. Among its members were Johann Matthias Schneuber, Professor of Poetry at Strassburg, and Georg Rudolf Weckherlin, but its life was short. The Teutschgesinnte Genossenschaft of Hamburg was the creation of that restless, orthographical crank, Philipp von Zesen (1643)†. It survived until 1705. Another Hamburg society was Der Elbschwanen Orden, which was founded by Johann Rist in 1660 and expired with him seven years later. The Pegnesischer Blumenorden‡, founded in 1644 by Georg Philipp Harsdoerfer at Nuremberg, is more important for us than the rest. Not only did many of its members travel in England at different times, but they made a special cult of pastoral poetry and we consequently find them very familiar with Sidney's *Arcadia*. For this reason I shall postpone further discussion of the Pegnesischer Blumenorden until I come to deal with the influence of Sidney in Germany.

In spite of the number of these societies their influence was really very slight. It cannot for a moment be compared with that of La Pléiade in France. In fact, it is no exaggeration to say that no member of any of them produced anything of sufficient merit to survive to our day. Of course, the earlier literary historians do not share this opinion. Herdegen[1], for example, says: "Just as the last century (i.e. the seventeenth)

---

* In the list of admissions for 1641 I notice the following interesting entry: "Octavio Piccolomini Aragona Hertzog zu Amalfi Der Zwingende. Die kleine Monraute. Zuentwafnen." (p. 272.)

† Born at Fürstenau, Anhalt, *c.* 1619. Lived chiefly in Amsterdam and Hamburg, where he died in 1689. Member of Fruchtbringende Gesellschaft (or Palmenorden).

‡ So called from the River Pegnitz at Nuremberg.

[1] Johann Herdegen (Amarantes): *Historische Nachricht von dess...Hirten und Blumen-Ordens...Anfang und Fortgang...* 1744. Bibl. 43.

is distinguished from other ages both by the large number of famous and learned men, who came forth like those heroes from the Trojan horse, and by the magnificent works they published as eternal memorials of their excellence, so also was it remarkable for the fact that many learned societies came into existence, some of which gradually died out, whereas others have made the progress they desired down to the present time." (I. p. 1.)

Perhaps the most interesting feature of these Sprachgesellschaften is the evidence they afford of a revival of interest in literature on the part of rulers and princes. ' " In the fourteenth and fifteenth centuries we see poetry gradually pass from the narrow circle of the nobility into the hands of the citizen guilds, in whose charge it receives an excellent cultivation during the sixteenth century. But with the commencement of the seventeenth scholars soon obtain almost entire possession of poetry and of every force that tends thereto, and while they are seeking to put themselves and their work under the protection of the German princes, we see poetry again falling under the influence and returning to the circle of the nobility." (H. M. Schletterer*.)

Literature, with the exception of religious lyrics, is no longer popular in spirit; it is merely a pastime for scholars and pedants, a means of currying favour with the great. Indeed, popular literature was almost an impossibility in the seventeenth century. For thirty years Germany was convulsed with one of the most disastrous of civil wars. In 1619, on the death of the Emperor Mathias, the Bohemians refused to acknowledge Ferdinand II as their king and chose instead Frederick V, Elector of the Palatinate and son-in-law of James I. The short struggle between the two princes, ending with the defeat of Frederick, the " Winter King," at the battle of Prague (1620), constitutes the first phase of the war. Frederick's marriage with the Princess Elizabeth (1612) is one of the most important connecting links between England and Germany in the seventeenth century and it seems more than

* Introduction to *Johann Rist, Das friedewünschende Deutschland und Das friedejauchzende Deutschland.* 1864.

probable that a thorough study of the movements of the numerous members of the Electoral house will add considerably to our knowledge of the dramatic and theatrical relations of the two countries*.

That these years of war were unfavourable to the interests of literature is obvious. Their effect on the language has been well summed up by Walter[1]. The Thirty Years' War was not the cause of the corruption of the German language, as might be supposed from the polyglot nature of the armies engaged. It merely brought to a head the importation of foreign words which had begun many years before. Signs of this decay are already apparent in Wolfram's *Parzival* and Williram's (d. 1085) *Paraphrase des hohen Liedes.* Aegidius Tschudi (1505—1578) holds the "Cantzler" and the "Consistorische Schryber" responsible for the irruption of foreign words into the vocabulary. Then comes the influence of Italian commerce and the Latinization of proper names. Walter observes: "Before the League of Smalkald (1530) the German princes used only Latin and German in their intercourse with France... But when this League fell into difficulties and the help of France was sought, then things changed. Francis I (d. 1547) wrote in French to the Elector Johann Friedrich of Saxony and from 1551 a knowledge of French was indispensable to the latter's Privy Councillors as well. The conscious pride in their language which the Germans had hitherto shown in their dealings with France was gone."

As other factors in the decay of German must be mentioned the decline of the Protestant universities and the emigration of German students to Italy and France, the rise of Calvinism, the translation of *Amadis* (1582), the spread of Roman law towards the end of the fifteenth century, the accession of Charles V and the consequent irruption of Spaniards and Italians into Germany. The war, owing to its disturbing effects on court and university life and the babel

---

* See Aloïs Brandl: *Zu " Shakespeares Totenmaske" und "Ben Jonsons Totenbild."* In the Shakespeare-Jahrbuch for 1911.

[1] Joseph Walter: *Über den Einfluss des 30-jährigen Krieges auf die deutsche Sprache und Literatur...* 1871. Bibl. 48.

of tongues spoken in its camps, served to accentuate these tendencies.

We cannot wonder, therefore, that during these terrible years literary intercourse with a comparatively distant country like England was reduced to a minimum, although sympathy with the Electress Elizabeth and her unfortunate husband caused the course of the war itself to be eagerly followed in this country* and its main incidents were, as we shall see, reflected in various ways in English literature. Moreover, when the Peace of Westphalia (1648) brought the long struggle to a close, England herself was in the throes of civil war and it became Germany's turn to assume the part of spectator. Hence, we must not be surprised to find that the literary relations of the two countries are of an extremely spasmodic nature. One or two movements, it is true, e.g. the influence of the English comedians, can be traced more or less continuously throughout the century, but as a rule we find that those English authors whose works were read in Germany (there is very little to say of German authors in England)† were translated into German, sometimes through the medium of French or Latin, achieved a sudden and furious popularity and were almost as rapidly forgotten. This is especially true of Sidney, Owen, and Barclay, although the latter has received occasional attention during the last two centuries[1].

Although the wars of the century caused a certain amount of emigration of men of letters to England, they interfered on the other hand with literary intercourse, inasmuch as they restricted the movements of travellers. For this reason it has

---

* A periodical, *Weekly News from Italy, Germany...*, published by Nathaniel Butter, Nicholas Bunne, and Thomas Archer, made its first appearance on May 23, 1622.

† I mention here once and for all a few books of a very miscellaneous character:

Conrad Gesner: *The Historie of the Foure-Footed Beastes...Translated by Edward Topsell.* 1607.

Adam Olearius: *The Voyages and Travels of the Ambassadors from the Duke of Holstein to the Duke of Muscovy and King of Persia*, 1632—1639. *Translated by John Davies.* 1662.

Numerous medical works are quoted by William London as being translated from German writers. See Bibl. 1. On the other hand, some English books of travel, e.g. by Raleigh, Robert Knox, were translated into German.

[1] See K. F. Schmid: *John Barclay Argenis...* 1904. Bibl. 136.

been found necessary to deal with travellers in two groups, representing the beginning and end of the century respectively. As far as English travellers in Germany are concerned, the middle years have nothing to offer, excepting a few reports of British officers who served in the continental armies.

In the first chapter, therefore, an attempt is made to estimate the value of the earlier travellers as literary intermediaries.

CHAPTER I

EARLY TRAVELLERS

.FROM all the events which tended to promote intercourse between England and Germany before the end of the Thirty Years' War Elze[1] singles out three as calling for especial attention. The first is purely commercial, viz. the establishment in the Middle Ages of Hansa trade centres in England, the subsequent growth of English commerce and the final invasion of Germany by English merchant-adventurers ("Die Wagenden") in the sixteenth century. The second is the persecution of Protestants in the reign of Mary, which caused colonies of English refugees to establish themselves at Frankfort, Strassburg, Duisburg and elsewhere, and the third the visits paid to the larger German towns, from about 1585 onwards, by the various companies of English comedians[2]. To these must be added a fourth, viz. the emigration of German Protestants to England to escape the oppression of the Catholic princes during the war.

The accounts of the principal foreign travellers in England before the death of James I have been collected and discussed by Rye[3]. In 1592 Duke Friedrich of Würtemberg, the "cozen garmombles[4]" and "Duke de Jamanie" of *The Merry Wives of*

[1] Karl Elze: *Die englische Sprache und Litteratur in Deutschland*, 1864. Bibl. 58.

[2] The discussion of the English comedians forms part of the dramatic relations of England and Germany, and has, for reasons given in the Preface, been omitted from this volume. For literature see Betz (Bibl. 12).

[3] William Brenchley Rye: *England as seen by Foreigners*, 1865. Bibl. 66. I have not seen the article by G. Binz (see Appendix C). He mentions, I believe, a certain Platter who witnessed a performance of *Julius Caesar*.

[4] I.e. Mompelgard, Mümpelgart, or Montbéliard, which passed from Burgundy to Würtemberg in 1419. Mentioned in First Quarto (1602) only.

1

Windsor, paid Elizabeth a visit in the hope that she would invest him with the Order of the Garter. An account of the journey was published by his secretary, Rathgeb, in 1602 with the curious title, *Beschreibung der Badenfahrt,* so called in memory of the terrible storm the party encountered on the outward journey[1]. The book contains a description of the Universities of Oxford and Cambridge by a certain Simon Bibeus (Bibby?), but Rathgeb nowhere mentions literature, although he does not forget to record that the Duke was much interested in a sheep with five legs at Uxbridge.

Prince Ludwig Friedrich, second son of the above, was despatched to England on a diplomatic mission in 1608, as assistant to Benjamin von Buwinckhausen[2]. It is probable that the latter's secretary, Georg Rudolf Weckherlin (of whom more in the next chapter), was also in England then. In 1610 the Prince, Buwinckhausen and Hippolytus von Colli[3] were sent as ambassadors to James I by the German Protestant party. Their secretary, Wurmsser, wrote a diary of the journey in French. On Monday, April 30th, we are told, "S.E. alla au Globe lieu ordinaire ou l'on joue les Commedies, y fut representé l'histoire du More de Venise." Beyond this there are no entries of literary interest.

Another German prince who visited the English theatre was Philip Julius, Duke of Pommern-Stettin. His tutor, Professor Friedrich Gerschow, wrote an account of the journey but it remained unpublished until 1892[4]. Their stay, although short (Sept. 10th—Oct. 3rd, 1602), was not uninteresting. On the 13th of September they saw a play which dealt with the capture of Stuhl-Weissenburg by the Turks and its reconquest by the Christians[5]. The next day a "Tragica Comoedia"

[1] Bibl. 62.
[2] Born 1571. On diplomatic service after 1595 and held in high esteem at Stuttgart. Died 1635.
[3] A Swiss lawyer of Zürich; Chancellor of Prince Christian of Anhalt.
[4] See H. Hager: *Diary of the Journey of Philip Julius...,* 1893. Bibl. 68. The diary was edited by Dr Goffried von Bülow and Wilfred Powell as Vol. vi of the *Transactions of the Royal Historical Society,* New Series, 1892. The MS is preserved at the Swedish University of Lund (Mscr. B 1), and is entitled *Des Durchleuchtigen Hochgeborenen Fürsten vnd Herren Philippi Julij Hertzogen zu Stettin, Pommern,...Rays, Durch Deutschland, Englandt, Franckreich vnd Italienn, Datum in E. F. G. Universitat zum Greiffswaldt Anno 1605.*
[5] See Chapter vi.

about Samson and half the tribe of Benjamin was given, which Bolte[1] considers to be the same as "the booke of Samson," for which Samuel Rowley and Edward Jubye received £6 from Henslowe on July 29th, 1602. On the 16th the party witnessed a performance by a company of children. The play dealt with the story of the "Casta Vidua," or "royal widow of England," which description Bolte thinks might apply to Anthony Munday's *The Whidow's Charm.*

Another visitor mentioned by Rye is one Justus Zinzerling, a native of Thuringia and Doctor of Laws of Basel, who recorded his impressions in Latin and alludes once to the theatres (*Theatra Comoedorum*) as being places for cock-fighting and the baiting of bulls and bears.

On the whole, these accounts, although interesting enough as historical documents, are of little use for our purpose. They contain small reference to English learning and none at all to literature. Even these scanty allusions to the theatre are unimportant, as we have no evidence to show that the visitors took away any lasting impressions. In fact, it is unreasonable to expect casual travellers to acquire any knowledge of English literature during a few crowded weeks of business and sightseeing.

Nor are the English travellers in Germany much more communicative. Francis Quarles (1592–1644) accompanied the Princess Elizabeth to Germany as cup-bearer in 1613 and apparently remained in her service for six or seven years. John Donne was there with Lord Doncaster in 1619. Sir John Suckling joined the Marquis of Hamilton's army and fought under Gustavus Adolphus at Leipzig and Magdeburg. Yet none of these has anything to say of German literature. Something, however, may be gleaned from the narratives of Thomas Coryat (1577–1617) and Fynes Moryson (1566–1630).

Coryat's *Crudities*[2] (1611) begin with an oration in praise of travel translated from the Latin of Hermann Kirchner[3]. Our author then describes how he left Dover on May 14th, 1608,

---

[1] Johannes Bolte: *Schauspiele in Kassel und London,* 1889. Bibl. 67.
[2] Bibl. 71.
[3] Professor of Eloquence at Marburg. Died 1620.

at eight a.m. and wandered from Calais *via* Amiens, Paris, Lyons, Chambéry, Turin, Milan, Mantua, Padua, Venice, Verona and Bergamo into Rhaetia (the Grisons). At this point he remarks: "But seeing that I am now come into that part of the Grisons country which speaketh Dutch (i.e. German), I wil here interrupt my description of it by the addition of a most elegant Latin Oration that I have annexed unto this discourse written in praise of the travell of Germany by that learned German Hermannus Kirchnerus, the author of the first German Oration that I have prefixed before my booke, and according to my meane skill rudely translated into our mother tongue by my selfe....I say with Kirchnerus, that Germany is the Queene of all other provinces, the Eagle of all Kingdomes, and the Mother of all Nations." Leaving Curic (Chur, Coire), he passed on to Ragatz and Zürich, where (he says) "it was my good fortune to enter into a league of friendship with some of the profound schollers of this worthy Citie; a thing that hath ministred no small joy and comfort unto me. This first epistle following is to that rare Linguist and famous traveller Gaspar Waserus." This letter contains an account of Coryat's wanderings after leaving Switzerland and is followed by a Greek epistle to the same person. Waser's reply is dated "Tiguri 16 Mart. 1610" and signed "Tui studiosissimus Gustavus Waserus, Professor sanctarum linguarum in schola Tigurina." In another letter, dated "pridie Calen. August. 1609," to "M. Rodolphus Hospinianus a learned Preacher and writer of controversies of the city of Zürich," Coryat mentions his ignorance of the German tongue: "Nam si memineris, consuluisti mihi digredi parum ex via ad videndum balnea prope Badenam vestram Helvaticam. Sed in multis profecto diverticulis & ignotis callibus erravi, antequam illa invenire potuerim, hac praecipue de causa, quoniam inscius vestrae linguae non potui Germanice percontari viam." Then follow a letter of the same date to Heinrich Bullinger the younger, and one to Marcus Buelerus, in which he enumerates the great men of Zürich. A reply from Buelerus, dated "8 Cal. April. Anno ultimi temporis 1610," is the last of these letters.

Coryat left Zürich on August 27th, and reached Strassburg

via Basel and the Rhine. Here he again interrupts his narrative to quote some verses in praise of Germany by a certain George Sidenham of Somerset. He then visited German Baden and Heidelberg. The Palatine library in the latter town excited his admiration, and he had a long conversation with Janus Gruter[1], the librarian, who was acquainted with Thomas James' Catalogue of the Bodleian and said that the Heidelberg library could boast a superiority of a hundred manuscripts. A certain Lingelshemius[2], formerly tutor to Elector Friedrich IV and a friend of Sir Henry Wotton, procured him admission to the palace. He also visited the University and gives a list of the principal *Alumni*.

In Frankfort, which he reached by way of Spires, Worms and Mainz, he met an Englishman named Thomas Row and was impressed by the extent of the book-trade. Of the other German towns he visited before reaching London in October, 1608, Coryat says nothing which can interest us.

References to German vernacular literature are, indeed, altogether absent from the accounts of these early travellers and remarks on the language are almost as rare. That cosmopolitan writer, John Barclay (see Chapter IV), in his satirical novel *Euphormionis Lusinini Satyricon*[3], has little praise to bestow on the people of Germany (Boeotia). He says they are more capable of manual than of intellectual work, somewhat stupid and violently addicted to drink—a vice, then as now, characteristic of almost any country except one's own. A chapter in his later work, *Icon animorum* (1614), is openly devoted to a discussion of Germany and the Germans. Their stolidity and vanity are held up to derision, but great emphasis is laid on their honesty and sound common-sense[4].

[1] Born in 1560 at Amsterdam. His mother, an Englishwoman, taught him Latin and Greek. He was taken to England while young, and studied at Cambridge and Leyden.

[2] See Alex. Reifferscheid: *Quellen zur Geschichte des Geistigen Lebens*, 1889. Bibl. 51.

[3] Part I, Paris, 1605. The passage is quoted at greater length by G. Steinhausen: *Die Deutschen im Urteil des Auslandes*, 1909. Bibl. 73.

[4] This book attracted considerable attention in Germany, and Barclay's denunciation of German manners and customs was received with indignation. A translation (Bibl. 63) by Johann Seyfert appeared in 1649, published by Erhard Berger of Bremen. The writer of the preface (Seyfert?) warns the reader that Barclay is not always reliable, e.g. in Chapter v; "Von den Teutschen;

The *Itinerary*[1] of Fynes Moryson, although the journeys recorded therein are of an earlier date than Coryat's, did not see publication until 1617. On the first of May, 1591, he sailed from Leigh-on-Thames and landed a few days later at Stade, whence he travelled *via* Hamburg, Lübeck, Lüneburg, Magdeburg and Leipzig to Wittenberg, where he matriculated. The legends in circulation about Faust and Luther interested him greatly. "They show a house," he says, "wherein Doctor Faustus a famous conjuror dwelt. They say that this Doctor Faustus lived there about the yeere 1500 and had a tree all blasted and burnt in the adjoyning wood, where hee practised his Magick Art, and that hee died, or rather was fetched by the Divell, in a village neere the Towne. I did see the tree so burnt; but walking at leasure through all the Villages adjoyning, I could never heare any memory of his end." After leaving Wittenberg he visited (1592) Meissen, Dresden, Prague, Pilsen, Amberg, Nuremberg, Augsburg, Lindau, Reichenau, Schaffhausen, Zürich, Baden and Basel. At this point he refers to Francis Hotman (d. 1590), John Oecolampadius (d. 1531) and Erasmus (d. 1536). Thence he travelled *via* Frankfort, Cassel, Brunswick and Hamburg to Emden and wintered in the Hague. In July, 1593, we find him again in Emden. In Lübeck he bought a copy of *Amadis* in German. From Lübeck he passed to Copenhagen, Danzig, Cracow, Vienna, Venice, Rome, Genoa, Padua (Dec. 4th, 1594), Chur, Zürich, Geneva, Strassburg, Paris and Dieppe, and reached London in May, 1595. In November he again set sail, this time in company with his brother Henry, and travelled *via* Flushing, Emden, Lüneburg, Bamberg, Nuremberg and Innsbruck to Venice. Thence he sailed to Palestine, where Henry died, visited Constantinople and returned to Venice on April 30th, 1597. Passing through Augsburg, Nuremberg and Brunswick to Stade he reached Gravesend in September.

vnd denen Völckern/die man heut zu tag Niderländer heist/auch deren Sitten vnd Eigenschafften." After a particularly offensive passage Seyfert inserts the words "garrit Barclajus." A revised edition of this translation was published by Berger in 1660, with a long preface by Hans Just Wynckelmann, who may also be responsible for the preface of 1649. The title is somewhat different (Bibl. 64). An edition of the Latin text appeared at Dresden in 1680, with notes by August Buchner, probably written as early as 1646.   [1] Bibl. 72.

It is clear from this short summary that Moryson knew more of Germany than any other Englishman of his day, but it cannot be said that his communications, as far as this earlier portion of his *Itinerary* is concerned, are of much value for our purpose. In the chapter Of Precepts for Travellers, he says: "My advice is, that in each Kingdome which he desires most to know, and the language whereof is of most use in his own Countrie, he goe directly to the best Citie for the puritie of language, namely, in Germany to Leipzig[1], Strasburg, or Heidelberg, and in France to Orleans, etc." In a later passage (III. pp. 453-8) he quotes a large number of German proverbs.

The Fourth Part of the *Itinerary* was finished about 1620 but never published by the author, although he obtained the necessary license in 1626. I quote the following passages from the modern edition by Mr Charles Hughes[2].

"Of the Germans Nature and Manners, strength of body and witt, manuall Artes Sciences Universities language... (p. 290).
...For Sciences : There is not a man among the Common sorte who cannot speake Lattin, and hath not some skill in Arithmaticke, and Musicke...(p. 300).
...All the Vniversityes labour and giue large stipends to drawe those of greatest fame to be Professors and Readers of the lawe in their Schooles...(p. 303).
...Germany hath some fewe wandring Comeydians, more deseruing pitty than prayse, for the serious parts are dully penned, and worse acted, and the mirth they make is ridiculous, and nothing lesse than witty (as I formerly haue shewed)."

Then follows a reference to a visit to Frankfort of "some of our cast dispised Stage players," whose performance wearied Moryson immensely.

"...One thing I cannot commend in the Germans, that for desyre of vayneglory, being yet without Beardes and of smalle knowledge, they make themselves knowne more than praysed by vntimely Printing of bookes, and very toyes, published in theire names. Young Students who haue scarce layd theire lipps to taste the sweete fountaynes of the Sciences, if they can wrest an Elegy out of theire empty braine, it must presently be Printed, yea if they can but make a wrangling disputation in the Vniversity, the questions they Dispute vpon, with the Disputers names, must also be Printed. Yea, very graue men and Doctors of the liberall Professions, are so forward to rush into these Olimpick games, for gayning the prise from others, as they seeme rather to affect the writing of many and great, then iudicious and succinct bookes, so as theire riper yeares and second Counsells (allwayes best) hardly suffice to correct the

---

[1] Nowadays about the last place one would visit for the purpose.
[2] *Shakespeare's Europe*, 1903. Bibl. 69.

errours thereof....The Printers of Germany, are so farr from giuing the Authors mony for theire Copies (which they doe in other Countryes) as feareing not to vent them with gayne, they dare not adventure to Print them at theire charge. So as the German Authors vse, ether to pay a great part of the charge leauing the bookes to the Printer, or to pay a crowne for the Printing of each leafe, keeping the bookes to themselues, which they commonly giue freely to frendes and strangers, as it were hyring them to vouchsafe the reading thereof..." (p. 304).

Then comes a long account of the German universities, more particularly of Wittenberg, where Moryson himself studied (pp. 306–20). Of the language itself he says:

"...The German language is not fitt for Courtship, but in very love more fitt rudely to commande than sweetly to perswade, it being an Imperious short and rude kynde of speech, and such as would make our Children affrayd to heare it, the very familyer speeches and pronuntiations sounding better in the mouth of a Tamberlin, then of a Ciuill man..."

This is the most definite pronouncement on the German language I have been able to discover in the narratives of these early English travellers. They seem to have paid as little attention to German literature as their contemporaries to English. Indeed, these years before the war produced only one man, Weckherlin, who can be justly termed a valuable intermediary between the two countries and he, as we shall see, had lived thirty years in England when his last volume appeared.

CHAPTER II

AT the beginning of the seventeenth century English music was at a high level and English musicians were to be found at many of the larger continental courts. We know, e.g. that Christian IV of Denmark, a liberal patron of the art, invited to his court not only native, but also German, Italian and English composers[1]. The collections of songs and airs by Philip Rosseter and William Corkine were probably the first to become known, but in 1642 we find one of John Dowland's airs, "Can she excuse my wrongs with virtue's cloak?" (1597), twice utilized in Germany. The melody occurs in part in Johann Rist's *Galathe* and again in Gabriel Voigtländer's[2] *Oden und Lieder* (No. 16). The latter was in the service of the King of Denmark after 1639 and must inevitably have been brought into contact with English musicians at the court. This is clear from the title of the collection: *Erster Theil Allerhand Oden vnnd Lieder / welche auff allerley / als Italienische / Frantzösische / Englische / vnd anderer Teutschen guten Componisten / ... Gestellet vnd in Truck gegeben / Durch Gabrieln Voigtländer... Sohra...1642.*

These details refer more properly to the history of *musical* relations, but in one case at least we have an actual translation of the English texts. In 1593 appeared Thomas Morley's *Canzonets, or little short songs to three voices*, which were published in Germany, in 1624, under the following title:

---

[1] Kurt Fischer: *Gabriel Voigtländer*, 1910. Bibl. 86. Fischer refers to Angul Hammerich: *Musiken ved Christian d. IV. Hof.* Copenhagen, 1892.

[2] Born 1601 (?); in Lübeck c. 1626–39. With Christian IV after 1639. Died 1642 (3?).

*Thomae Morlei Angli Lustige und Artige Dreystimmige Welt
liche Liedlein: Wie sie durch Johan von Steinbach mit Teudt-
schen Texten unterleget, Itzo wiederumb auffs newe ubersehen,
und in besserer, artiger und anmutigerer Form zu drucken
verordnet. Von M. Daniele Friderici. Gedruckt durch Johan
Richels Erben. In verlegung Johan Hallervordes, Buchhändlers
daselbst. Im Jahr M.DC.XXIV.*[1] His *Ballets to five voices*
(1595) had already been published with original German texts
by V. Haussmann at Nuremberg in 1609, but in the case of
the Canzonets we have to deal with actual translations from
the English. In the preface, addressed to Johan Sesemann of
Lübeck, Friderici says he was requested to prepare the book
for publication owing to Steinbach's edition, published about
ten years before, having become so rare that copies were no
longer obtainable. This earlier edition, says Bolle, is probably
the one mentioned by Gerber (*Lexikon der Tonkünstler*) in his
article on Morley: "*Tricinia, darin dem Text so erstlich Englisch, auch in teutscher Sprache sein rechter sensus verborum
gelassen worden. Kassel, 1612.*" Morley's collection contains
24 songs, of which I quote the third, together with the German
version as reprinted by Bolle.

Cruel, you pul away to soone your daintie lips,
 when as you kisse mee;
But you should hould them still,
 and then should you blisse mee.
Now or eare I tast them,
 strayt away they hast them;
But you perhaps retire them
to move my thoughts thereby the more to fyre them.
Alas! such baytes you need to fynd out never:
if you would let mee; I would kisse you ever.

Feins Lieb, du zeuchst zurück zu bald dein rothes Mündelein,
wenn ich dich wil küssen;
ach nein es stille halt,
sonst thuts mich sehr verdriessen.
denn eh ichs berühret,
hastu mirs entführet,
doch dencke ich, du thusts vieleicht, destu dadurch die Liebe wilst
 vermehren:
Ach nein, ach nein! fürwahr, denn solche ist gar nicht von nöten:
So du nur woltest lassen mich, wolt ich dich hertzen,
freundlich mit dir schertzen.

[1] Quoted by W. Bolle: *Die gedruckten englischen Liederbücher bis* 1600, 1903. Bibl. 85.

There is another trace of English influence in Zincgref's[1] anthology of German poetry (1624). Poem No. 40, written by himself, is entitled "Adonis Nachtklag vor seiner Liebsten Thür. Ex Anglico." It consists of seven verses, each of eight lines, as follows:

> Mag dann, ach schetzlein,
> Von euch keiner Gnaden schein
> Widerfahren mir,
> Der ich lig vor ewrer Thür,
> Vnd netze diese Schwell
> Mit manchem threnenbach,
> Die ich doch wieder schnell
> Mit Seufftzen brücken mach...

I have not been able to discover the English original.

Leaving these fragments we can now turn to the only man whose works at once betray a familiarity with the lyrics of the reigns of Elizabeth and James I.

Georg Rudolf Weckherlin was born on September 15th, 1584, at Stuttgart[2] and in 1601 entered the University of Tübingen as a student of law. From March to November, 1604, he was travelling in Saxony and in 1606 he visited Montbéliard, Lyons, Orleans and Paris. In October, 1607, we find him again in Paris, in close relation with Benjamin von Buwinckhausen, Statthalter of Alençon. It is probable that he went with Buwinckhausen to England the same year, where they were joined in 1608 by Prince Ludwig Friedrich of Würtemberg (see Chapter I). Or he may have been attached to the second mission in 1610. At any rate, we know that by 1616 he had spent three years in England. In 1613 the Electress Elizabeth left England for her new home in Heidelberg, and the next we hear of Weckherlin is that he spent about six years in the service of the Duke of Würtemberg as secretary to the Board of Domains. In 1616 appeared his *Triumf Newlich bey der F. Kindtauf zu Stutgart gehalten*, published at Stuttgart by Johan-Weyrich Rösslin. The occasion

---

[1] Julius Wilhelm Zincgref: *Auserlesene Gedichte deutscher Poeten*, 1624. Bibl. 80.

[2] See Höpfner: *Weckherlin's Oden und Gesänge*, 1865, Bibl. 79, and Fischer: *Georg Rudolf Weckherlin's Gedichte*, 1893 and 1897, Bibl. 83. I have used Fischer's edition throughout for the purpose of quotation.

was the christening of Friedrich, son of the reigning Duke, Johann Friedrich, and Barbara Sophia, daughter of Elector Joachim Friedrich of Brandenburg. The festival lasted from the 10th to the 15th of March (old style) and among the guests were the Princess Elizabeth and her husband, Friedrich V, Elector of the Palatinate. In her honour Weckherlin published simultaneously an English version of the same work, entitled *Triumphall shews set forth lately at Stutgart*. The dedication to the Electress is dated "Stutgart day of John Baptist 1616," and the preface (To the Reader) runs: "Gentle Reader, Behold here a smalle booke written in English by a German, and printed in Germanie. Therefore if thou art too daintie a reader, I doe intreat thee, to seeke somewhere els fit food, to bee pleased withall, as, I know, there is greater store of in England, then in any other countrie. As for me, beeing fully acquainted with mine incapacitie, I willingly would crave pardon for this rude relation, if I did set it forth by boldnesse. But to obey the commandement of my Soveraigne (his Highness of Wirtemberg) I was glad to/find out all my best English, I had learned within three yeares, I lived in England. Therefore I pray thee, to take it in good part, and so, as I doe meane it, though I do not say, well: and kindly to reforme by thy judicious reading the faults either of the erring author, or of the unwitting Printer, who, good man, never in his life saw, nor perhaps will see more English together. Thus I shall indevor the more, to honour in German the gallant English Nation, whereof (verely) I make more account, then I can utter (though with truth) without getting the name of a flatterer. Farewell." This English version is somewhat shortened, especially towards the end.

Another similar volume appeared in 1618 in celebration of the christening of Johann Friedrich's next child, Ulrich, and of the wedding of Prince Ludwig Friedrich and Elisabeth Magdalene of Hesse. This was entitled *Kurtze Beschreibung, dess zu Stutgarten bei der Fürstlichen Kindtauf vnd Hochzeit, Jüngstgehaltenen Frewden-Fests* and published by Dieterich Werlin at Tübingen. It contains nothing of interest for our purpose except perhaps some tricks of versification which, according to Bohm[1], betray the influence of Owen, e.g. No. 21 (ed. Fischer):

> Mensch, wilt du wissen was dein Leben?
> So merck das Wörtlin Leben eben:
> Liss es zu ruck, so würstu sehen,
> Was es, und wie es thut vergehen.

Weckherlin's first important work, the First Book of the *Oden und Gesänge* (1618), begins with a prefatory poem in imitation of Spenser's well-known lines "To His Booke," prefixed to the *Shepheardes Calender* (1579). It will be seen that the beginning and end agree literally[2].

> Go little booke: thy selfe present,
> As child whose parent is unkent:
> To him that is the president
> Of noblesse and of chivalrie:
> And if that Envy barke at thee,
> As sure it will, for succour flee
>
> Under the shadow of his wing:
> And asked; who thee forth did bring,
> A shepheards swaine say did thee sing,
> All as his straying flock he fedde:
> And when his honour hath thee redde,
> Crave pardon for my hardy-head.
>
> But if that any aske thy name,
> Say thou wert base begot with blame:
> For thy[3] thereof thou takest shame.
> And when thou art past ieopardie,
> Come tell mee, what was sayd of mee:
> And I will send more after thee.
>   Immerito.

>   An mein Buch.
> Wolan, Büchlein, du must es wagen,
> Zeuch hinauss mit getrostem muht:
> Weil unser gewissen gantz gut,
> So gilt es gleich was man wirt sagen.
>
> Deemüthig-küssend zu begrüessen
> Einer mächtigen Göttin hand,
> Soll Dich Missgunst und Unverstand
> Weder verhindern noch verdriessen.
>
> Gefallen solt du gar nicht allen,
> Vihlen gefallen ist zuvihl:
> Hast also dein gewisses spihl,
> Das du wenigen wirst gefallen.

---

[1] W. Bohm: *England's Einfluss auf G. R. Weckherlin*, 1893. Bibl. 82. Many of Bohm's parallels are rightly rejected by Fischer on the ground that in many cases both Weckherlin and his alleged English model borrowed from the same French source.

[2] Cf. also Valentin Löber's *Fahr hin/du kleines Buch/und lass dich irren nicht*, prefixed to his translation (1653) of Owen's epigrams (Bibl. 147).

[3] Another reading is "why."

Dieser (wie wenig ihrer seyen)
Seind gar gnug, weil Sie gut und fromb;
Und Sie, bei denen du willkomb
Werden dich schon vor unfall freyhen.

Wan du nu, so wol aufgenommen,
Auch vor andern kämest herfür,
So wollen frölich bald nach dir
Mehr schönere geschwistrigt kommen.

Poems 42 and 43 (in Fischer's edition) are both addressed to the Princess Elizabeth. In the first, the Latin, English, French and German muses speak in turn in their own language. No. 52, *Kennzaichen eines Glückseligen Lebens* is a translation of Sir Henry Wotton's *Character of a happy life* (c. 1614).

How happy is he born and taught
That serveth not another's will;
Whose armour is his honest thought
And simple truth his utmost skill!

Whose passions not his masters are,
Whose soul is still prepared for death,
Not tied unto the world with care
Of public fame, or private breath:

Who envies none that chance doth raise
Nor vice; who never understood
How deepest wounds are given by praise;
Nor rules of state, but rules of good:

Who hath his life from rumours freed,
Whose conscience is his strong retreat;
Whose state can neither flatterers feed,
Nor ruin make accusers great;

Who God doth late and early pray
More of His grace than gifts to lend;
And entertains the harmless day
With a well-chosen book or friend;

—This man is freed from servile bands
Of hope to rise, or fear to fall;
Lord of himself, though not of lands;
And having nothing, yet hath all.

Wie glückselig ist dessen leben,
Dem keines andern will gebeut;
Der ohn neyd missgunst oder streit
Sicht andrer glück fürüber schweben.

Der selbs seine begird regieret,
Dessen frumb und redlicher muth
Ist sein beste rüstung und hut;
Dessen gewissen triumfieret.

Welcher keines geschrays begehret,
Dem die Warheit die gröste kunst;
Den des Fürsten noch Pöfels gunst,
Weder hofnung noch forcht bethöret.

Der die Fuchsschwäntzer fort lasst gehen,
Und nicht speiset von seinem gut;
Und dessen fall oder armut
Kan seine hässer nicht erhöhen.

Der selbs nicht waist, wie übel schmürtzet
Des bösen lob, des frommen fluch;
Dem ein guter freund oder buch
Seine schadlose zeit verkürtzet.

Dessen gemüht sich vor nichts scheyhet,
Als allzeit berait für den Tod;
Der ernstlich früh und spaht zu Got
Mehr umb gnad, dan umb güter schreyhet.

Der mensch besorgt sich keines falles,
Sondern ist gantz frey, reich und gross,
Sein selbs Herr, ob Er wol Land-loss,
Und habend nichts hat Er doch alles.

Two other poems of this volume *may* also go back to English sources, but there is great uncertainty in both cases. Bohm compares *Amor betrogen* (No. 57) with Spenser, Epig. 3 (Globe edition, p. 586), but Fischer quotes Marot, Epig. 103 (ed. Jannet), and it is quite certain that Spenser translated Marot. The dialogue *Liebliches Gespräch von der Liebe, Myrta und Filidor* (No. 70) is based on either Drummond, *Pastoral Song,* or Jean Passerat, I. 141 (ed. Blanchemain).

The Second Book of *Oden und Gesänge* appeared in 1619. The first ode is addressed to the Princess Elizabeth and the tenth to Sir Henry Wotton[1]. The twelfth ode, *Brautlied Zu Ehren der Hochzeit Filanders und seiner Chloris* (No. 87), is based, according to Bohm, on Thomas Carew (1589–1639), *A Rapture. Die Lügin* (No. 104) is a poor rendering of Joshua Silvester (1563–1618), *The Soul's Errand,* and *Ulysses und Sirene* (No. 106) is an imitation of *Ulysses and the Siren,* by Samuel Daniel (1562–1619). This last parallel was first noticed by Herder.

The same year also saw the publication of another English

---

[1] Wotton spoke German fluently and was for several years the ambassador of James I at the court of the Elector Friedrich. He studied in the archives of the Hansa towns and collected material for a Life of Luther.

work by Weckherlin, viz. *A Panegyricke to the most honourable
and renowned Lord, The Lord Hays¹ Viscount of Doncaster His
Majesties of Great-Brittaine Ambassadour in Germanie Sung by
The Rhine Interpreted by George Rodolphe Weckherlin Secr. to
his High. of Wirtemberg...Printet at Stutgart by John-Wyrich
Rosslin.   Anno M.DCXIX.*

In 1616 Weckherlin had already married an English wife,
Elizabeth Raworth, and by 1622 he had left Stuttgart.   His first
letter from England is dated "April 3. 1624" and he was appointed
an Under-Secretary of State the same year.   From 1629–1632
he was secretary to the Earl of Dorchester and subsequently
(until 1640) to Coke.   He died in London in 1653.

The *Gaistliche und Weltliche Gedichte* first appeared at
Amsterdam in 1641, although the preface is dated "den letzten
Tag Herbstmonats 1639. an dem Königlichen Hofe in Engel-
land."   The following sonnet (No. 162 in Fischer's edition),
entitled *Traum*, is a paraphrase of Spenser, *The Ruines of
Time*, lines 491–504, as Bohm points out (p. 64).

> Ich sah in meinem schlaff ein bild gleich einem Got,
>   Auff einem reichen thron gantz prächtiglich erhaben,
>   In dessen dienst und schutz zugleich auss lust und noht
>   Sich die Torrechte leut stehts hauffen weiss begaben.
>
> Ich sah wie dieses bild dem wahren Got zu spot
>   Empfieng (zwar niemahl sat) gelübd, lob, opfergaben ;
>   Und gab auch wem es wolt das leben und den tod,
>   Und pflage sich mit raach und bossheit zuerlaben.
>
> Und ob der himmel schon offtmahl des bilds undanck
>   Zustrafen, seine stern versamlete mit wunder ;
>   So war doch des bilds stim noch lauter dan der dunder :
>
> Biss endlich, als sein stoltz war in dem höchsten schwanck,
>   Da schlug ein schneller plitz das schöne bild herunder,
>   Verkehrend seinen pracht in koht, würm und gestanck.

> I saw an Image, all of massie gold,
> Placed on high upon an Altare faire,
> That all, which did the same from farre beholde,
> Might worship it, and fall on lowest staire.
> Not that great Idoll might with this compaire,
> To which th'Assyrian Tyrant would have made
> The holie brethren falslie to have praid.

---

¹ James Hay; 1606, Baron; 1615, Lord Hay of Sawley; 1618, Viscount
Doncaster; subsequently first Earl of Carlisle.   Probably passed through Stuttgart in June, 1619, while on diplomatic service.

But th'Altare, on which this Image staid,
Was (O great pitie!) built of brickle clay,
That shortly the foundation decaid,
With showres of heaven and tempests worne away;
Then downe it fell, and low in ashes lay,
Scorned of everie one, which by it went;
That I, it seeing, dearlie did lament.

The volume also contains forty epigrams, five of which may with certainty be traced to Donne, one to Harrington, one to Sir Thomas More and four to Owen. Bohm suggests other more doubtful parallels. Further reference will be made to Weckherlin's epigrams in Chapter v. Bohm decides in favour of English sources for the sonnets, *Sie ist gantz lieblich und löblich* (No. 209) and *Schöne haar* (No. 219), but Fischer thinks Ronsard (i. 25, No. xlii) and Du Bellay, *L'Olive*, No. 10, more likely.

The final edition of the *Gaistliche und Weltliche Gedichte* (Amsterdam, 1648) contains little of interest for our purpose except 88 epigrams, of which nine or ten may be traced to Owen, one to Harrington and one to Sir Thomas More. In some cases it is almost impossible to discover the original.

On the whole, the influence of English literature on Weckherlin is not as strong as Bohm would have us believe. It is more prominent in the *Gaistliche und Weltliche Gedichte* than elsewhere, but always less important than that of French. It usually takes the form of the translation or paraphrase of a complete poem, whereas Weckherlin's wider knowledge of other literatures is proved by numerous quotations and more or less unconscious allusions. Still, he is the only German of his time in whose works any considerable influence of English literature can possibly be discovered.

CHAPTER III

SIDNEY'S "ARCADIA" IN GERMANY

THE popularity of pastoral poetry in Germany in the seventeenth century is chiefly due to the influence of Italian literature. Any attempt to trace its evolution would be beyond the scope of this volume. Suffice it to say that the principal classical models were Theocritus and Vergil, of whose idylls and eclogues the Italian pastoral of the sixteenth century is an expansion. The principal example of the non-dramatic type is the *Arcadia* (1504) of Sannazaro, the dramatic type being best represented by Tasso's *Aminta* (performed at Ferrara in 1573) and Guarini's *Pastor Fido* (1590). All these had a lasting influence.

The best known example of pastoral literature in England[1] is the *Arcadia* of Sir Philip Sidney. It betrays the influence not only of Sannazaro and Montemayor[2], but also of the great prose romance, *Amadis*, and of certain Greek sources, viz. the *Æthiopica* of Heliodorus, the *Leucippe and Clitophon* of Achilles Tatius and the *Chaireas and Calirrhoë* of Chariton[3]. Sidney began the *Arcadia* in 1580 on being banished from court by Elizabeth, after addressing to her a letter of remonstrance against her suspected policy of marrying the Duke of Anjou. The book was written for the entertainment of his sister, the Countess of Pembroke, with whom he was then living at Wilton House. It remained unfinished on his death in 1586, but was

---

[1] W. W. Greg: *Pastoral Poetry and Pastoral Drama*, 1906.
[2] Jorge de Montemayor, a Portuguese poet, author of the famous romance *Diana Enamorada* (1524).
[3] See K. Brunhuber: *Sir Philip Sidney's Arcadia und ihre Nachläufer*, 1903. Bibl. 107.

published in 1590. In the seventh edition (Dublin, 1621), wrongly called the fifth, appeared a "Supplement of a defect in the third part..." by Sir William Alexander, and the ninth edition (Dublin, 1627), wrongly called the sixth, contained a Sixth Book, by Richard Beling, which had been published separately in 1624. Further complete editions appeared in 1633, 1638, 1655, 1662 and 1674[1].

The popularity of the *Arcadia* was not confined to England. Two French translations appeared in 1624 and 1625, the first by a certain Baudouin, the second the joint work of "Vn Gentilhomme Francois" and a lady, Geneviefve Chappelain, the former translating the first two Books, the latter the last three[2]. As we shall see, it was largely owing to these translations that the work became known in Germany.

It must not be forgotten that Sidney himself had travelled widely on the continent. He was in Paris on the night of the massacre of St Bartholomew, August 24th, 1572. Thence he passed through Lorraine to Strassburg and Heidelberg, reaching Frankfort in September, where he stayed with Wechel, a printer, and made the acquaintance of Hubert Languet, the Reformer. They travelled in company until September, 1573, and met again a few weeks later in Vienna. Then Sidney visited Hungary and Italy, where he spent the winter. On the homeward journey he again spent some time with Languet, visited Frankfort, Heidelberg and Antwerp and returned to England in May, 1575. The next year, although he was only twenty-two, he was sent by Elizabeth as ambassador to console with the Emperor Rudolf II on the death of Maximilian II[3].

The *Arcadia* itself does not seem to have become known in Germany before about 1620. Opitz[4], in the dedication of *Die*

[1] *Arcadia* (ed. Baker), 1907. Bibl. 95.
[2] The entry in the British Museum Catalogue is as follows: "...vn Gentilhomme Francois (i.e. Geneviefve Chappelain)...." If this is meant to imply that Geneviefve Chappelain was a man, it is a mistake. The prefaces to the three parts clearly state that the translation is by two hands and also explain that the lady spent seven years in England in the suite of the Countess of Salisbury. Bibl. 96: *Larcadie De La Comtesse De Pembrok....*
[3] This is the mission referred to by Merian in his preface to the German translation of 1629. See p. 22.
[4] Martin Opitz, b. Bunzlau, 1597. Hailed by his contemporaries as the greatest poet of his own or any other age. Paul Fleming says, "Tasso, Petrarch, as well as the neo-latinists Bartos, Sidney, Sannazar, must give way when Opitz

2—2

Schäfferey Von der Nimfen Hercinie to Hans Ulrich Schaff-Gotch, mentions as writers of pastorals "Theocritus, Virgilius, Nemesianus, Calpurnius; Sannazar, Balthasar Castilion, Lorenzo Gambara, Ritter Sidney, d'Urfé and others." In the edition of 1645 (Amsterdam) this dedication is dated "Glatz zu Aussgang des Jahres 1622," but in the first edition (Breslau, 1630) the date is 1629[1]. The date 1622 in the later edition must therefore be a misprint. It is, however, quite certain that Opitz was familiar with the *Arcadia* long before 1629. Lemcke[2] says Sidney is mentioned in *Aristarchus*[3] but is apparently unaware that this is true only of the second edition (Strassburg, 1624). The first edition, published at Beuthen between the autumn of 1617 and the spring of 1618 (see Witkowski[3]), certainly contains a passage which includes the names of several writers of pastorals, but Sidney is not mentioned: "Cum Italia tot Petrarchas, Ariostos, Tassos; Gallia Marottos, Bartasios, Ronsardos & alios Poëtas praeclaros in dedecus nostri & exprobationem eduxerit: Belgae quoq; eadem virtute stimulati id ipsum tentaverint." In the edition of 1624, however, two additions appear: *Sannazarios* is added after *Tassos*, and *Anglia Sidneos* after *Ronsardos*. From this it is clear that Opitz became acquainted with the *Arcadia* between 1617 and 1624, probably while at Heidelberg in 1619.

Goedeke[4] cites the following sentence as occurring in the preface to the *Buch von der Deutschen Poeterei*: "Dess Edlen Herrn Sidney Arcadia macht die Engelländer fast Stolz mit jhrer Sprach." This seems to be a mistake. At any rate,

---

sings." At Marien-Magdalenen-Gymnasium, Breslau, 1614–7; at Schönaichianum, Beuthen, 1617. Then tutor to sons of Tobias Scultetus. Studied French, Dutch and Italian. At University of Frankfort o/O, 1618. In Heidelberg, 1619; tutor to sons of G. M. Lingelsheim (see p. 3). Met Janus Gebhard, Balthasar Venator, Jul. W. Zincgref, Caspar Barth, Heinr. Alb. Hamilton. Visited Strassburg and Tübingen. In Holland with Hamilton, 1620; met Heinsius. Then in Jütland; Lübeck and Silesia (1621); held post in Gymnasium at Weissenburg (1622); then in Liegnitz; met Buchner in Köthen (1625); then in Dresden, Silesia, Vienna; private secretary to Hannibal, Burgrave of Dohna; ennobled in 1628 (M. O. von Boberfeld); member of *Fruchtbr. Gesellsch.* (1630); on diplomatic journey to Paris, 1635; in Thorn and Danzig same year; died of plague at Danzig on August 20th, 1639.

[1] Bibl. 102. [2] Bibl. 47.
[3] Georg Witkowski: *Martin Opitzens Aristarchus...und Buch von der Deutschen Poeterei*, 1888. Bibl. 106.
[4] *Grundriss der deutschen Dichtung*, Vol. III. 1887[2]. Bibl. 36.

I failed to discover the passage either in Fellgibel's edition (Breslau, 1690 ?) or in Witkowski's reprint of the original of 1624[1]. Borinski's[2] theory that the treatise is largely based on Sidney's *Apologie for Poetry* (1589) is rejected by Witkowski on the ground that when Opitz borrows, the agreement is not merely one of ideas but of words, witness his use of Ronsard and Scaliger.

The next date of importance is 1629, when a German translation of the *Arcadia*, from the pen of a certain Valentinus Theocritus, was published by Matthaeus Merian at Frankfort. A portion of the lengthy title-page[3] runs as follows: "Arcadia of the Countess of Pembroke....Described at first in English by that noble, eloquent and celebrated English Earl and Knight, the late Sir Philip Sidney; afterwards translated by various famous persons into French; and now carefully and faithfully translated from both languages into our High German tongue by Valentinus Theocritus of Hirschberg...." This page is dated 1629, but there is also a secondary title-page dated 1630. The publisher's dedicatory epistle, portions of which I translate, is a typical specimen of its kind and begins thus:

"Der Durchleuchtigen/ Hochgebornen Fürstin und Frawen/ Frawen Sophien Leonora/ Geborner auss Churfürstlichem Stamme zu Sachsen/ Jülich/ Cleve/ vnd Bergen Hertzogin/ Landgräfin zu Düringen/ zu Meissen/ Burggräfin zu Magdeburg/ Vermählter Landgräfin zu Hessen/ Gräfin zu der Mark/ Ravenspurg/ Mörss/ Catzenelnbogen/ Dietz/ Ziegenhain vnd Nidda/ &c. Meiner Gnädigen Fürstin vnd Frawen...."

Merian then proceeds to discuss the merits of the *Arcadia* and its author. The translator is apparently of no importance.

"...When the present Heroic and extraordinarily ingenious, charming and elegant work of the late Sir Philip Sidney, a very noble knight of Great Britain, who wrote it in the English language and called it the *Arcadia of the Countess of Pembroke*, had already been several times translated by various great minds from the original, viz. English, into French, published in

---

[1] Bibl. 106.
[2] Karl Borinski: *Die Kunstlehre der Renaissance in Opitz' Buch von der deutschen Poeterei*. Munich, 1883.
[3] *Arcadia Der Gräffin von Pembrock...*, 1629. Bibl. 97.

many places and read by many with great pleasure, profit and delight, a few gentlemen of eminence and learning, well versed in such Poetical and historical inventions, recommended it to me so strongly and so often, with the assurance that its like had never been seen in any language, not to mention our own High German, that I finally allowed myself to be persuaded by their manifold exhortations, after obtaining the opinion of other equally qualified persons, to take upon myself the expense and trouble of having the same translated into our German tongue, adorned with exquisite copper-plates by my hand[1] and published for the benefit of our beloved Fatherland, in such a form, I hope, (now, thank God, brought to a happy conclusion) as to bear inspection and invite perusal.

"That this work, gracious Princess and Lady, contains nothing common or low, but that everything is very lofty and magnificent, yes, in a word, princely, we see at once from the Argument or Matter, which treats of pure, virtuous and constant love between very noble persons (although under the assumed names of shepherds), whose actions are entirely praiseworthy and admirable, or from the Countess, in whose honour the poet applied his pains and his energy, intending to publish his *Arcadia* under her exalted name, or finally from the Author himself, who was not only of very noble family and enjoyed great eminence, being of the line of the noble Earls of Warwick, who deserved well of the kingdom of England, but was also held in such esteem by Queen Elizabeth of pious memory, that he, Philip Sidney, notwithstanding his youth, filled the first and most distinguished position in the embassy which the noble Queen sent to His late Imperial Majesty, Rudolf the Second, and not only did he discharge his mission to the general satisfaction but also to the astonishment of many great lords, so that he was called a paragon of virtues and an example of a great genius. Hence it would in no wise become me to choose for this work an insignificant patron and protectress.... Frankfort, 1 September, 1629.
Matthaeus Merian."

---

[1] Merian forgets to mention that he appropriated most of the plates from the French edition of 1625 (Bibl. 96). They are 21 in number and were used again in the edition of 1638 (Bibl. 98).

This dedication closes with much sickly flattery and a further reference to the copper-plates, which Merian evidently regarded as the most important part of the work. The preface of the translator, who is not mentioned by Merian, is longer and more interesting. The following is a translation of the more important portions:

"Short Preface of the Translator to the kind reader.

"Dear Reader, on the completion of this work it seemed fit and proper to say a few words on several points, and I hope you will take everything in good part, for so it is meant. Know therefore, firstly, that it was by no means my own conceit which moved me to the translation of this Arcadian poem of the late, famous English knight Sidney, etc., nor any peculiar love of amorous adventures; but simply and solely a hearty liking for foreign languages, in which I have some little skill, which I did not wish to lose, but rather the more exercise in my hours of leisure from official duties by the translation of some elegant work.

"The generous and candid reader, therefore (for I cannot forbid Zoilus his sneers), will silently attribute the pains I have taken to no wantonness nor wicked trifling, but to the above-mentioned honourable motives. All the more so as this *Arcadia* is not a lewd or pernicious book, but on the contrary most ingenious, moral and edifying; in short, a book of such a nature that not only was its first Author, that noble and well-tried English Earl and Knight, the late Sir Philip Sidney, not ashamed of it, but he gave it the Countess of Pembroke's exalted name, and finally several distinguished knights and other noble persons in France ventured to translate this admirable work from the English original into their native tongue and, in addition, to dedicate the published copy to persons of rank. If, I say, those eminent persons were not ashamed of the work, and rightly so, for there is more good than evil to be found therein, much less then can I be justly reprimanded for this German version, translated from the English and the French...."

The translator then proceeds to apologize for the large number of foreign words in his version. He points out that it is the fashion, German being largely a mixture of French,

Spanish and Italian. Still, their insertion is to some extent intentional, as he wishes thereby to symbolize the prevailing confusion and disorder in the land. He fears he has not translated the various technical terms with sufficient accuracy, being a poor courtier and a worse soldier, lawyer, hunter or lover. Finally, he regrets the inadequacy of his poetical renderings.

"Fifthly, I must apologize for the German verses, for I am a bad poet[1]. They are indeed based on the French versions, and made as concise as possible while preserving the full meaning of the Author, although (even in the English and French) he is occasionally somewhat obscure and hard to understand. Let anyone who would find fault, himself try to translate verses from foreign languages into German, retaining the original number of syllables without mutilating the sense; I know he will agree with me that it is not so easy, and that I am therefore to be all the more readily excused for my bad rhymes. I have nowhere allowed myself so much license (except where it could not be otherwise), as to deserve a just reproach. I will therefore point out that no man can truthfully accuse me of being, with regard to this work, a Demagoras (which disgraceful charge was actually made against one of the French translators) or mischievous defacer of the form of this *Arcadia*, for the ingenious work remains entirely unmutilated, even if everything is not quite as elegantly expressed as by the Author in the English original, unless the sense has been distorted, a crime of which I know I am innocent. If any mistake has been made, it must have happened inadvertently and be in addition so unimportant that the kindly reader (with whom alone I have to deal) will indulgently excuse it...."

The book is not to be read as an amusement but as a lesson in the practice of virtue and the avoidance of vice.

"...The book does not aim at lewdness nor the corruption of the young but really at their encouragement in virtue and the honest entertainment of their mind; nor is there anything foul or unchaste therein, otherwise the publisher would certainly have put his money to a more useful purpose and I should never have translated the work. I hope the kind reader will believe

---

[1] As we shall see, this modesty is not out of place.

and trust me and receive Valentinus Theocritus into his hearty favour, whose identity, if perchance the insignificant person be known to him, I trust he will in friendly confidence keep to himself....

"Abtsberch in der Wawte 20 Jul. MDCXXIX."

Merian was apparently satisfied with the success of his venture, for in 1638 we find him busy with a second edition, revised, as we see from the title-page, by Martin Opitz von Boberfeld: *Arcadia of the Countess of Pembroke, written by Sir Philip Sidney in English, then translated into French, and from both for the first time into German by Valentinus Theocritus of Hirschberg; now revised and improved throughout, the poems and rhymes made quite different and translated by the noble M.O.V.B*[1].

There is no translator's preface to this edition, but Merian again waxes loquacious. Addressing himself to the same lady he repeats many of his former observations and adds:

"...Gracious Princess and Lady, as this *Arcadia* was originally dedicated by the Author himself, as already mentioned, to a noble Countess, and as I therefore eight years ago humbly addressed and dedicated to Your Highness this German translation, which received, I hope, Your Highness' satisfied acceptance, and as, when the first edition was exhausted, I had this *Arcadia* newly revised and improved by the noble M.O.V.B. and the poems altered and newly translated, as may be easily seen by comparison with the previous version, I have therefore, Gracious Princess and Lady, with due respect and humility again desired to solicit your former princely protection and favour and again dedicate and present this work to Your Highness, with the humble request that you will be graciously pleased to accept and remain, as hitherto, my gracious Princess and Lady...." (Then follow the usual pious wishes for the welfare of the lady and her family, and the date, "Frankfort, 1 Febr. 1638.")

We are now in a position to compare the two editions and examine the precise nature of Opitz' revision.

The translation of 1629 already contains Sir William Alexander's "Supplement of a defect in the third part," which first

---

[1] Bibl. 98.

appeared in the Dublin edition of 1621, but not Richard Beling's
Sixth Book, published separately at Dublin in 1624 and added
to the ninth edition (wrongly called the sixth) in 1627. Consequently the first German translation is based on either the
seventh English edition (Dublin, 1621) or the eighth (London,
1623), and of course, as V. Theocritus himself states, on a French
version.   The introductory and final notes to Sir William Alexander's "Supplement," which covers some twenty pages in
Baker's edition (1907) and includes one poem (*More dangerous
darts than death, love throws I spy*), are omitted.

The revised translation of 1638 contains the Sixth Book,
although Opitz apparently knew nothing of Richard Beling, as
is clear from the special title-page, which I here translate:

"The Sixth Book of the Countess of Pembroke's *Arcadia*;
written in English by Sir Philip Sidney, Earl and Knight, and
now for the first time put into German by an especial admirer
of the Arcadian inventions."

Opitz allowed the heading of Book V (Das Fünfft vnd letzte
Buch) to stand but omitted the concluding paragraph, in which
Sidney expresses the hope that others will continue the histories
of the different characters.   He is presumably responsible for
the short life of Sidney (two pages) at the end and for the note:
"Liese von jhm sonderlich Justum epist. II. Centur. ad Famil."

As regards the quality of the translations there is little
difference, if we leave the poems out of the question for the
moment.   Opitz' alterations are confined to minor corrections of
style or spelling, not always for the better, although the printer
may be largely responsible for the chaotic state of the latter.
For the sake of comparison the first paragraph of Book I is
quoted from the translation of 1629, together with the corrections made by Opitz in the edition of 1638.

"It was in the time that the earth begins to put on her new apparel
against the approach of her Lover, and that the Sun running a most even
course, becomes an indifferent arbiter between the night and the day,
when the hopeless Shepherd Strephon was come to the Sands, which lie
against the Island of Cithera; where viewing the place with a heavy kind
of delight, and sometimes casting his eyes to the Isleward, he called his
friendly Rival, the Pastor Claius unto him; and setting first down in his
darkned countenance a doleful Copy of what he would speak.   O my
Claius, said he, hither we are now come to pay the Rent, for which we
are so called unto by over-busie Remembrance, Remembrance, restless

Remembrance, which claims not only this duty of us, but for it will have us forget ourselves. I pray you, when we were amid our flock, and that of other Shepherds some were running after their sheep, strayed beyond their bounds; some delighting their eyes with seeing them nibble upon the short and sweet grass; some med'cining their sick Ewes; some setting a Bell for an Ensign of a sheepish squadron; some with more leisure inventing new games of exercising their bodies, and sporting their wits; did Remembrance grant us any Holy-day, either for pastime or Devotion? nay either for necessary food or natural rest? but that still it forced our thoughts to work upon this place, where we last (alas that the word Last should so long last) did grace our eyes upon her ever-flourishing beauty, did it not still cry within us? Ah you base minded Wretches! are your thoughts so deeply bemired in the trade of ordinary worldlings, as for respect of gain some paltry Wooll may yield you, to let so much time pass without knowing perfectly her estate, especially in so troublesom a season? to leave that shore unsaluted from whence you may see to the Island where she dwelleth? to leave those steps unkissed wherein Urania printed the farewel of all beauty? Well then, Remembrance commande, we obeyed, and here we find, that as our remembrance came ever cloathed unto us in the form of this place, so this place gives new heat to the feaver of our languishing remembrance. Yonder, my Claius, Urania lighted, her very Horse (methought) bewailed to be so disburdened: and as for thee, poor Claius, when thou went'st to help her down, I saw reverence and desire so divide thee, that thou didst at one instant both blush and quake, and instead of bearing her, wert ready to fall down thy self. There she sate, vouchsafing my cloak (then most gorgeous) under her: at yonder rising of the ground she turned her self, looking back towards her wonted abode, and because of her parting, bearing much sorrow in her eyes, the lightsomness whereof had yet so natural a cheerfulness, as it made even sorrow seem to smile; at that turning she spake to us all, opening the cherry of her lips, and Lord how greedily mine ears did feed upon the sweet words she uttered! And here she laid her hand over thine eyes, when she saw the tears springing in them, as if she would conceal them from other, and yet her self feel some of thy sorrow. But wo is me, yonder, yonder, did she put her foot into the Boat, at that instant, as it were dividing her heavenly beauty, between the Earth and the Sea."

1629. Der Erdboden begundte nunmehr ein frische Zierd anzunemmen/
1638.   eine   Zier   anzunehmen/
wegen herbey nahung seines liebsten Buhlen / vnd gab die Sonn ein
                                        und die Sonn gab einen
vnparteyischen Schiedsmann zwischen Tag vnd Nacht / als der trostlose
Schäfer Strephon anlangt bey dem sandigen Meerufer / so stracks gegen
Schäffer   bey dem sandigen Meerufer / so stracks gegen der Insul
der Insul Cythera vber gelegen. Demnach er aber an solchem Ort sich
Cythera vber gelegen anlangete.   Orte
vmgesehen / auch seine Augen gegen gedachter Insul mit frölicher gestalt
vmbgesehen   Gestalt
schiessen lassen / ruffet er seinem lieben Gesellen / vnd liess ihn erstlich
           ruffete
in   seinem Angesicht lesen den Unmuth / welchen er in Hertzen hatte /
auss   Angesichte
darauff wider jn sagend: Sihe da / mein liebster Claius, wir seyn nunmehr
sagete darauff wider ihn: Clajus
hieher kommen zu bezahlen vnd ausszurichten den Tribut / welchen wir
            vnnd

vnserer Erinnerung schuldig seyn! Ach / verdriessliche Erinnerung / die
nicht allein diese Pflicht von vns erfordert / sondern noch darzu haben
wil / dass wir drüber vnser selbsten vergessen sollen! Ich bitte dich / als
will   vnserer
wir mitten vnter vnseren Herden / theils jhren verjrrten vnd zerstreuwten
                              den
Schafen nachlieffen; theils jren hertzlichen Lusten hatten / dieselbige im
                                          hertzliche Lust
grünen Grass hüpffen vnd springen zu sehen; etliche dero Kranckheiten
       Grase
vnd Uffstossung heilsame Artzney beybrachten; andere dem Widder in
vnnd
der Herd ein Schelle an Halss henckten / zum Zeichen dess gesampten
          Herde eine Schelle zum Zeichen dess gesampten wolletragenden Hauffens /
wollechten Hauffens: Widerumb andere mit mehrer muss vnd besserer
an den Halss henckten;   Musse
Weil tausendterley kurtzweilige neuwe Spiel erdachten / so wol zur vbung
Weile   anmutige   newe   Ubung
der Leiber / als ergetzung jhres Gemühts: Under währendem solchem
                 Ergetzung dess Gemühtes
allem (sag ich) hat vns auch jemals diese schmertzliche Erinnerung / ein
einiges Stündlein zu vnserer Zeitvertreibung / oder ein einigen Augenblick
                                                         einen
zu vnserer Ruhe vergönnet / darinnen sie nit auffs wenigst vnsere
Gedancken genötiget hette täglich zu besuchen diesen Orth / an welchem
                                    zubesuchen
vnsere Augen das letztemal (O / dass doch diss Wort das letztemal mein
                                                         letzte mal
letztes were!) so selig gewesen seyn / zu betrachten die schneeweisse
Lilien ihres holdseligen Angesichts? Ach trawrige / ach vnruhige Erinnerung! welche vns nachmalen ohn vnderlass in den Ohren schreyet; Jr
                                                         ! Ihr
Unglückselige! Seyn denn alle euwere Gedancken so gar in schlechten
                                  ewere
vnnd heillosen Dingen verwickelt vnd vertiefft / dass ihr vmb spöttlichen
vnd
Gewinns willen / betreffend ein kleines bisslein Wollen / so viel guter zeit
                                                                      Zeit
verfliessen lasset / vnd darinnen nicht mit mehrerer Sorgfältigkeit nach-
                        vnnd
forschet / wohin sie eigentlich kommen seye? Habt jr auch ein so
              eygentlich   ihr
verzagtes Hertz / dass jr hie dörfft fürbey passiren / ohne begrüssung
                                                         Begrüssung
dess lieblichen vnd schönen Gestads / von welchem auss man ferner
betrachten kan die Insul so diesen vberköstlichen Schatz in verwahrung
                        /   Verwahrung
hält? vnnd ohne küssung der Fussstapfen warinnen die schöne Vrania
        vnd   Küssung
gestanden / damals / als sie von diesen orten jren Vrlaub nam? Sihe / diss
                                      Orthen
commandirte vns vnser erinnerung / vnnd wir haben ihr folg geleistet.
befahl   Erinnerung   folge
Befinden aber nun mehr / dass gleich wie vnns Vrania an diesem so
                                      vns
gestaltem orth tägliche Gesellschafft gehalten / also verdoppelt desselbigen
          Orte   gelaystet

betrachtung in vnserem krancken vnd matten Gedächtnuss / die brennende
Betrachtung
Hitz seines Fiebers. Dorten war es / mein lieber Claius, da Vrania
Hitze
abstiege / vnd es das gäntzliche Ansehen hatte / als ob auch ihr
vnvernünfftiges Pferdt seufftzet vnnd trawerte / sich sehend einer so
　　　　　　　　　　 seuffzete vnd
köstlichen Bürde entladen seyn. Dich aber betreffend / arbeitseliger
　　　　　　　　　　　　 in dem er sich sahe
Claius! als du jhr woltest herunter helffen / trieben dich die Ehrerbietung
Clajus
vnnd Begierdt dermassen / dass ich dich zu einer zeit sahe zittern vnnd
　　 Begierde　　　　　　　　　　　　　　 Zeit　　　　　　 vn̄
Schamroth werden. Ja an statt dass du sie halten soltest / fielest du
bey nahe selbsten zu boden. Hie war es / da sie auff mein Mantel sasse
beynahe
(welcher sich sehr gut vnd ruhmwürdig bedaucht / jhren ein solchen
　　　　　　　　　　　　　　　　 bedauchte　 jhr　 einen
Dienst zu erweisen) vnnd von dannen jhr Gesicht hin vnd wider wandte /
　　　　　　　　 vnd　　　　　　　　　　　　　 vnnd wieder
noch einmal zu beschauwen den orth jhrer Wohnung / welchen sie
　　 einmahl　　　　　　　 Orth
verlassen solte. Ob nun wol jhre äuglein offenbarlich bezeugten / dass
　　　　　　　　　　　 äuglein
sie wegen solches Abschiedes hefftig bekümmert / so erschien nichts desto
weniger dero Klarheit mit solchem vnnachlässlichem hellen Glantz / dass
　　　　　　　　　　　　　　 (　　　　)
sichs ansehen liess / als wolten sie dem jenigen Vnmuth selbsten / der
auss jhrem Angesicht zu verspühren war / ein sonderbare Gratien vnd
　　　　　　　　　　　　　　　　　　　　　　　　　　　　 vnnd
Lieblikeit geben. Gleich damit öffnet sie jhre schöne Corallenfarbe
Leiblikeit　　　　　　　　　　　　　　　　　　　 Corallenfarbene
Lefftzlein / vmb mit vns zu reden. Ach jr Götter! was holdseliger
Lippen　　(　)　　　　　　　　　　 jhr
Süssigkeit haben damals meine Ohren vernommen? Sihe da noch den
Ort / da sie jhre zarte Händlein auff deine in Thränen fast versunckene
Orth　　　　　　　　 Hände
Augen legt / eben als ob sie dieselbige vor andern verbergen wolte / aber
　　 legte　　 alss　　　　　　　　　　　　　　　　　　　　　　 ;
nichts desto minder jhres theils ein hertzliche Begierd hette deines
　　　　　　　　　　　　　　　 eine　　　　 Begier　 hatte
bittern Schmertzens theilhafftig zuseyn. Etwas weiters hievon / O
Vnglück! etwas weiters hindan / sag ich / setzt sie jhren Fuss ins Schiff /
　　　　　　　　　　　　　　　　 setzte
sampt were sie willens jhre vortreffliche Schönheit / mit Wasser vnd
Land / Meer vnd Erdboden gleichmässig zu theilen[1].
Lande

---

[1] The following is a portion of the same passage from the French translation of 1625. See Bibl. 96.

"La Terre commençoit à prendre sa nouvelle parure pour l'approche de son Amant, & le Soleil estoit indifferend Arbitre entre la nuit & le iour. Quand Strephon ce berger desesperé vint sur les sables qui regardēt l'isle de Cithere, ou courāt ce lieu de ses yeux, & les jettāt vers l'isle auec vne espece de joye il appella son cher riual, & luy faisant premierement lire en sa face le mescontentement qu'il auoit: cher Claius (luy dit il) nous voicy donc arriués pour payer la rente que nous deuons à nostre resouuenir. Helas! fascheux resouuenir, qui n'exige pas seulemēt ce deuuoir de nous, mais qui veut encor nous faire oublier nous mesmes. Ie vous prie, lors qu'au milieu de nos troupeaux

We are now in a position to discuss the question of authorship. Who was Valentinus Theocritus[1]? He tells us himself in his preface of 1629 that he writes under an assumed name. The town "Hirschberg" seems to imply that he was a Silesian. So was Opitz. For this reason, apparently, most scholars have assumed that Theocritus and Opitz are the same. Goedeke[2] includes the translation of 1629 in his list of Opitz' works. Carl Vogt[3], in his article on Schupp, says, "In 1629 Opitz had published a German version of Sir Philip Sidney's *Arcadia*." Brie[4] and Max Koch[5] make the same assumption. The catalogue of the Berlin University Library has the entry: "Theocritus, Valentinus. Pseud. s. Opitz." In the catalogue of the British Museum Library the book is quoted under "Sidney," with "Martin Opitz" in parenthesis after "Valentinus Theocritus." Other writers, e.g. Koberstein[6], Ernst Martin[7], assume that the translations are by two hands. Borinski[8] is somewhat more explicit. He states that Opitz was required by the Fruchtbringende Gesellschaft to give a formal assurance that the translation had been revised by him.

One fact which seems to indicate that this second view is correct is the appearance of both "Valentinus Theocritus" and "M.O.V.B." (i.e. Martin Opitz von Boberfeld) on the title-page of 1638, but an examination of the poems places the matter beyond dispute. The difference between the prose specimens already quoted is too slight to enable us to say whether Opitz was revising his own work or that of another man, but this is not the case with the poems. The difference is one of quality

les vns couroient apres leurs brebis esgarees : que les autres prenoient leur plaisir à les voir sauteler sur l'herbe, les autres à mediciner leurs maladies, les autres à mettre vne clochette au col du maistre belier, comme pour le signal de l'escadron laineux ; & les autres auec plus de loisir inuētoient mille jeux nouueaux pour exercer leurs corps, & recréer leurs esprits : Pendāt tout cela, dis ie, ce triste resouuenir nous a-t'-il jamais permis vne seule heure pour nostre passetemps, ny aucun moment pour prēdre nostre repos ?..."

[1] I cannot understand why Brunhuber (Bibl. 107) refers to him as Theocritus Valentinus.

[2] Bibl. 36.

[3] Carl Vogt: *Johann Balthasar Schupp...*, 1910. Euph. 17, p. 484. Bibl. 22 and 185.

[4] Friedrich Brie: *Das Volksbuch vom "gehörnten Siegfried" und Sidney's "Arcadia,"* 1908. Bibl. 108.

[5] Vogt und Koch: *Geschichte der deutschen Literatur*, II. p. 12, 1904. Bibl. 39.

[6] Bibl. 35.   [7] Bibl. 37.   [8] Bibl. 50.

and not of quantity, for both translators make precisely the same omissions, as will be seen from the following scheme:

		No. of poems in original	No. translated by V. Theocritus	No. translated by Opitz
Book	I.	5 and 5 in Eclogue	5 and 5	5 and 5
„	II.	16 and 10 in Eclogue	12 „ 8	12 „ 8

(There is a gap in both translations, three long poems and a short one of six very difficult lines being omitted. In the Eclogue the dialogue between Philisides and Echo is mentioned but not translated, and Zelmane's second song, "Reason, tell me thy mind, if here be reason," is omitted.)

„	III.	27 and 6	25 and 6	25 and 6
„	IV.	1 and 3	1 „ 3	1 „ 3
„	V.	1	1	1
„	VI.	1 „ 4		1 „ 4

Single stanzas of two or four lines have not been included in the above scheme.

I now proceed to give a few specimens, with the object of proving that Valentinus Theocritus and Martin Opitz are two entirely different persons. The first is a short poem from Book I.

The Shepherds' Brawl.

We love and have our love rewarded.
We love, and are no whit regarded.
We find most sweet affection's snare.
That sweet, but sour, despairful care.
Who can despair, whom hope doth bear?
And who can hope that feels despair?
As without breath no pipe doth move,
No music kindly without love.

This is neatly rendered by Opitz (1638):

Wir lieben, und nicht unvergolten.
Wir lieben, doch nicht ungescholten.
Sehr süsse sind der liebe Stricke.
Zwar süsse, doch nicht sonder Tücke.
Wer doch verzagt den Hoffnung nähret?
Wer hofft weil die Verzagung wehret?
Durch blasen muss man pfeiffen vben:
Die Music lebet auch durch lieben.

Are we to believe that Opitz is also the author of the following appalling doggerel?

Wenn man liebt recht trewlich
Thuts AMOR stets remunerirn
Wir glauben festiglich
Ein blosser Blick kan kein curirn

AMORIS Reytzung macht
　　Die Augen Lusts vnd Frewden voll.
Die Seel fühlt Tag und Nacht
　　Dass daher rührend leiden woll
Allzeit man haben soll
　　Im lieben ein gute Speranz
Hoffnung dient uns nicht woll /
　　Venus hat zur Hülff kein Apparenz.
Gleich wie ein Sackpfeiffen man sicht /
Unauffgeblasen lautten nicht /
　　Und ohne Wind all Nutzn verliern :
Also kein Music die man vbt /
　　Kan jhr Gesang recht animirn,
Wann Amor seine Zierd nicht gibt.
(V. THEOCRITUS, 1629.)

It will be remembered that Valentinus Theocritus himself recognized the inadequacy of his poetical translations and stated, moreover, that they were based on the French versions. To make this clear I quote the poem in its French form of 1625 :

Dialogue des Bergers.

En aymant loyaument,
Amour tous les iours nous guerdonne,
Nous croyons fermement,
Qu'vn regard ne guarit personne.
Les dous appas d'Amour,
Sont agreables à la veuë
L'ame sent nuict et iour,
Leur mal qui vient à l'impourueue.
Il faut toujours auoir
En son amour de l'esperance,
Mais que nous sert l'espoir,
Quand on n'y veoid nulle apparence.
Ainsi que l'on veoid la Musette,
Faute d'haleine estre imparfaitte,
Et ne pouvoir former les sons :
La musique aussi quoy qu'on face,
Ne peut animer ses chansons,
Si l'amour ne luy sert de grace.
(By "Vn Gentil-homme Francois.")

This single example should suffice, but the following specimen from Book III is even more ludicrous. I again quote the French of 1625 for the sake of comparison.

Beauty hath force to catch the human sight ;
Sight doth bewitch the fancy evil awaked,
Fancy we feel includes all passion's might
Passion rebell'd oft reason's strength hath shaked.

No wonder then, though sight my sight did taint,
And though thereby my fancy was infected,
  Though, yoked so, my mind with sickness faint,
Had reason's weight for passion's ease rejected.

But now the fit is past; and time hath giv'n
Leisure to weigh what due desert requireth.
All thoughts so sprung, are from their dwelling driv'n,
And wisdom to his wonted seat aspireth;
  Crying in me: eye-hopes deceitful prove;
  Things rightly priz'd: love is the band of love.

Opitz (1638):

Wenn Schönheit nur auss zweyen Augen blicket /
Und sich dadurch in Hertz vnd Sinnen dringt /
Verursacht sie dass alles missgelingt
  Was die Vernunfft jhr gleich entgegen schicket.
Es wirdt Gehirn vnd Sinn darvon verstricket /
Der ferner nun den Willen nicht mehr zwingt /
Der vbersteigt / vnd auss dem Schrancken springt /
  Und alles Ziehl der Weissheit vnterdrucket.

Mich haben auch zwo Sonnen so verletzt /
Dass ich verstand gar weit hindan gesetzt /
  Und einig mich bemühe mit beschwerden.
Doch ehr' ich auch die Ursach meiner pein /
Und grabe diss in meinem Hertzen ein /
  Durch lieben pflegt man auch geliebt zu werden.

V. Theocritus (1629):

Die Schönheit einer jungen Damen /
Durch vnzehliche Blick voll Flammen
  Kan dess Buhlers Augen wol blendn:
Wardurch die Gedancken also bald /
Auch werden offendirt mit Gwalt /
  Dann sie keins wegs widerstehn köndn

Ferrner solche das Hirn turbirn /
Thun gar tyrannisch drinn regirn /
  Wollen zähmen die Passion.
Doch endlich diese Schmaichlerin
Macht sich der Vernunfft Meisterin /
  Vberwindt die Affection.

Mir han mein Gsicht zwo Sonnen klar
Mit jhren Strahlen verletzet gar;
  Vnd mein Gedancken inficirt.
Ich sih / dass mein Vernunfft sich breit
Gibt vnter den Gwalt der Schönheit
  Ist von Amor gar disarmirt.

Aber ich erkenn die Meritn
Meinr schönen vnd lieben Caritn,
  Die mir allein den Tag gebihrt.
Tieff hab ich mir ins Hertzen Schrein /
Meinr Flamm Secret gegraben ein /
  Dass Lieb durch Lieb gewonnen wirt.

Geneviefve Chappelain (1625):

Vers de Zelmane.

La beauté d'vne jeune Dame,
Par mille traits tous pleins de flame
Peut charmer les yeux d'vn amant,
Et puis aussi-tost les pensees
Par leurs charmes sont offencees,
Sans resister aucunement.

Les pensers brouillent la ceruelle,
Et d'vne maistrise cruelle,
Veulent dompter nos passions,
Puis les passions flateresses
De la raison sont les maitresses,
Pour vaincre nos affections.

Deux beaux Soleils a l'impourueuë,
De leurs rays ont blessé ma veuë,
Mon penser en est infecté,
Et ie voy ma raison charmee
Se rendre toute desarmee
Sous ce pouuoir de la beauté.

Mais ie recognois le merite
De ma belle et chere Carite,
Qui seule me donne le jour:
Et i'ay bien graué dans mon ame
Ce rare secret de ma flame,
Qu'amour se gaigne par amour.

If we remember that in 1624 Opitz had already published his *Teutsche Poëmata* and *Buch von der Deutschen Poeterei* and was crowned with laurel the next year by Ferdinand II at Vienna, it is ridiculous to imagine him capable of the above versions of 1629. Besides, why should he wish to conceal his identity? He was not ashamed to publish a translation of Barclay's *Argenis* under his own name in 1626. But further argument is unnecessary. The ludicrous contrast between the two German versions proves beyond all doubt that Valentinus Theocritus and Martin Opitz are two entirely different persons. Who the former really was we may perhaps never discover. The first part of the name sounds genuine; the second is of course that of the Greek pastoral poet. It may also be a literal translation of some German name, e.g. Gottscheid. A careful examination of the records of Hirschberg—if such exist—might solve the question[1].

---

[1] Herdegen, in his *Historische Nachricht...*, 1744 (Bibl. 43), attributes the translation to Merian himself (Kap. I. p. 5): "Es ist A 1629 von Matth. Merian /

The popularity of the *Arcadia* in its revised German form is proved by the fact that it was reprinted at Amsterdam in 1640 and 1659 and at Leyden in 1642 and 1646[1]. Throughout the century I find only one uncomplimentary reference. That sturdy pedagogue, Johann Balthasar Schupp, observes ironically in his *Orator Ineptus* (1638)[2]: "...To make your ordinary speech superior to that of the common people you can always mix with it the embellishments and inventions of poets, and other pompous words from the *Amadis* or the *Arcadia of the Countess of Pembroke.*"

In 1644 an event took place in which the *Arcadia* played no small part. This was the establishment of an important Language Society, the Pegnesischer Blumenorden, at Nuremberg, where it still flourishes. According to Herdegen[3], the occasion of the foundation of the society was a marriage festival at Nuremberg. Georg Philipp Harsdoerfer and Johann Klai were asked to compose poems for the occasion and a wreath of flowers was promised to the author of the best. The result of their efforts was a joint-poem, *Pegnesisches Schäfergedicht in den Berinorgischen* (i.e. Noribergischen) *Gefilden, angestimmt von Strephon und Claius.* Neither Harsdoerfer nor Klai would have the garland but, taking each one flower as an emblem, they dedicated it to a society of poets they determined then and there to found. In the preface to the poem Harsdoerfer mentions Sidney in company with Theocritus, Vergil, Ronsard, Tasso, Lope de Vega, Opitz and Fleming. Birken[4] quotes this passage in his *Pegnesis* (1673) and adds that Harsdoerfer and Klai took their names, Strephon and Claius, from the *Arcadia.*

des berühmten Engländers Herrn Philipp Sidney Arcadia...in teutscher Sprach übersetzet/...worden." This may be mere carelessness. At any rate I can find no evidence to support the statement. I have had no opportunity of consulting Burckhard-Werthemann's article on Merian (see Appendix C).
[1] Bibl. 99 and 100.
[2] Translated from the Latin as *Der ungeschickte Redner* by Balthasar Kindermann in 1659. Contained in Bibl. 178. See also Carl Vogt, Bibl. 185, and W. W. Zschau, Bibl. 184.
[3] Bibl. 43.
[4] Sigmund von Birken (Betulius): *Pegnesis...*, 1673. Bibl. 104. See also his *Teutsche...Dichtkunst...*, 1679. Bibl. 105. Birken, son of an evangelical preacher, Daniel Betulius, was born at Wildenstein bei Eger on May 5th, 1626. He studied law and theology at Jena. Elected member of Pegnitzorden, 1645 (Floridan). Ennobled in 1655 and changed his name to "von Birken." Died June 12th, 1681, at Nuremberg.

Throughout the century the *Arcadia* was always regarded as one of the masterpieces of pastoral literature. Harsdoerfer devotes some space to the subject in the second part of his *Poetischer Trichter* (1648), a manual of poetry in twelve lessons(!). In the last lesson, p. 13, he observes: "As for the names of these persons (i.e. characters in pastoral literature) they are partly taken from foreign languages, from the *Arcadia, Diana, Astrea, Ariana,* &c., partly invented in imitation of old German names....The names ought to indicate the qualities of the persons, and some art, virtue or science is often implied. Hence Strephon's love in the *Arcadia of the Countess of Pembroke* is called Urania, which means the contemplation of heavenly things[1]." David Schirmer, in the dedicatory epistle to his *Poetische Rosengepüsche*, 1657 (first edition 1650), declares that Germany can now boast a band of poets, e.g. Werder, Opitz, Buchner, Dach, Fleming and others, who are in no way inferior to the greatest poets of other countries. He gives a long list but mentions only one Englishman—Sidney[2]. I have already quoted from Birken's *Pegnesis*. In the dedication to his *Teutsche Rede-Bind- und Dichtkunst* (1679) the same author discusses pastoral poetry with particular reference to the *Arcadia* of Sidney and Lope de Vega and the *Diana* of Montemayor[3]. There is another reference to Sidney's novel as a model of its kind in Chapter XI. K. H. Viebing says (1680): "It is an art to present princes and noblemen in the guise of shepherds, and the noble Sir Philip Sidney, in his incomparable *Arcadia*, has produced a masterpiece[4]."

So much for the popularity of the *Arcadia* itself in Germany. There still remains something to say about its influence on German literature.

[1] Bibl. 103.   [2] Bibl. 145.

[3] Bibl. 105. In the preface to the same work Birken gives a list of famous poets, among whom he includes an Englishwoman, Jane Weston. Her Latin poems were published at Prague with the title: "Parthenicon Elisabethae Ioannae Westoniae, Virginis nobilissimae, poëtriae florentissimae, linguarum plurimarum peritissimae, Liber I. operá ac studio G. Mart. à Baldhoven, Sil. collectus; & nunc denuò amicis desiderantibus communicatus. Pragae, Typis Pauli Sessij." There is no date, but the copy in the Göttingen University Library (P lat. rec. II 6352) has the following MS note opposite the title-page: "Elisabeth Johanna, Vxor Johannis Leonis, in Aula Imp[ii] Agentis & ex familia Westoniorum Angla. Pragae 16 Augusti Ao 1610."

[4] Quoted by Max von Waldberg in *Die deutsche Renaissancelyrik*, 1888. Bibl. 181.

Brie[1] points out that the duel between the two cowards in the chapbook *Vom gehörnten Siegfried* is an almost exact repetition of that between Dametas and Clintas in the third book of the *Arcadia*.   In both books the episode is very loosely connected with the plot, serving in the original to amuse Basilius and Philoclea, in the Volksbuch as a sort of entertainment at Siegfried's wedding.   Brie quotes parallel passages which show, sentence for sentence, an almost perfect agreement both in incident and expression.   Von Bloedau[2] discovers another parallel in *Simplicissimus* (1668), II. 25.   Simplicius, disguised as a girl, is in the employ of a cavalry captain's wife and is pursued with the attentions of both his mistress, who penetrates the disguise, and of his master, who does not.   Similarly in the *Arcadia*, both the old king, Basilius, and his queen, Gynecia, make love to the youth Pirocles, who is disguised as an Amazon and has taken the name of Zelmane.   The same writer also thinks that the presence of songs and eclogues in Philipp von Zesen's *Adriatische Rosamunde* (1645) betrays the influence of Sidney.   Finally Brunhuber[3] mentions an Italian opera, *Il Rè Pastore, overo: Il Basilio in Arcadia. Drama per musica.* 1691 *da Flaminio Parisetti. Wolffenbüttel. 3 Acte. Musica del Sig^re Gio. Battista Alveri.*   The Italian libretto was translated into German by a certain F. C. Bressand, who lived at the court of Duke Ulrich of Brunswick.   The music for this German text was written by Reinhard Keiser (1673–1739) and the opera was published at Hamburg as *Der konigliche Schäfer oder Basilius in Arcadien in einer Opera.   Auf dem hamburgischen Schauplatze vorgestellt im Jahre· 1694.   Hamburg, gedruckt bey Conrad Neumann, Hochweisen Raths Buchdrucker.*

[1] Bibl. 108.
[2] Carl August von Bloedau: *Grimmelshausens Simplicissimus und seine Vorgänger*, 1908. Bibl. 138.
[3] K. Brunhuber. Bibl. 107.

CHAPTER IV

THE LATIN NOVEL

As Latin was the international language of the seventeenth century, books written in that tongue had a far better chance of becoming known throughout Europe than those written in English or German. Indeed, some English authors, e.g. Bacon, might have remained unknown on the continent for years but for the Latin editions of their works.

Of the books originally written in Latin, three novels call for especial attention, viz. More's *Utopia*, Hall's *Mundus alter et idem* and Barclay's *Argenis*.

(a) Sir Thomas More's *Utopia*.

The first edition of the *Utopia* appeared at Louvain in 1516, and others followed at Paris, Basel and Vienna during the author's lifetime. Ralph Robinson's English translation was published in 1551, but by this date a French, an Italian, and a German version, the latter by Claudius Cantiuncula (Basel, 1524), were already in existence. The Latin text was again published in 1601 at Frankfort, and in 1613 at Hanau, the latter edition being a simple reprint of the former[1]. Both contain prefatory epistles by Erasmus, Budaeus, Hieronymus Buslidius and Petrus Aegidius (i.e. Peter Giles) and commendatory verses by Gerardus Noviomagus and Cornelius Graphaeus. A complete edition of More's works, with extracts from Stapleton's *Life* and several epistles of Erasmus, was published at Frankfort and Leipzig in 1689, the contents being as follows[2]:

---

[1] *Vtopia....* Bibl. 109, 110.   [2] *Opera omnia....* Bibl. 113.

I. Vita & obitus Thomae Mori e Thomae Stapletoni Tribus Thomis, Duaci Anno MDCLXXXIX.
II. Doctorum virorum varia epigrammata in Laudem & Mortem Thomae Mori.
III. Historia Richardi Regis Angliae ejus nominis Tertii....
IV. Thomae Mori Responsio ad convitia Martini Lutheri....
V. Thomae Mori Expositio Passionis Christi....
VI. Quod pro Fide mors fugienda non sit....
VII. Precatio ex Psalmis....
VIII. Thomae Mori Utopia, sive de optimo Reipublicae Statu Libri Duo.
IX. Thomae Mori Poemata....
X. Thomae Mori Dialogi Lucianei e Graecis in Latinum Sermonem conversi....
XI. Thomae Mori Epistolae....
XII. Erasmi Epistolae ad Morum.
XIII. Erasmi Epistola ad Huttenium de vita Mori.

Another German translation appeared at Leipzig in 1612, and this was followed the next year by *Mundus alter et idem*, with the secondary title *Utopiae Pars II*. Both versions are by the same hand, but the translator disguises his name in Utopian hieroglyphics which have hitherto not been definitely interpreted[1]. The volume contains portraits of More[2] and Erasmus, and the first part, i.e. the *Utopia* proper, begins with the translator's preface, of which I translate a portion:

"Almost a hundred years have passed since that great and noble man, Thomas Morus, formerly Royal Counsellor and Chancellor in England, wrote this careful account of the new island of Utopia,—a book which gave great pleasure to almost all the learned and upright men of his day who saw it and was hailed by the majority of them with such applause and jubilation that shortly afterwards the great Erasmus of Rotterdam was compelled to have the work printed, and so it was published, on his recommendation, by Johann Frobenius at Basel in 1517[3]. What Erasmus thought of this treatise may easily be gathered from the title he prefixed to it, which runs: *De optimo Reip. statu, deq; nova Insula Vtopia, libellus vere aureus, nec minus salutaris, quam festivus, &c.* That famous man, Guilielmus Budaeus,...likewise praised this work very highly in an epistle which has been printed with it.... Other eminent men as well have been loud in their praise, e.g. Gerhardus Noviomagus, Petrus Aegidius, Hieronymus Buslidius, Cornelius Graphaeus, Johannes Bodinus and many others whose names it would be unnecessary and tedious to quote here. That this book was popular with foreign nations may be easily inferred from the fact that it was gradually translated into various languages, and so the famous jurist, Claudius Cantiuncula, thought it worthy of being translated into German. For these reasons I was recently moved, for the reader's sake, to undertake such a version and to devote to it those hours which others spend in walking, play or sleep.... 1. Januar Anno 1612."

[1] Bibl. 111.
[2] More's portrait is missing from the copy in the Königlich-Preussische Bibliothek, Berlin.
[3] This is an error; the date should be 1518.

After the index to the sixteen chapters (the original is divided into two books) comes a verse of four lines in the Utopian language, but Latin characters, followed by Latin and German translations. There is also a diagram with the complete Utopian alphabet and the same verse written in these characters, although one word in the first line is incorrectly printed and the first half of the last line omitted. A comparison of this key with the translator's pseudonym gives the following unsatisfactory result:

SMDYGMW(?) IROHDRH
.MW(?) ISODM

Baumgarten[1] apparently gave up the problem at this point. He remarks: "On both title-pages (i.e. *Utopia*, 1612, and *Mundus...* 1613), before the place of publication, are two lines of Utopian letters which should stand for the translator's name. They are, indeed, taken from the alphabet given by More, but quite at random, for More's key gives no possible name, but unpronounceable words." Flögel[2] mentions the unknown characters but does not attempt a solution. If Baumgarten had examined the title-page of *Mundus...* more carefully, he would have found that the characters differ somewhat from those on the title-page of *Utopia*, although the number is the same in both cases. In the case of *Mundus...* the key gives a fairly intelligible solution, viz.:

GREGORIUM, HUEMU
MER(?) UIUM.

The fact is the characters were printed backwards in the *Utopia* of 1612, and the page must be held up to the light before the key can be applied. The result then is

GREGORIUM HYEMS
MENSIUM.

Apparently, the same types were used for the title-page of *Mundus* in 1613, but in a somewhat damaged condition.

After arriving at the above solution, I found that the compiler of the entry "More" in the Catalogue of the Library of

---

[1] *Nachrichten von merkwürdigen Büchern*, 1752–8, I. 556 ff. Bibl. 19.
[2] *Geschichte der komischen Litteratur*, 1784–7, II. 346 ff. Bibl. 120.

the British Museum had already interpreted the hieroglyphics more or less correctly as "Gregorium Hyemsmensium" and "Gregorium Huemumenium." Petherick[1] interprets the second correctly as "Gregorivm Hvemvmervivm," but seems to have ignored the title-page of *Utopia* altogether. No attempt seems to have been made to discover the translator's real name. "Hyemsmensius" is simply a barbarous translation of "Winter-monat." Gregorius Wintermonat was an obscure historian who published an ecclesiastical history[2] in 1614 and several minor chronicles at later dates[3].

After the appearance of this translation references to the *Utopia* in Germany are not frequent. It was apparently not even a financial success, for in 1704 we find the same firm of publishers trying to dispose of the old stock. This edition[4] was not even a reprint, for the old copies were simply supplied with a fresh title-page and offered for sale. An expurgated Latin edition appeared at Cologne in 1629, under strictly Roman Catholic auspices, as is clear from the title: *T. Mori Utopia, a mendis vindicata et juxta Indicem libror. expurgat. Card. et Archiep. Toletani correcta*[5]. I have come across only one other reference during the seventeenth century. Johann Balthasar Schupp, in *De Arte Ditescendi*, 1648[6], pictures Bacon as conducting a party of German exiles to an island like Utopia: "Insula haec ita comparata est, ut si Thomae Moro nova Utopia describenda esset, hanc veluti ideam & exemplar sibi proponeret."

(b) JOSEPH HALL'S *Mundus alter et idem.*

It is now generally assumed (e.g. the *Cambridge History of English Literature*, IV. xvi. 336, 1909) that *Mundus alter et idem* is the work of Joseph Hall[7], but the evidence is by no

---

[1] *On the Authorship and Translations of Mundus alter et idem*, 1896. Bibl. 122.

[2] *Historia Ecclesiastica Romana. Newe Bäpst Chronica: oder Römische Kirchen Historia.... In vorlegung Henning Grossen / dess Eltern...* Leipzig, 1614. (Kgl.-Pr. Bibl. Cd 2111.)

[3] See Catalogue, Kgl.-Pr. Bibl. Berlin.

[4] Bibl. 112.   [5] Brit. Mus. 718 a 22.   [6] Bibl. 176.

[7] Joseph Hall, b. July 1, 1574, at Bristow Park, Leicestershire. Entered Emmanuel, Camb. 1589; Fellow, 1595; Rector of Halstead, Essex, 1601; 1605 in Spanish Netherlands with Sir Edmund Bacon. D.D. *c.* 1612. Dean of

means conclusive. The literature on the subject has been discussed by Petherick[1], who gives an admirable summary of the
claims of Hall and Alberico Gentili[2], without being able to
come to a definite decision. The most we can say is that the
balance of probability is in favour of Hall. To enter fully into
the question of authorship would be beyond the range of these
studies, so I will content myself with giving the principal facts
of the book's history.

Mundus alter et idem is a "moral satire in prose, with a
strong undercurrent of bitter gibes at the Romish Church and
its eccentricities, which sufficiently betray the author's main
purpose in writing it. It shows considerable imagination, wit
and skill in latinity, but it has not enough of verisimilitude to
make it an effective satire, and does not always avoid scurrility"
(*Dict. of Nat. Biog.*). Hallam[3] calls it "an imitation of the
weaker volumes of Rabelais," and Warton[4] "a pleasant invective
against the characteristic vices of various nations." The first
dated edition appeared at Hanau in 1607[5], and the next at
Utrecht in 1643. Petherick mentions another edition (Munich,
1664), which I have not seen. There is also an undated edition
which appeared at Frankfort[6]. This must be the one entered
in the Stationers' Register by John Porter, June 2nd, 1605, as
the Hanau edition is announced in *Catalogus Universalis pro
Nundinis Francofurtensibus autumnalibus de anno* 1606, *sect.
Hist. Polit. et Geogr.* The author signs himself "Mercurius
Britannicus," and dedicates the book to Henry, Earl of
Huntingdon, as follows:

"Honoratissimo Domino nec minus virtute sua quam splĕdore generis
illustri Dom. Henrico Comiti Huntingdoniae, Mvndvm suum supplex
vouet Mercvrivs Britannicvs."

Worcester, 1617; Bp. of Exeter, 1627; Norwich, 1641. In Tower, 1641-2;
ejected from see, 1643. Retired to Higham, near Norwich. Died 8th Sept.,
1656.
    [1] Bibl. 122.
    [2] Alberico Gentili, b. Jan. 14, 1552, at Sanginesio. Protestant. Educated
at Univ. of Perugia. Forced to leave Sanginesio owing to religion. Fled to
Carniola; persecuted by Inquisition. Fled to Tübingen, thence to Heidelberg
and England. In Oxford, 1580 (recommended by Earl of Leicester). Reg.
Prof. of Civil Law, 1587. Admitted to Gray's Inn, 1600. Died June 19, 1608.
    [3] *Literature of Europe*, 1839, III. 684.
    [4] *History of English Poetry*, 1781, IV. 52.   [5] Bibl. 116.
    [6] Bibl. 115.

"Supplex" implies that the person addressed was still living when the dedication was written. Consequently, if it refers to Henry Hastings, third Earl of Huntingdon, the book must have been written before his death in 1595. This earl was a benefactor of Emmanuel College, and Hall was indebted to him for his Fellowship, although Huntingdon died two days before Hall's formal election. George, the fourth earl, was succeeded by another Henry, to whom Hall subsequently refers (dedication to the *Contemplations...*, 1612) as "the first patron of my poor studies." Now *Mundus alter et idem* was published, if we are to believe William Knight, who wrote the first preface, against the author's wish, as we learn from the following paragraph:—"Verum illius author, mundique ignoti explorator, qui iam pridem Musis (quarum insignis fuerat cultor) vale dicto, ad Theologiae sacra se contulerat (iisque iam totus vacat) haec, & nonnulla alia sua commenta Philologa luce & laude dignitissima, tanquam leuia aut vana aspernatus, nullis precibus induci potuit, vt permitteret in publicum exire. Excusabat autem, se iuuenili quidem aetate otioque Academico huiusmodi proprii exercitii & oblectationis gratia composuisse ; sed nūc quasi nugas inutiles reiicere, abdicare, nec dignare vt suo nomine vnquam sub aspectum hominum veniant...."

The words "iuuenili...aetate" imply that the book had been written several years before. The first edition, as we have seen, appeared in 1605. Consequently, the dedication can hardly refer to Henry, the *fifth* earl, who did not succeed to the title until 1604. Moreover, if the author really regarded his work with contempt, he would not have troubled to add a new dedication even if the book itself were old. It seems most probable to me that *Mundus alter et idem* was written before 1595 and dedicated to Henry, *third* Earl of Huntingdon.

William Knight[1] tells us that he published the book on his own responsibility, the manuscript having been entrusted to him by the author, who had abandoned literature for theology.

---

[1] William Knight, a native of Arlington, Sussex. Entered Christ's Coll., Camb., July 1, 1579; B.A. 1583; M.A. 1586. Friend of Hall. Rector of Barley, Herts., 1598. M.A., Oxford, July 12, 1603. Author of *A Concordance Axiomatical, containing a Survey of Theological Propositions, with the Reasons and use in Holy Scripture.* London, 1610.

This preface is the strongest argument in favour of attributing the work to the bishop, whose other satires[1] also appeared before 1600.

Let us now turn to Alberico Gentili. In the index to the edition of 1607, the heading of Lib. II. c. 2, is "Quid Alberico Gentili a Gynaecopolitis factum fuerit," which reappears in the German translation by Gregorius Wintermonat (1613) as "Wie die Weiber zu Frauenheim mit Alberico Gentili seind umgangen." The Frankfort edition, however, has "Quid mihi factum a Gynaecopolitis." As may be seen from the title-page of the German translation[2], Wintermonat attributed the book unhesitatingly to Gentili. It seems to have been first assigned to Hall by Thomas Hyde, who gives a reference from "Mercurius Britannicus" to "Joseph Hall" in his catalogue of the Bodleian, 1674. Blaufuss[3] thinks it strange that Thomas James, who knew Hall, did not include *Mundus* among the latter's works in the first catalogue of the Bodleian, 1620, and suspects Knight of wishing to put people on a false scent. He considers the presence of Gentili's name in the index decisive. Baumgarten[4] says Wintermonat is wrong in ascribing the work to Gentili. The author is beyond doubt Joseph Hall. A more detailed discussion is promised, but I have not discovered any further reference in Baumgarten's writings. Flögel[5] says : "Some have thought that this satirical account of an ideal state was written by Albericus Gentilis, because his name appears on the title-page of the German translation. Blaufuss was also of this opinion, because of the heading to Chapter II in the edition of 1607....This is also found in the German translation...but in the second Latin edition, which I have before me, stands simply (p. 100): 'Quid mihi factum a Gynaecopolitis.' No matter how the name Albericus Gentilis came into the book, the real author is nevertheless Joseph Hall, as Thomas Hyde, who was in a position to know and must have

[1] See Konrad Schulze: *Die Satiren Halls, ihre Abhängigkeit von den altrömischen Satirikern und ihre Realbeziehungen auf die Shakespeare-Zeit.* Berlin, Mayer and Müller, 1910. (Palaestra CVI.)
[2] Bibl. 117.
[3] Jacob Wilhelm Blaufuss: *Vermischte Beyträge zur Erweiterung der Kenntnis seltener und merkwürdiger Bücher*, 1753–6, p. 329. Bibl. 119.
[4] Bibl. 19, Vol. I. p. 588.   [5] Bibl. 120, Vol. II. p. 348.

done so, expressly states (*Catal. Bibl. Bodleyan.* p. 319)." On the other hand, the Berlin copy[1] of the Utrecht edition (1643) contains a note in manuscript to the effect that Mercurius Britannicus is Alberico Gentili, and a reference to some book which might be instructive if it were only legible. Petherick quotes the following interesting entries from the Admission Register of Gray's Inn:

1592. Ascanius Rialme, an Italian.
1598. Mar. 17. Henry Lord Hastings, heir-apparent to the Earl of Huntingdon.
1600. Albericus Gentilis, Doctor of Civil Law, Regius Professor at Oxford.
1615. Nov. 1. Joseph Hall.

It is curious that both the Frankfort and Hanau editions were published "apud haeredes (sumptibus haeredum) Ascanij de Renialme[2]." Moreover, the Gulielmus Antonius mentioned on the title-page of the Hanau edition published no less than four of Gentili's works, e.g. *De legationibus Libri tres*, 1607.

The clues to the authorship provided by internal evidence are very slight. The book is introduced by an imaginary dialogue between the author and two friends, Drogius and Beroaldus: "E reliquis postquam mihi multus sermo cum meo Beroaldo Gallo, & Drogio Belga de peregrinationis utilitate subortus fuisset...." Drogius[3] is unknown to me, but Beroaldus is François Beroalde de Verville, who also wrote an account of an imaginary voyage[4]. It would be interesting to discover whether Hall or Gentili knew Beroaldus or had read his works. At any rate *Mundus* was written by a man with a wide knowledge of foreign countries and languages. Petherick states that of the foreign (i.e. non-Latin) words in the text, 39 are Spanish, 29 Italian, 28 Greek, 28 French, 15 German, 6 English and 1 Hebrew. I have not tested these figures except for German, where I can make a few additions. The Glossary or Index Nominum Propriorum (compiled by Knight?) contains the following entries, "Y" signifying that the words occur in the second part of Book I, i.e. Yuronia:

[1] Kgl.-Pr. Bibl. Xf 12156.   [2] Bibl. 115, 116.
[3] He is not mentioned in G. Kalff: *Geschiedenis der Nederlandsche Letterkunde*. Groningen, J. B. Wolters, 1906.
[4] *Le Voyage des princes fortunez*. Paris, Guerin La Tour, 1610.

Y Auffzeichner / German. Registrarius.
Y Beachera vrbs. Germ. Poculum. vnde nos Angl. a Beacker.
Y Kotzunga. v. Germ. kotzen / vomere. hinc vomitio, kotzunga.
Y Krugtopolis, a German. krugt / Amphora.
Y Gesundheits. Germ. quod nos Angli. Healths.
    Nuchtermagen : Germ. stomachus ieiunus.
Y Schlauchberga. v, a Germ. Schlauch. vtre. dempto c.
Y Schaum fl. Germ. spuma.
Y Traubena, a Germ. Trauben. vina, racemus.
    Traurigi montes, a Germ. Trawrig.
    Zornus fl. Germ. Iratus, furiosus.
Y Zouffenberga, a Germ. Zauffen, quod sig. Gall. carouser.
    Zuckerii coll Germ. pro saccharo, zucker.

The following expressions occur in the text but are not included in the glossary:

    p. 62...Burgomagistrorum...
    p. 66...Sprützwall...
     „ ...Faesseram, vrbem...
    p. 74...Trinkenius...
     „ ...Zaufenius...
    p. 90...Houbeloniam...(the third province of Viraginia).

The first book deals with the land of Crapulia, which is divided into two provinces, Pamphagonia (i.e. Gluttony) and Yuronia (Intemperance). The first is of about the same length and breadth as England, the second as Germany. Book III, Moronia (i.e. Land of Fools), deals with the various provinces of the Roman Church; Orgilia (Chap. v) is Spain, Bavaria (Chap. vi, Fr. baver) is France and the capital, Parrivilia, is Paris.

At the end of the work comes the subscription: "Hos ego homines, hos mores, has urbes vidi, stupui, visi ; annoque demum tricesimo itineris tanti laboribus fractus in patriam redii."

An English translation, by John Healey, was entered in the Stationers' Register on Jan. 18, 1609. A fragment, Book I, Chaps. I–VI, and two lines of Chap. VII, was translated by William King[1] and published in *Miscellanies* (1732). Wintermonat's German version (1613) was re-issued, together with the *Utopia* (see p. 39), in 1704[2], and reprinted at Frankfort and Leipzig in 1730. Alberico Gentili left instructions that his

---

[1] Henry Morley: *Ideal Commonwealths*..., 1885. Bibl. 121. William King was born in 1663. Educated at Westminster and Christ Church, Oxford; M.A. 1688; LL.D. 1692. Judge of High Court of Admiralty, Ireland, 1702. *Art of Cookery*, 1709.

[2] Bibl. 118.

unpublished MSS should be burned, except *Hispanicae advocationis libri duo*, published posthumously at Hanau in 1613. This wish was not carried out, and at the beginning of the nineteenth century fifteen volumes, which to my knowledge have never been properly examined, were transferred from Amsterdam to the Bodleian. It is possible that they might throw some light on the authorship of *Mundus alter et idem*.

(c) JOHN BARCLAY'S *Argenis*.

The Barclays were a Scottish family of Gartly, Aberdeenshire, and related to the Leslies, Gordons and Ogilvies[1]. After the imprisonment of Mary Stuart (1569), John's father, William, settled in France and studied law at Bourges under Donneau. In 1577 he became Professor of Law at Pont-à-Mousson (Lorraine), and subsequently Dean of the Faculty. He married a Lorrainian lady of good family, Anne de Malavilliers, and John was born on January 28th, 1582. He was educated at the Jesuit college of his native town and published a Commentary on the *Thebais* of Statius before leaving school. In 1603, William Barclay resigned his position owing to a disagreement with the Jesuits, who seem to have controlled the University, but he was still at Pont-à-Mousson in July of that year. On the accession of James I, John Barclay wrote a congratulatory poem, which was printed at Paris. Both father and son paid a short visit to England in the autumn, but as it was impossible for Catholics to obtain public appointments they returned to France and were in Paris in December. On the 15th of January, 1603, William Barclay was appointed Professor at Angers, where he died on July 3rd, 1608[2].

It is generally supposed that John Barclay published the first part of *Euphormionis Lusinini Satyricon* during his visit to London in 1603, although no copies of this date are known to exist, the earliest extant edition being that of Paris (1605).

---

[1] Philipp August Becker: *Johann Barclay*, 1582–1621, 1904. Bibl. 137.
[2] One of William Barclay's books, *De regno et regali potestate adversus Buchanum, Brutum, Boucherium et reliquos monarchomachos*, 1600, created a sensation. He is mentioned in a letter, quoted by Reifferscheid (Bibl. 51), from Grotius to G. M. Lingelsheim, Sept. 8, 1617.

The book is a rogue-tale and betrays the influence of Petronius and the Spanish picaresque novel. Its influence on Grimmelshausen's *Simplicissimus* is considerable[1]. The second part, which is largely autobiographical, whereas the first is pure fiction, was published at Paris in 1607.

In 1605 Barclay married Louise Debonnaire, of Paris, and left soon after for London, where he became Royal Chamberlain in 1606, enjoying the favour of James I for many years. His first volume of poems, *Sylvae*, appeared at London in 1606. This was followed in 1614 (London and Paris) by *Icon Animorum*, a series of psychological sketches[2], and in 1615 by *Poëmatum Libri duo*. These poems were afterwards edited by M. Bernegger and published at Cologne in 1626, the year of Opitz' translation of the *Argenis*. Reifferscheid[3] quotes a letter from Bernegger to Opitz, dated Strassburg, 26 March, 1626: "Interim in vicem pulcherrimi mihique valde preciosi muneris tui mitto munusculum, Barclaiia carmina, forsan tibi necdum visa."

In September, 1615, Barclay, who was regarded as a foreigner in England and allowed to attend the Roman Catholic services at the French or Spanish embassies, left for Rome with his family. He stayed in Paris until the summer of 1616 and then travelled to his destination *via* Marseilles, Leghorn and Florence, where he completed his *Paraenesis ad Sectarios* (see Chap. VIII).

During these years in Rome, 1617–1621, Barclay was occupied with his most famous work, *Argenis*. The dedication to Louis XIII of France is dated "1 July 1621," and on the 28th the license to publish was granted to Nicholas Buon, of Paris. On August 1st Barclay caught the fever and on the 12th he died. He was buried in the Church of Sant' Onofrio at Rome. The publication of the book was supervised by his friend, Peiresc, and it appeared the same year.

The *Argenis* is a political novel written expressly for the guidance of the young French king. It deals in the form of

---

[1] I have not gone very fully into this question, as, according to Becker, a special dissertation is in course of preparation at Strassburg.

[2] Bibl. 63, 64, 65. See also Introduction, Chapter I, and Chapter VII.

[3] Bibl. 51.

a romance with numerous serious religious and constitutional questions, but it is not a systematic allegory of French history, as there is absolutely no allusion to the Massacre of Saint Bartholomew, the murder of Henry III and other equally important events, the omission of which would be impossible[1]. Still, there are numerous personal reminiscences. Dunalbius is Roberto Ubaldino, Antenorius, is Antonio Querenghi, Hierolander is Hieronymus Aleander, and Nicopompus is Barclay himself. Nor is there any doubt that Poliarchus is Henry IV, and Ibburanes, Pope Urban III.

That the *Argenis* was one of the most popular books of the century is proved by the following list of editions, compiled from Becker, Schmid[2] and other sources:

Paris.   1621, 1622, 1623, 1624[3], 1625.
London.   1622 (two).
Strassburg.   1622, 1623.
Frankfort.   1622, 1623, 1626, 1630, 1634, 1676 (Summary only).
Venice.   1626, 1637, 1643, 1656, 1657, 1675, 1682.
Leyden.   1627[4], 1630, 1659[5], 1664 (and Amsterdam).
Amsterdam.   1630, 1642, 1655, 1659, 1671, 1674.
Segovia.   1632.
Oxford.   1634.
Leipzig.   1659.
Cambridge.   1673, 1674.
Nuremberg.   1673, 1687, 1693, 1703, 1724, 1769, 1776.

The number of translations is equally astonishing, no less than twenty-seven having appeared before the close of the eighteenth century and one in the nineteenth. The following is a complete list with the various editions[6]:

French.
P. de Marcassus, Paris, 1622, 1626, 1632.
N. Guibert, Paris, 1623, 1624, 1625, 1633, 1638.   Rouen, 1632, 1643.
N. Coëffeteau (Summary), Paris, 1624, 1626, 1628, 1662.   Rouen, 1641.
L. Pierre de Longue, Paris, 1728.
Abbé Josse, Chartres, 1732, 1734, 1764.
M. Savin, Paris, 1771.

---

[1] See Becker, Bibl. 137.
[2] Karl Friedrich Schmid: *John Barclay, Argenis,* 1904.   Bibl. 136.
[3] First edition with "Tabula nominum fictorum in Argenide."
[4] First edition with the "Discursus in Argenidem" (usually referred to as "Clavis in Argenidem"). This is a discussion, by B. Rivinus, of the "Tabula nominum fictorum."
[5] First Latin edition divided into chapters.
[6] For this list I am chiefly indebted to K. F. Schmid, who discusses both editions and translations at length.   Bibl. 136.

English.
  Kingsmill Long, 1625, 1636.
  Le Grys and May, 1629.
  Clara Reeve, 1772.
Italian.
  Fr. Pona, Venice, 1629, 1634, 1644 (Padua?), 1651, 1663, 1669, 1675, 1682.
  C. A. Cocastello, Turin, 1630.   Venice, 1631, 1636, 1663, 1671.
Spanish.
  Pellicer de Salas, Madrid, 1626.
  Gabriel de Corral, Madrid, 1626.
German.
  Martin Opitz, Breslau, 1626.   Amsterdam, 1644.
  A. Friderici (from the French of Coëffeteau), Leipzig, 1631.
  August Bohse (Talander), Leipzig, 1701, 1709.
  Anon., Augsburg, 1770.
  J. Chr. L. Haken, Breslau, 1794.
  G. Waltz, Munich, 1891.
Greek.
  Anon., Leyden, 1627.
Dutch.
  Glazemaker, Amsterdam, 1643, 1680.
Polish.
  Potocki, Warsaw, 1697.   Leipzig, 1728.   Posen, 1743.
  Anon., (Summary) 1704.
Swedish.
  J. Malmborg, Stockholm, 1740.
  J. Ehrenström, Stockholm, 1741.
Danish.
  Paus, Copenhagen, 1746.
Russian.
  Tredjakowskij, 1751.
Hungarian.
  A. Fejér, Erlau, 1792.
  K. Boér Sandor, Klausenburg in Hermannstadt, 1792.

Three other translations were made but never published:

English.
  Ben Jonson, 1623 (lost).
Icelandic.
  J. Einarsson, 1694.
Modern Greek.
  Anon. (No year.)

Let us now confine ourselves to the history of *Argenis* in
Germany.   In spite of the enormous popularity of the book,
there were many who regarded Barclay's Latin as a source
of danger to the study of the language, and until about 1740,
when he began to be forgotten, it was a bone of contention
between scholars[1].   Still, the absorbing interest of the book

---

[1] The literature on the subject is discussed by Schmid, Bibl. 136.

made the question of its latinity immaterial to the majority of readers.

The first reference to Barclay seems to be in a letter, dated "Heidelberg, 23 May, 1615," from Jan Gruter, librarian to the Count Palatine, to Julius Wilhelm Zincgref[1]: "Ei vos quoque plurimam a me salutem, ut et dn. Barclaio: quamvis hunc de scriptis solum noverim, non etiam vultu. Praestantissimum esse ingenium patriae suae, iam fidem fecit[2]." Zincgref seems to have read the *Argenis* before Gruter, for on March 20, 1622, the latter writes from Tübingen to G. M. Lingelsheim: "Sed et avide videbo Argenida Barclaii, de qua ante mihi scripserat Zincgrefius noster." Lingelsheim apparently sent a copy to Gruter, who again writes from Tübingen on June 19th: "Multum tibi debeo de Barclaii Argenide, quam a capite ad calcem totam uno impetu perlegi. Invehitur quidem duobus locis in Hyperephanios satis acriter: verum non videtur totam fabulam ideo exorsus esse: sed potius ut sub ea boni malique principis proponeret exemplar. Interim pag. 436 et seqq.[3] totus est in laudandis Jesuitis. Ad eam fere faciem est Aranea[4] mea, in qua tamen plura regum delicta notantur, quam celebrantur benefacta, uti etiam plura peccant, quam agunt benigniter aut ex officio." The edition of Barclay's poems, sent to Opitz by M. Bernegger from Strassburg on March 24, 1626, has already been noticed (p. 48). That Opitz' Strassburg friends were at this time anxiously awaiting the appearance of his German translation is clear from a letter of Balthasar Venator of the same date: "Quantum autem voluptatis speramus ex Argenide, ex Psalmis, ex aliis?" On August 8th, Kristof Koeler (Colerus)[5] writes to the same effect: "Desiderio Barclai tui flagramus omnes, quam solus Germanice loqui potes docere." In the meantime (Boleslaviae Silesiorum, XIII Cal.

---

[1] Born June 3, 1591, at Heidelberg; studied at Univ. from 1607. In Basel, 1611. After 1612, in France, England and Holland. Back at Heidelberg, 1617. In Heilbronn, 1620. Appointed judge-advocate to garrison of Heidelberg. Fled to Frankfort after siege, Sept. 1622. Became interpreter to French Embassy at Strassburg. Subsequently in Stuttgart, Worms and Kreuznach in Alznei. Died of plague at St. Goar, Nov. 12, 1635.

[2] All these letters are quoted by Reifferscheid, Bibl. 51.

[3] I.e. in Book V.   [4] Never published.

[5] Born at Bunzlau, Dec. 1, 1602. Vice-principal of a school in Breslau. Died April 19, 1658.

Martiis 1626) Opitz writes to Venator to say that the translation is in the press: "Est et sub incude Argenis, nostro
sermone, non tam iudicio meo quam voluntate meorum, reddita,
sed ad umbilicum non adhuc deducta." On the 9th of June he
writes to Buchner[1] in a similar strain: "Argenis typographo
tradita est fere tota, quae prostabit nundinis auctumni." It
appeared in due course at Breslau and apparently had a rapid
sale, for in 1627 (Propridie Cal. Maii Juliani) we find Koeler
complaining in a letter to Opitz that he has been unable to
obtain a copy: "Argenis tua, quam tandem ab his nundinis
adventuram speravi, ad nos non venit. Aiunt bibliopolae nostri,
se tantum unicum exemplar, quod aere redimendum non fuisset,
Francofurti vidisse." In June, 1627, a certain Senftleben writes
from Breslau to Bernegger: "Argenidem misissem, sed qui illa
suscepit, haec renuit, altera tamen vice, si apud vos emanserit,
quod per Colerum certior fieri volo, transmittam." In September,
1628, Koeler is still without a copy, for he writes to Opitz as
follows: "Nam inter aliud agendum Argenidem et nuper
Laudes Martis, doctum, grave, severum atque prudens carmen
vidimus. Exemplar anxie a nundinis Francofurtensibus expecto; sin in mercatum nullum veniet, a te unum peto."
Finally, on May 4th, 1628, Opitz, apparently in answer to an
inquiry, writes from Breslau to Balthasar Venator to explain
that he translated the *Argenis* while on his travels and used
the Latin original and a French translation alternately:
"Argenis et mea est et non mea. Esse meam, ex paucis carminibus coniicere potuisti, quorum me profecto non poenitet.
Fabulam ipsam tum Germanice reddidi, cum aut in itinere fui,
aut ob strepitum eorum, cum quibus fui, aliud agere non potui.
Interdum autem Latinum, interdum Gallicum exemplar ad
manum non erat, ita ut haec pagina ex illo, altera ex isto versa
sit. Qua re nihil excuso. Iniuriam autem mihi bibliopola
fecit, cum in praefatione a nescio quo advocato conscripta dicere
ausus fuit, argento se librum a me emisse (*sic*). Est, unde vivam,
et quidem ita, ut pauci meae conditionis in hac urbe homines."

---

[1] Born 2 Nov. 1591, at Dresden. In Schulpforta after 1604. In Wittenberg,
1610. Professor of Poetry, 1616. Professor of Eloquence, 1631. Senior of the
University, 1649. Died 12 Dec. 1661.

The publisher, David Müller, dedicated the book to Georg, Ludwig, Rudolf and Christian, Dukes of Silesia, and wrote a lengthy preface, a portion of which I translate : "Scholars are well aware how many different books Johannes Barclaius wrote and published. Last of all, in 1621, appeared his *Argenis*, which was so delightful and so well thought of by scholars that it has been not only reprinted several times in Latin but also elegantly translated into French and is now to be found in everybody's hands, both high and low. Indeed, it is not improbable that its like will nowhere be met with in Latin, as Barclaius himself remarks at the beginning of his preface to the Most Mighty and Christian King of France, Louis the Thirteenth of that name. For, not to mention the beauty of the language and the excellence of the disposition which the author has been careful to employ, it is astounding how cleverly Barclay has brought in each and every scrap of worldly wisdom, so that the careful reader grows not only more and more anxious to learn, although unconsciously, the historical facts from the allegory, but also to recognise thereby the virtues and vices of persons of high and low degree.... For these reasons I undertook, on the advice of men of intelligence and learning, to entrust Herr Martin Opitz with the translation of this excellent book of *Argenis* and published it at my expense...."

As to the merits of the translation opinions seem to differ. According to Schmid, the rendering is faithful ("Die Wiedergabe ist eine getreue "), but Borinski[1] says it is very free ("Opitzens Übertragung ist sehr frei, schmückt viel aus und ist daher länger als das Original "). It is not sufficient to compare the German with the Latin; it must not be forgotten that much was translated directly from the French. Consequently, the German sometimes appears free as compared with the former, but faithful when the latter is taken into account. Schmid points out a few mistakes and also an addition of Opitz' own invention at the end of Book I, Chapter VI. Only seven of the numerous poems are translated[2]. Attention is drawn to this fact in a postscript: "Owing to other business, he who

---

[1] Karl Borinski: *Die Hofdichtung des 17. Jahrhunderts*, 1894. Bibl. 52.
[2] These versions are included in Opitz' *Poetische Wälder*, I. Buch.

translated this book into German was unable to correct either his own manuscript or the printed copy. Consequently, there will doubtless be here and there a mistake, which you will correct for yourself. Moreover, only those poems which are to be found in the French version have been translated, seeing that the omission of the remainder interfered little or not at all with the disposition of the work."

Seventeenth century criticism is almost without exception favourable to Opitz' version. He was regarded as the Homer of his age, and everything he wrote was inimitable. Nevertheless, one or two dissenting voices were raised. Johann Balthasar Schupp[1], who lectured on Barclay at Giessen in 1638-9, finds considerable fault with Opitz in *Der teutsche Lehrmeister*, 1667 (written 1658), and *De Opinione*, 1639[2]. Morhof[3] observes a great difference in the quality of the poetical renderings.

In 1631 another German version, by A. Friderici[4], appeared at Leipzig. The author dedicates the volume to Frau Anna Elisabeth, Countess zu Bappenheim, and compares her perfections with those of Argenis. He did not use the Latin original but merely translated the French summary of N. Coëffeteau.

After Barclay's death three continuations of the *Argenis* appeared; the first, in French, by A. de Mouchemberg in 1625, the second, in Spanish, but based on Mouchemberg, by Pellicer de Salas in October, 1626, and the third, again in French, by Bugnot in 1669. Mouchemberg's version was translated by Opitz and published at Breslau by David Müller in 1631 as *Der Argenis anderer Theyl, verdeutscht durch Martin Opitzen...*" These continuations need not detain us.

References to Barclay in German literature are numerous[5].

[1] See Carl Vogt: *Johann Balthasar Schupp*, 1909-10. Bibl. 185.

[2] See W. W. Zschau: *Quellen und Vorbilder in den "Lehrreichen Schriften" Johann Balthasar Schupps*, 1906. Bibl. 184.

[3] Daniel Georg Morhof: *Unterricht von der Teutschen Sprache*, 1682. Bibl. 255.

[4] Bibl. 127. See also Schmid, Bibl. 136, who seems to have been the first to discover Friderici's work. I had no opportunity of examining Bohse's translation (1701), but as it lies just outside our period it will be sufficient to refer again to Schmid, who has carefully discussed all existing versions.

[5] There are also several books, chiefly university dissertations in Latin, e.g. *Joh. Barclaii Thesaurus Argenideus...*, 1669, which deal exclusively with Barclay. As these have already been enumerated by Schmid, I have not thought it necessary to discuss them.

Schupp, who possessed a copy of the original edition of the *Argenis*, introduces him as a character in *De arte ditescendi* (1648) along with Bacon[1]. After the latter has outlined a scheme of emigration to an unknown island, Barclay rises and makes several criticisms: " Adhuc ita loquebatur Baconus, cum Johann Barclayus, ille qui nuper Romam Romano docuit ore loqui, surgeret atque ita responderet..." (p. 26). The same work contains several quotations from and reminiscences of the *Argenis.* Several of Schupp's other works betray the same familiarity, e.g. *Der rachgierige Lucidor* (1657), I. 287; *Der Hauptmann zu Capernaum* (1666, written 1657 ?), II. 201; *Der Lobwürdige Löwe* (1654), I. 836, and others[2]. Harsdoerfer, in the first part of *Frauenzimmer Gesprächspiele*[3], 1641, observes: " We must remember one thing: it is well known that Lords and Princes hear the truth with impatience. Now there is no more skilful means than to employ fictitious persons to convey it, as the world-renowned Barclay did in a most masterly manner in his *Argenis...* " (XLVII. 15). The same writer quotes *Argenis* (II. 134) in his *XII Andachts-Gemähle*[4] and in *Nathan und Jotham*[5], 1659, he states that Barclay by his plain speaking and unmasking of hypocrisy had made many enemies in France (*Jotham*, I. p. 10). Buchner[6] says that among the poets who teach by means of images and pictures may be mentioned " Erasmus in his *Moria*, or Eulogy of Folly, More in his *Utopia*, and John Barclay in his various excellent works." Birken[7] discusses the nature of romances like " Sidney's *Arcadia*, Biondi's *Eromena*, Barclay's *Argenis*, the *Ariana* and *Diana*, which have been translated into German from the English, Italian, Latin, French and Spanish." Michael Kongehl makes Barclay the subject of a poem in his *Sieg-Prangender Lorbeer-Hayn*[8], 1700:

> Johannes Barclajus / der Nettschreibende.
> Wer nettgesezt Latein / und schön-verblühmte Sachen /
> in einem Kunst-Roman / das nach der Kunst verstekt /
> und dem / der grübelt nach / viel grosse Ding' entdekt;

[1] Bibl. 176.
[2] See Zschau, Bibl. 184.
[3] Bibl. 128 *a*.
[4] No year. Bibl. 128.
[5] Bibl. 129.
[6] *August Buchners Poet...*, 1665. Bibl. 131.
[7] *Teutsche Rede-Bind- und Dicht-Kunst...*, 1679. Bibl. 105.
[8] Bibl. 133.

Wer schöne Vers' und Sprüch' Jhm recht bekandt will machen /
der less' und lese wol Barclajen Argeniss ;
Da het Er / was Er sucht / da findet Ers gewiss ;
Schad! dass der Edle Mann so bald der Welt entgangen ;
Barclajen Nach-Ruhm muss in stetem Wolseyn prangen!

Then follow a short life of Barclay in Latin and further admiring references to the *Argenis* and to Sidney's *Arcadia*.

Buchner prepared a school edition of the *Argenis* and inspired Paul Fleming[1], the best lyric poet of the century, with the idea of a *Margenis*, which, however, was never written. The plan is mentioned in the seventeenth ode of the Fourth Book, *An Herrn Magnus Schuwarten*, 1633[2].

Künftig will auch ich was melden
von den Taten unsrer Zeit
und die ritterlichen Helden,
so man rühmet weit und breit,
in ein solches Buch verleiben,
dass sie sollen ewig bleiben....

Lasse mich nächst nach dir gehen,
Barklai, und verzeih mir diss!
Meine Margenis[3] soll stehen
neben deiner Argenis,
Argenis, dem schönen Wesen,
das so ferne wird gelesen.

Fleming mentions Barclay more briefly in *Poetische Wälder*, III. 6 (April, 1635), and IV. 23 (Nov. 1634).

Barclay's actual influence on German literature has not yet been completely traced. Bloedau[4] has discussed the novel of the seventeenth century, and the part played by Barclay in its development is fairly estimated. In 1660 appeared Balthasar Kindermann's *Kurandor's Unglückselige Nisette*[5], an imitation, as Bloedau points out, of the *Argenis* in both matter and construction. "The plot of both novels is laid in the same century and both deal with insurrections in Sicily. The rebel leaders are very much alike, especially in the speeches they make to their troops before the decisive battle. Moreover, smaller points agree, e.g. the parting of Argenis and Poliarchus resembles that

[1] Born at Hartenstein, 5 Oct. 1606; died at Hamburg, 2 April, 1640.
[2] *Paul Flemings Deutsche Gedichte*, ed. Lappenberg, Stuttgart, 1865. Bibl. 134.
[3] Margenis, i.e. Germania.
[4] *Grimmelshausens Simplicissimus und seine Vorgänger*, 1908. Bibl. 138.
[5] Bibl. 130.

of Dorisophe and her lover, and the rescue of Poliarchus from a rock in the sea is like that of Seusippus." But it is from a technical point of view that Barclay's influence is most marked. The construction of the plot at the beginning, not only in *Nisette* but also in Zesen's *Assenat* (1670), is modelled on *Argenis*. With reference to Grimmelshausen's *Simplicissimus* (1660), Bloedau remarks: "The author makes far more use of secondary characters than of the narrator as a mouthpiece for his learning and his views. Like Barclay, Grimmelshausen employs for the purpose, with but one exception, characters we already know." Again, "the anagnorisis is one of the essentials of the idealistic novel. It is present in the *Arcadia*, *Argenis*, and *Nisette*, and it is therefore probable that Grimmelshausen borrowed the motive from that sphere before he worked it out, as it is unknown in the picaresque novel." Bloedau is, however, in error when he says that among the idealistic novels "Barclay's *Argenis* and its imitation, *Nisette*, stand somewhat apart owing to their division into chapters." As a matter of fact the first twenty-six editions of the former are divided simply into five books, the first edition to show division into chapters appearing at Leyden in 1659. We may notice one last point of resemblance in the conclusions of the books, "which Grimmelshausen, following the example of the *Argenis*, always fixes in a fresh group of scenes. He indicates the progress of the narrative by unfolding new features of character in the new book."

The most obvious product of Barclay's influence on German literature is Christian Weise's drama *Von der sicilianischen Argenis*, 1684[1]. It was published with two other plays, *Vom verfolgten David* and *Von der verkehrten Welt*, under the title of *Neue Jugend-Lust*, but has a separate title-page as well. In his preface to the volume he remarks: "As regards the second play, *Argenis*, a little necessary information will be given later. At present I will only mention the fact that I have so treated the pagan myths that little use is made of idolatrous sacrifices and other blasphemous ceremonies. Nor can I commend Barclay for introducing prayers and hymns to false gods in his description

[1] Bibl. 132. Weise's plays were written for performance by his scholars at the Gymnasium in Zittau.

of a heathen rite. For although he was obliged to be consistent with the religion of the people in the story itself, yet this singing might have been omitted without detriment to the general charm of the book. For this reason, instead of making Argenis a priestess who has to bless the whole nation with her rod, I have made her sit in public and receive the petitions to her royal father." A portion of the special preface runs as follows: "Least of all have I been able to imitate Barclay's wonderfully charming style, for his plot is so skilfully woven that one emotion must inevitably follow upon the other. But as the *series naturalis*, the simple narration of fact, as it were, must persist in the play, much of that elegance for which the author is most renowned disappears, and one is consequently obliged to think of other good points which may be embodied in a dramatic plot. Nicopompus, really one of the wisest characters in Barclay's story, here plays the part of a grotesque court-poet. There are also deviations in other small matters, but it will be clear from the remainder that from beginning to end little has been omitted."

The play begins with a prelude of twelve scenes: Act I has 17; Act II, 15; Act III, 24; Act IV, 16; and Act V, 14. Then follows a Nach-Spiel of seven scenes. Fortunately, they are all short[1].

---

[1] These notes on the influence of Barclay on German literature make no pretence to completeness. Dr K. F. Schmid, of Munich, has for some years been engaged on a volume to be entitled *Barclays Einfluss auf die Literatur*, and kindly offered to place his manuscript at my disposal. He has much new material to bring forward.

CHAPTER V

THE EPIGRAM

THE cult of the epigram in the seventeenth century is a phenomenon in the history of German literature. Pechel[1], in his critical edition of Wernicke, writes: "The epigram was perhaps the most pleasant feature of the century. Pithy brevity instead of tiresome and trifling prolixity, pungent wit instead of stale and dreary moralizing, malicious fun instead of dry respectability, make the epigram particularly salutary. Its nature would endure neither the emptiness of thought nor the unbearable stiltedness and discursiveness of the other branches of literature. It embodies the sum-total of the wit and acumen of this curious century. Moreover, a delight in epigram had been awakened by the polemics of the Renaissance. Old models were copied and a mighty international borrowing began. The Greek Anthology and Martial were the principal store-houses, but later the influence of Owen became predominant, in spite of his dryness. Unfortunately, all poets felt themselves called upon to write epigrams and the art consequently degenerated into a stale juggle with words....The principal form of verse was the alexandrine, which readily lends itself to playing with antitheses on account of its division into hemistichs. On the other hand, it must be noticed that it is precisely the regular movement of the alexandrine which often prevents it from doing justice to the abruptness of the epigram..."

Reference has already been made to a few English epigrams which attracted the attention of Weckherlin, but the Latin

---

[1] Rudolf Pechel: *Christian Wernicke's Epigramme*, 1909. Bibl. 264.

epigram is far more important. We occasionally meet with a few scraps from sixteenth century authors, such as Buchanan[1] and More, but it was John Owen[2] who created the real vogue. His first volume, *Epigrammatum Iohannis Owen Cambro-Britanni Libri Tres*[3]. *Ad illustrissimam D. Mariam Neuille, Comitis Dorcestriae filiam Patronam suam*, was twice published in 1606. In 1607 appeared a single book entitled *Epigrammatum Ioannis Owen Cambro-Britanni Ad Excellentissimam & doctissimam Heroinam, D. Arbellam Stuart, Liber Singularis*[4]. Two more volumes were published in 1612, *Epigrammatum Ioannis Owen Oxoniensis, Cambro-Britanni, Libri Tres*[5]. *Ad Henricvm Principem Cambriae Dvo. Ad Carolum Eboracensem unvs*, and *Epigrammatum Ioannis Owen Cambro-Britanni Oxoniensis. Ad Tres Mecaenates, Libri Tres*[6]. After Owen's death a collection of moral and political distichs from other writers, *Monosticha, quaedam ethica & politica veterum sapientum*, found its way into many editions[7].

Owen's influence on German writers has been discussed by Urban[8], who gives a long list of parallels and examines the professed translations. Unfortunately, he is content to place the number of each German epigram side by side with the number of the original in Owen and quotes no specimens. This defect I propose to remedy in the present chapter.

The following is a chronological list, compiled from Urban's treatise, of all German authors of the seventeenth century whose works contain epigrams imitated from Owen. The professed translations are denoted by a *T*. Except in these cases I have disregarded Urban's distinctions between imitations and translations and have also incorporated his appendix of less important authors with the main list.

---

[1] Two of Buchanan's epigrams were translated by Opitz in *Florilegium variorum epigrammatum*, 1638.
[2] Born 1563 (4?) at Armon, Carnarvonshire. Educated at Winchester and New College, Oxford. Fellow, 1584. Subsequently schoolmaster at Warwick. Died in 1622 and was buried in St Paul's.
[3] Hereafter referred to as Books I–III.
[4] 　　,,　　　,,　　　,,　　Book IV.
[5] 　　,,　　　,,　　　,,　　Books V–VII.
[6] 　　,,　　　,,　　　,,　　Books VIII–X.
[7] E.g. the Amsterdam edition of 1657. Bibl. 146.
[8] Erich Urban: *Owenus und die deutschen Epigrammatiker des 17 Jahrhunderts*, 1900. Bibl. 148.

Heinrich Hudemann.
    1625. *Teutsche Musa*, Hamburg. 3.
Johann Rist (1607–1667).
    1632. *Musa Teutonica*, Hamburg. 10.
    1638. *Poetischer Lust-Garte*, Hamburg. 15.
    1646. *Poetischer Schauplatz*, Hamburg. 4.
Zacharias Lund (1608–1667).
    1636. *Allerhand artige Deutsche Gedichte*, Leipzig. 2.
Ernst Christoph Homburg (1605–1681).
    1638. *Schimpff- und Ernsthaffte Clio.* 17.
T. Bernhardus Nicaeus Ancumanus.
    1641. *Rosarium Das ist / Rosen-Garten*, Emden[1]. *c.* 500.
Paul Fleming (1606–1640).
    1641. *D. Paul Flemings Poetischer Gedichte...Prodromus*, Hamburg. 1[2].
August Augspurger.
    1642. *Reisende Clio*, Dresden. 19.
Andreas Tscherning (1611–1659).
    1642. *Deutscher Getichte Früling*, Breslau. 20.
    1655. *Vortrab des Sommers*, Rostock. 1.
T. Johann Peter Titz (1619–1681).
    1643. *Florilegii Oweniani Centuria*, Danzig[3]. 100.
T. Simon Schultz.
    1644. *Centuria Epigrammatum e Martialis et Ovveni Libris selectorum*, Danzig[4]. 50.
Georg Greflinger (1620–1677).
    1645. *Deutscher Epigrammatum Erstes Hundert.* Danzig.
    1663. *Celadonische Musa.* (In all) 113.
Johann Francke (1618–1677).
    1648. *Poetischer Werke Fünftes Buch, Deutsche Epigrammata*, Frankfort o/O. 18.
Georg Rudolf Weckherlin (1584–1653).
    1648. *Gaistliche und Weltliche Gedichte*, Amsterdam. 14.
David Schirmer (*c.* 1623–after 1682).
    1650. *Poetische Rosen-Gepüsche*[5]. 11.
T. Valentin Löber (1620–1685).
    1651. *Epigrammatum Ovveni Drey Bücher*, Hamburg[6].
    1653. *Teutschredender Owenus*, Hamburg[7].
Wencel Scherffer von Scherffenstein (?–1674).
    1652. *Geist- und Weltlicher Gedichte, Erster Teil*, Brieg. 1.

---

[1] Bibl. 140.
[2] This is the only addition I have been able to make to Urban's list.
                     Aus dem Owen, i. 13.
    Die Liebe kommt mit Lust, geht wieder weg mit Trauren.
    Süss ist ihr Anfang wol, das Ende doch der Sauren.
                        Venus.
    Principium dulce est, at finis amoris amarus;
      Laeta venire Venus, tristis abire solet.
    Flumina quaesitum sic in mare dulcia currunt:
      Postquam gustarunt aequor, amara fluunt.
[3] Bibl. 141.   [4] Bibl. 142.   [5] Bibl. 145.
[6] Bibl. 143.   [7] Bibl. 147.

Friedrich von Logau (1604–1655).
    1654. *Salomons von Golaw Deutscher Sinn-Getichte Drey Tausend,*
        Breslau[1]. 99.

Daniel Czepko von Reigersfeld (1605–1660).
    1655. *Sexcenta Monodisticha Sapientum.* 4.

Logau marks the culminating point in the history of the epigram in the seventeenth century. Subsequent writers are mere slavish imitators of Owen and never rise above mediocrity.

Georg Martini.
    1654. *Deutsche Epigrammata und Sonette*, Bremen. 39.

Jacob Schwieger.
    1654. *Überschrifften*, Stade. 9.

Justus Sieber (1628–1695).
    1658. *Poetisierende Jugend.* 17.

Eduart Gärtener.
    1659. *Anbind-Brieflein*, Bremen. 2.

Johann Georg Schoch.
    1660. *Neu-erbauter Poetischer Lust- und Blumen-Garten*, Leipzig.
        25.

Andreas Gryphius (1616–1664).
    1663. *...Trauer-Spiele auch Oden und Sonnette*, Breslau. 4.

Anon.
    1663. In *Christian Hofmanns von Bresslau Spielersinnliche Ster-*
        bens-Gedancken. 4.

Martin Kempe (1637–1682).
    1665. *Poetischer Lust-Gedancken, Anderer Teil*, Jena. 5.

Quirinus Kuhlmann (1651–1689).
    1671. *Unsterbliche Sterblichkeit*, Jena. **3.**
    1671. *Himmlische Libes-Küsse*, Jena. 1.

Christian Knittel.
    1674. *Kurtz-Gedichte*, Frankfurt o/O. 5.

Gottfried Feinler (*c.* 1650–after 1704).
    1677. *Poetische Lust-Gärtgen*, Zeitz. 39.

Johann Grob (1643–1697).
    1678. *Dichterische Versuchsgabe*, Basel. 2.

Daniel Georg Morhof (1639–1691).
    1682. *Teutsche Gedichte*, Kiel. 3.

Michael Kongehl (1646–1710).
    1683. *Belustigung bey der Unlust*, Stettin[2]. 6.
    1694. *Lust-Quartier*, Danzig. 19.

Christoph Kaldenbach (1613–1698).
    1683. *Deutsche Lieder und Getichte*, Tübingen. 1.

---

[1] Bibl. 144.

[2] Urban says he was unable to discover a copy of Part II of this work. It was published at Königsberg (no year) and contains odes and sonnets but no epigrams. There is a copy in the Kgl.-Pr. Bibl., Berlin, numbered Yi 7451.

Anon.
  1695. *Herrn von Hofmannswaldau und anderer Deutschen aus-
         erlesener und bissher ungedruckter Gedichte siebenter
         theil. 5.*
Joannes Käyser.
  1698. *Parnassus Clivensis,* Cleve. 7.

Owen's ten books contain altogether some 1500 epigrams, the exact number in each being 173, 218, 208; 276; 111, 100, 124; 101, 100, 103[1]. The spurious book of Monosticha, which comes between Books IV and V, is divided into two parts, containing respectively 90 and 37, but as these are not Owen's work I shall give them little attention. Book I seems to have been the most popular with the German writers mentioned above, for no less than 126 epigrams (I neglect, of course, the professed translations of Nicaeus, Titz, Schultz and Löber) were taken from it. The other books supplied respectively 70, 106; 76; 78, 22, 19; 35, 22, 29. The least popular book, therefore, was the seventh, if we except the Monosticha, only 17 of which obtained a German dress. Book III is pre-eminently serious and Book VI topical, whereas the others are more general.

Let us now turn to the translations. The *Rosarium*[2] of 1641 is dedicated to the city fathers of Bremen and contains a preface from which we gather that the author was a clergyman. He says:

"The great English theologian, Joseph Hall, well says in his *Meditationibus et votis,* There is nothing more distressing to a pious heart than idleness, for the body, not to mention the prosperity and welfare of our estate, is preserved by exercise from sickness and the mind cheered and refreshed. I have indeed discovered the truth of this.

For when about three years ago it pleased Almighty God to visit me with a painful and tedious bodily weakness, so that for some time I was unable either to conduct the service or attend to my official duties, I could not remain idle but studied and meditated a little as soon as my sickness became less violent, so that I might not only pass the time more comfortably but recover all the more quickly and permanently, by dint of this exercise and with God's help, my previous bodily and mental strength. But when my weakness made continual application to more serious studies impossible I was obliged to vary it with lighter reading, so that I might thereby be relieved and not oppressed, in accordance with the well-known lines

Interpone tuis interdum gaudia curis,
Ut possis animo quemvis sufferre laborem.

[1] I quote the Amsterdam edition of 1657 (Bibl. 146).
[2] Bibl. 140.

To this end, especially at night when I could not sleep, and after a heart-felt prayer to God and other devout contemplations, I picked up the epigrams of that pious, learned and ingenious poet, John Owen, and let my eyes and mind wander through his lovely pleasure-garden or *Viridarium* and refreshed my weary spirit thereby not a little. And in order to enjoy this pleasure all the longer and let others share it with me—*Nullius boni sine socio jucunda possessio*, as Seneca testifies—I thought it well to construct from this same *Viridarium* or great "pleasure-garden" a *rosariolum* or rose-garden and translate some of the best and aptest epigrams into verse in the manner of Hans Sachs...."

The collection contains 623 epigrams, including almost the whole of the Monosticha, the serious nature of which would naturally appeal to a man of the translator's temperament. There is no attempt to preserve the original order or even the division into books, but the great majority are taken from the first four. The following is a specimen from Book I:

Orbis.

In mundo nil constat : in orbem vertitur orbis.
Quid mirum, recti quod fit in orbe nihil? Owen, i. 49.

Die runde Welt.

Nichts in der runden Welt besteht /
Die Welt stets wie ein Rad umbgeht.
Was ist denn wunder / wenn man sicht /
Dass in der Welt nichts Recht geschicht.

The advantages and disadvantages of this kind of metre are apparent. The shortness of the line makes expansion of the original inevitable, but it has a piquancy and a brightness which are very enjoyable.

We now come to Titz[1] and Schultz[2]. The former discusses the merits of Owen at some length in a Latin dedication (1643):

"Longe vero jucundissimum fructuosissimumque scribendi genus est, Epigramma. Nam & breve est ; itaque sine taedio legitur : & varium ; unde gratissima rerum diversitate avidum semper Lectorem allicit ac tenet : & argutum, atque acuminibus refertum ; propterea mire animum afficit atque oblectat. Quamobrem e veteribus praeclarissima multa ingenia gloriam hoc Carminum genere sibi quaesivere. Quorum pulcherrima inventa cum Germano Lectore, communicare, operae, credo, sit nec inutilis, nec injucundae. Ego, ut periculum aliquod facerem, JOH. OWENI, etsi recentioris, Poëmata primo mihi proposui : cujus festivissimi atque eruditi lepores non immerito Martialis Britannici nomen Parenti suo pepererunt. Ex amoenissimo illo horto Flores aliquot decerpsi, atque in Centuriam collectos, Teutonicae linguae coloribus, ut potui, expressi..."

[1] Bibl. 141.   [2] Bibl. 142.

The translations, which are in alexandrines throughout, are from Books I (56) and II (44). The following is a specimen:

Prophetae, Poëtae.
Illi de rebus praedicere vera futuris;
Hi de praeteritis dicere falsa solent.   Owen, I. 31.

Propheten, Poeten.
Propheten pflegen wahr vom künfftigen zu sagen;
Poeten falsch von dem / was sich schon zugetragen.

The alexandrine has the advantage that it allows the antithesis to be properly balanced, but its length is at times apt to drag.

Schultz says in his preface that in translating Martial and Owen he is following the lead of Opitz, Tscherning and Titz. He translates from all the books (except the first), bestowing most attention on VI (9) and VII (10), and, like Titz, employs the alexandrine throughout. His version of the popular Job motive will be quoted presently.

In 1651, Valentin Löber, a student of medicine, published a volume entitled *Epigrammatum Ovveni Drey Bücher*[1]. The title is very misleading, as the book is divided into two parts and contains five books together with the Monosticha, which follow Book I. Each part has a separate title-page, but as the pages are not numbered it is not clear whether the parts were published separately or together. Both bear the same date. The first contains Book I, the Monosticha, Book II, and an appendix which comprises the first quarter of Book III. The second part contains the remainder of Book III and Books IV and V. The translations are not as complete as in the *Teutsch-redender Owenus*, which appeared in 1653. After the translations from Book V come about a dozen epigrams which I have not been able to locate. Indeed, I doubt whether they are Owen's.

Löber's volume of 1653[2] is practically complete, although there are omissions even here. He prefixes a short poem, the first line of which—Fahr hin/ du kleines Buch/ und lass dich irren nicht—reminds one strongly of Spenser's "Go little Booke[3]...."

---

[1] Bibl. 143. Urban says he was unable to examine this book. There is a copy in the Kgl.-Pr. Bibl., Berlin (Xe 1258).
[2] Bibl. 147.   [3] See p. 13.

His preface begins:

"Kind Reader, we all have something to which our inclination draws us. On this occasion I have been seized with a desire to turn Owen into German and see whether his gay epigrams could not be translated with the same brevity in verse, so that in this kind of poetry the Latin language, with its pleasing terseness, might not alone bear away the prize (for German has the evil reputation of being too diffuse) but that the Germans also might have something from which to compose verses of this nature independently. Behold! I have ventured; the mountain is climbed and you, O reader experienced in German, will soon observe the merits of my performance. My predecessor in this kind of translation was the famous and industrious Opitz, who put into German not only the *Trojan Women*, Cato's *Disticha*, etc., but also many of Martial's epigrams. His example may protect me from the reproaches of those who regard such productions as forced, disagreeable, and contrary to the spirit of the German language... Farewell...V.L."

The translations are in alexandrines. Here are two specimens, the first on the stock subject of matrimony:

Amor conjugalis.
Plurimus in coelis amor est, connubia nulla:
  Conjugia in terris plurima, nullus amor. Owen, ix. 21.

Eheliche Liebe.
Viel Lieb im Himmel ist / und gantz kein Eheband /
auf Erd ist schlechte Lieb / und mancher Ehestand.

The alexandrine shows here to a disadvantage; "gantz" is mere padding, and the effect altogether is tame.

Ad Philopatrum.
Pro patria sit dulce mori licet atque decorum;
  Vivere pro patria dulcius esse puto. Owen, i. 48.

Philopatri, an die Liebhaber des Vaterlandes.
Süss ist es / in den Todt fürs Vaterland sich geben:
noch süsser aber / für dasselb in Ruhe leben.

Greflinger and Logau treated the same subject, the latter's version being:

> Fürs Vaterland sein Blut vergissen /
> Hat weiland man zu rühmen wissen:
> Das Blut dem Vaterland ersparen /
> Ist jetzt ein Ruhm bey vnsren Jahren.

One of the most popular subjects of epigram is the Job motive:

Miseria Iob.
Divitias Jobo, sobolemque, ipsamque salutem
  Abstulit (hoc Domino non prohibente) Satan,
Omnibus ablatis misero, tamen una superstes,
  Quae magis afflictum redderet, uxor erat. Owen, iii. 199.

I give below the translations of Schultz and Löber, and the versions of Hudemann and Logau. The subject is also treated by Feinler, whose epigrams I have been unable to obtain.

Des Jobs Elend.

Der Satan brachte Job vmb Wolfahrt / Kinder / Geld /
Weil sich der Höchste hier dawider nicht gestellt.
Nach allem ist sein Weib jhm hinterstellig blieben /
Die diesen armen mann hat sollen mehr betrüben. (Schultz.)

Jobs Elend.

Gesundheit / Kind und Gut und was ihm lieb nur war /
nahm Satan Hiob weg / nach Gottes Willen zwar.
Doch / ob der Bösewicht nichts schont / als seiner Seelen /
liess er ihm noch sein Weib / das kunte Job mehr quelen.
(Löber.)

Jobs Unglück.

Ich habe offt / und viel von Jobs Unglück gelesen /
Und achte / dass jhm sey ein gross Unglück gewesen /
Als jhm sein Güter all / vnd seine Kinder feyn
Sampt seines Leibes Krafft gantz weggenomen seyn /
Noch aber glaub ich (wiewohl ichs nicht erfahren /
Vnd wollte solche Gunst Fraw Glück an mir nur sparen)
Dass grösser Vnglück jhm in solchem seinem Leyd
Gewesen sey sein Weib mit taglicher Bössheit. (Hudemann.)

Des Jobi Weib.

Wann der Satan gieng von Job / ist sein Anwalt dennoch blieben
Jobs sein Weib; er hatte nie keinen bessern auffgetrieben.
(Logau, III. 2. 49.)

Logau makes Job the subject of two other epigrams:

Auff Hornutum.

Hornutus las : Was Gott Job habe weggenommen
Sey duppelt jhm hernach zu Hause wieder kummen /
Wie gut / sprach er / war diss / dass Gott sein Weib nicht nam /
Auff dass Job ihrer zwey / für eine nicht bekam. (I. 2. 7.)

Von Jobs Weibe.

Wie kam es / dass / da Job hatt alles eingebüsset
Was jhm ergetzlich war / dass er sein Weib nicht misset?
Es steht nicht deutlich da / warumb sie übrig blieb /
Allein ich schliesse fast / er hatte sie nicht lieb. (I. 2. 8.)

References to Owen are numerous in German authors of the century. Heinrich Hudemann contributes two laudatory Latin poems, both quoted by Urban, in his *Divitiae poeticae*, Hamburg, 1625[1]. Schupp, though he wrote no epigrams himself, quotes

---

[1] Bibl. 139.

him frequently, e.g. in *De arte Ditescendi*[1], p. 148 (1648), *Antwort auff M. Schmids Discurs*, I. 747 (1659, Altona), *Almosen-Büchse*, II. 360 (1667, written 1659?), and *Der Bekehrte Ritter Florian*, II. 36 (1667)[2]. Moscherosch, in his *Gesichte Philanders von Sittewald* (1645), quotes the following epigram from Book I,

> Pompejanus ero si vicerit omnia magnus,
> Omnia si Caesar Caesarianus ero.

Birken[3] has a chapter on the epigram, in which he observes: "The learned Muretus well says of this kind of verse that its real charm is that, like the bee, it wounds with its tail and leaves the sting behind. Herein the ancient poet, Martial, and in more modern times Angelus Politianus, and finally the Englishman Owen, especially the last-named, are incomparable. Of the Germans, Samuel (*sic*) von Golaw has proved himself the equal of these Latin writers...." (Chap. IX). Morhof[4] also has a few words on the subject in a paragraph entitled "Von den Epigrammatibus": "The translations of foreign epigrams, especially of those which derive their *acumina ex fonte allusionum*, are heavy. Consequently, Löber's attempt to translate the epigrams of Owen is not particularly praiseworthy, for the effect of putting into German, without discrimination, all the epigrams which spring from Latin *allusionibus* is sometimes very poor...." Morhof also refers to a collection of 300 proverbs expressed in epigrammatic form by John Heydon. Gottfried Feinler, in his *Poetische Betrachtung der IV letzten Dinge oder Geistliche Madrigalen*, Jena, 1692, says: "A madrigal is nothing but an epigram, (in the composition of which in olden times Martial, in our own day Owen, were especially happy)...." One great writer of epigrams, Wernicke, seems to have escaped the influence of Owen[5].

[1] Bibl. 176.   [2] See Zschau, Bibl. 184.
[3] *Rede-bind- und Dicht-Kunst*, 1679. Bibl. 105.
[4] *Unterricht von der Deutschen Sprache*, 1682. Bibl. 255.
[5] See Pechel, Bibl. 264.

CHAPTER VI

HISTORY IN LITERATURE

(a) German History in English Literature.

THE knowledge of German history displayed by English
dramatists of the seventeenth century is extremely rudimentary.
" The *Alphonsus* is merely a crude and sanguinary travesty
of an imperial election dispute, in which the chief interest
attaches to a wholly mythical love affair. The *Hector of
Germany* (1615), professedly dealing with a contemporary of
the Black Prince, is an audacious revision of the history of
the fourteenth century in the spirit of the seventeenth. *The
Costlie Whore*, though it falls in a period when the war had
already made Germany relatively familiar, is nevertheless
merely a combination of the legend of Hatto with a scarcely
less romantic story of a duke of Saxony; Chettle's *Hoffman*
lays at Lübeck the scene of a tragic story in which dukes and
emperors take part, but which is a palpable coinage of the
Elizabethan brain. *Evordanus* (1605) and *A defiance to Fortune*
(1590) are romances attached in the loosest manner to German
localities[1]." Of the plays dealing with earlier periods of German
history *The Costlie Whore* may be taken first. The scene is
laid in " Meath," i.e. Mainz[2], but the plot is taken from a story
in Greene's *Planetomachia*. Greene's source was an anecdote in
Aelianus, Ποικίλη Ἱστορία, and in Strabo. There is a reference
in the play to Archbishop Hatto (850–913), elder brother of

---

[1] Herford, Bibl. 59.

[2] Emil Koeppel: *Quellen-Studien*, 1897. Bibl. 167. Koeppel also mentions Richard Brome's comedy, *The Novella* (1632), in which a German,
Swatzenberg, speaks a few sentences in that language fairly correctly.

the "duke of Saxonie." The *Alphonsus* (1654), which is almost certainly not the work of George Chapman, as Elze[1] takes for granted, deals with the period of the great inter-regnum, 1257–1273, and the rivalry of Richard of Cornwall and Alphonso X of Castile for the imperial dignity. The Princess Hedewick speaks German throughout the play and two peasants speak Low German. From this Elze conjectures that the author was familiar with the plays of Heinrich Julius of Brunswick, who also makes his servants and clowns speak Low German, whereas his principal characters speak High German. Elze considers that the author displays a good knowledge of German customs and suggests that he had the assistance of a German collaborator. This hypothesis is taken up by Parrott[2], who suggests Weckherlin.

With the outbreak of the great war, however, English interest in Germany becomes more lively. Reference has already been made (see Introduction) to the periodical *Weekly News from Italy, Germany, etc.*, which was first published on May 23rd, 1622, and a long list of similar publications is given by Herford (IV. 174). I quote the following from Hazlitt[3]:

*Newes out of Germany of the most bloody murders that ever were committed...*1607.

*A true Relation of all Battailes as hath been fought in the Pallatinate, since the King of Bohemia's arrivall there, untill this 27. of May, Stilo nouo...*1622.

*A booke called a Lamentable List of Certaine hideous signes in the Ayre in Germany, &c....*1638.

*A Trve Relation of the taking of Alba-Regalis, in the German Tongue, called Stullweissenburgh, the Chiefe Cittie in Nether Hungarie, which was taken by the Christian Armie, the Twentieth of September last past, 1601. Truely translated out of the German Tongue...*1601.

*The Lamentations of Germany. Wherein, as in a Glasse, we may beholde her miserable condition, and reade the woefull effects of Sinne. Composed by Dr. Vincent Theol., an eye-witnesse thereof...*1638.

*Lachrymae Germaniae: Or, The Teares of Germany. Vnfolding her woefull Distresse by Jerusalems Calamity. In a Sermon preached at a Generall Assembly in the Maiden-Towne of Nuremburg, &c. Translated out of the high Dutch Coppy...*1638.

[1] Karl Elze: *George Chapman's The Tragedy of Alphonsus*, 1867. Bibl. 160.

[2] Thomas Marc Parrott: *The Tragedies of George Chapman*, 1910. Bibl. 169. For Chettle's *Hoffman* (1631) see Richard Ackermann: *The Tragedy of Hoffman*, 1894. Bibl. 166.

[3] W. Carew Hazlitt: *Handbook to the...Literature of Great Britain*, pp. 226–7, 1867. Bibl. 6. Also *Collections and Notes*, II. 246–7 (1882) and III. 94 (1887). Bibl. 7.

The story of Stuhl-Weissenburg was dramatized and, as·we have already noted (see Chapter I), performed at least as early as September, 1602. On September 20th, 1601, the fortress was captured by the imperial general, Count Russworm, from the Turks, in whose hands it had been since 1553. However, as Bolte[1] points out, it had again changed hands at the time of the performance in London, having been retaken by the Grand Vizier, Hassan, on August 29th, 1602.

We may also note two more serious works which deal with contemporary German history. They are *A Discourse of the Empire of Germany* (1659) by James Howell and *The Present State of the German and Turkish Empires* by a certain D...A...M.D.[2]

The lukewarm attitude of James I towards the fate of his daughter and son-in-law was not shared by his subjects. Thousands of volunteers left these islands to fight against the Catholic oppressor. Six hundred Scots fell with Colonel Lindesay at Neubrandenburg. Such disasters are lamented in numerous popular ballads, one of which, quoted by Hoenig[3], begins:

> Oh, woe unto these cruel wars,
> That ever they began,
> For they have reft my native isle
> Of many a pretty man.
>
> First they took my brethren twain,
> Then wiled my love from me,
> Oh woe unto these cruel wars
> In Low Germanie.

The Swedish army contained thirteen Scottish regiments, with 1000 officers, one of whom, Alexander Leslie, ranked next to Gustavus Adolphus himself. They distinguished themselves particularly at Leipzig. Many of them left accounts of their experiences, one of the most interesting of these chronicles being Monro's *Expedition*, which has been discussed at some length by Hoenig. The title fully explains the nature of the book:

---

[1] Johannes Bolte: *Schauspiele in Kassel und London*, 1889. Bibl. 67.
[2] The date has unfortunately been cut away in the Berlin copy, which forms one volume with Howell's treatise. I have seen no other.
[3] B. Hoenig: *Memoiren englischer Offiziere im Heere Gustav Adolfs*, 1902. Bibl. 168.

Monro His Expedition with the worthy Scots Regiment (called MacKeyes Regiment) levied in August 1626 by Sir Donald MacKey, Lord Rhees, Colonell for his Majestie's Service of Denmark, and reduced after the Battaile of Nerling to one Company in September 1634 at Wormes in the Paltz.

Discharged in severall Duties and Observations of service; First under the magnanimous King of Denmark, during his wars against the Emperor; afterward, under the Invincible King of Sweden, during his Majestie's life time; and since under the Rex-chancellor Oxensterne and his Generalls.

Collected and gathered together at spare hours, by Colonell Robert Monro, at first Lievetenant under the said regiment etc.

To which is annexed the Abridgement of Exercise, and divers practicall Observations etc.   London, 1637.

Hoenig also mentions similar memoirs by Sir John Hepburn and Sir James Turner[1].

In the rich Wallenstein bibliography compiled by Georg Schmid[2] I find (p. 78) a Latin chronicle by an Irishman, a certain Carve Thomas:

Carve Thomas, Tipperariensis; Sacellanus maj. in legione Colonelli D. Walt. Deveroux. Itinerarium in fortissima juxta et nobilissima legione Domini Colonelli Deveroux sub S. C. Majest. stipendia merentis cum historia facti Buttleri, Gordoni, Lesly et aliorum.   Moguntiae 1639.   Editio tertia auctior et correctior.   Ibidem I et II. 1640–1641; Spirae III. 1646.

This of course shows the other side of the picture. A German translation appeared in 1640, entitled:

Carve Thomas, Irrländers, dess Edlen Gestrengen Walteri Deveroux, Kays. May. wohlbestellten Obristen, Feldt Caplans.   Reyssbüchlein.   Darinnen allerley glaub- vnd denckwürdige Historien vnd Kriegsverlauff vom Jahr 1630 biss 1638 verfasset... Auss dem Latein ins Teutsch vbersetzt durch P. K.... Mayntz....   Im Jahr Christi 1640.

Another work by the same author is:

Rerum germanicarum ab anno 1617 ad annum 1648 gestarum epitome. Editio altera et cum priore continuata.   s. l. 1654.

Among the additions made by Loewe[3] to Schmid's bibliography are

The great and famous battle of Lützen fought betweene the renowned king of Sweden and Waldstein... Here is also inserted an abridgement of the king's life and a relation of the king of Bohemia's death.   Faithfully translated out of the French Coppy.   No place, 1633.

---

[1] Published by the Bannatyne Club, 1829.   On p. 193 is "A letter from Don Francisco of Quevedo to Philander of Sitwald, who wrote the continuation of Quevedo's Visions, etc.   In the year 1659, Englished out of the Hie Dutche."

For other similar chronicles, e.g. Sydnam Poyntz: *A True Relation of these German Warres*, see the Bibliography to Vol. VII of the *Cambridge History of Eng. Lit.* 1911.

[2] *Die Wallenstein-Literatur*, 1879.   Bibl. 162.

[3] Victor Loewe: *Die Wallenstein-Litteratur*, 1896, 1902.   Bibl. 163.

and

The relation of the death of the Great Generalissimo (of his Imperial Maiestie) the Duke of Mecklenburg, Fridland, Sagan and great Glogaw etc. Together with the cause there of. London, 1634.

Koeppel[1] gives numerous quotations from the English drama with reference to the war, e.g. the soldier in Middleton's *The World Tost at Tennis* (1619–20) cries, " I'll over yonder to the most glorious wars That e'er fanned Christian kingdom "; Shirley alludes to the victories of Gustavus Adolphus in *The Opportunity* (1634) and to those of Tilly and Wallenstein in *The Example* (1634), and Massinger also mentions the latter in *The Bashful Lover* (1655, performed 1636).

This brings us to the most important portrayal of Wallenstein in contemporary English literature—Henry Glapthorne's *Tragedy of Albertus Wallenstein*, 1639.

The play was probably written in 1634, as the introductory poem by Alexander Gill, *In caedem Alberti Wallenstenii, ducis Fridlandiae*, bears this date. The first copies were published in 1639 and a re-impression appeared the next year. Sufficient has been written on the subject by Vetter[2], Elze[3] and others to render criticism superfluous here, but I quote Elze's summary of the play to give the reader an idea of Glapthorne's conception of Wallenstein: "The plot of Glapthorne's tragedy partly turns on the intention of Wallenstein's younger son Albertus to marry Isabella, a virtuous chambermaid of his mother, which incites the father to display a most tyrannical cruelty 'in king Cambyses' vein. He is willing at length to allow the marriage, on condition that Albertus will engage to murder his young wife with his own hands on the morning after the wedding. At this moment the Duchess enters and accuses Isabella of having stolen a precious jewel, afterwards found in her own drawer. Wallenstein, in spite of her protestations, orders her to be hanged, and as the guards are laying hold of her, one of them is killed by Albertus in defence of his

[1] Emil Koeppel: *Quellen-Studien zu den Dramen George Chapman's, Philip Massinger's und John Ford's*, 1897. Bibl. 167.
[2] Theodor Vetter: *Wallenstein in der dramatischen Dichtung des Jahrzehnts seines Todes...*, 1894. Bibl. 165.
[3] Bibl. 160, and in *The Plays and Poems of Henry Glapthorne*. London, 1874. Bibl. 161.

innocent bride. Wallenstein in a rage stabs his son and
Isabella is hanged. Afterwards Wallenstein also kills a page,
who, sent by the Duchess, awakens him against his orders. In
the fifth act Wallenstein goes to Eger in order there to celebrate
the wedding of his elder son Frederick with Emilia, daughter
to the Duke Saxon-Weimar, one of the Protestant leaders.
Exactly as in Schiller's celebrated tragedy, the Earls of
Tertski and of Kintzki, Colonel Newman and Marshall Illawe,
are shot by some soldiers at a feast prepared for them by
Gordon (governor of Eger), Leslie, and Butler, upon which the
conspirators hasten to Wallenstein's chamber, where Gordon
instantly despatches him[1]."

Glapthorne's tragedy seems to have found its way to
Germany. The Landschaftsbibliothek at Stettin possesses an
old programme[2] which announces a performance of a play
dealing with Wallenstein in the Rathaus at Berlin on "Monday,
September 3rd." Bolte[3] points out that, according to the
Julian calendar, which was still followed in Brandenburg in
the seventeenth century, September 3rd fell on a Monday in
1690. The same writer reprints the programme and makes it
clear that we here have to deal with a performance of Glapthorne's work. Loewe[4] adduces evidence of another performance
at Lüneburg in 1666.

(b) *English History in German Literature.*

The events of English history figure largely in German
literature during this period. The fate of Charles I naturally
receives the largest share of attention, but he is by no means
the only royal personage to appear in German drama.

The divorce and death of Catherine of Arragon are treated
in Joh. Christoph Hallmann's *Sterbende Unschuld*, published in
1684 in a volume entitled *Trawer- Freuden- und Schäfferspiele*[5].

[1] Elze refers of course to the sequence of events. Schiller's Gordon is a
very different character from Glapthorne's.
[2] Reprinted in *Baltische Studien*, III. 2, 254–7. Stettin, 1836.
[3] *Eine englische Wallensteintragödie in Deutschland*, 1887. Bibl. 164.
[4] Victor Loewe: *Die Wallenstein-Litteratur*, 1902. Bibl. 163.
[5] Bibl. 156.

The author remarks in his preface: " In my *Catharina* (the subject of which required very discreet treatment) is depicted a queen, who, though mortally insulted, reveals herself as most patient and magnanimous. Her inconstant husband repudiates her in defiance of law and justice, defies the Church and the Emperor, executes some of the most innocent persons in England, tears asunder the indissoluble bond of holy wedlock and raises to the throne a handmaid and servant called Bolena, in place of a born Queen who has been solemnly crowned ! In the treatment of this fruitful subject I have followed as far as possible the most credible and dispassionate historians. For these reasons I submit the result of my labours (more particularly the account of England's century of misfortune, depicted by Catharina's ghost in twelve prophecies, which have indeed come true) to the impartial judgment of the learned reader, who will not, I hope, find fault with me for attributing to this much wronged queen, by a pardonable *fictio comica* and with the object of emphasizing the bitterness of her sufferings, an actual intention of putting Bolena, her rival, out of the way. For this (although we can never know her actual thoughts) in no wise detracts from her much lauded patience, because in the face of such poignant *mortificationes* Patience herself, let alone a woman's, must become impatient, as Germany can well testify from a recent and similar example." The dedication to Johann Georg, Freiherr von Fürst, is dated " 4 May, 1684." We are informed that, in accordance with the dramatic unity of time, the tragedy begins at dawn, lasts the whole day and finishes after midnight. The following is a short account of the plot:

ACT I. Queen Catherine has had a disturbing dream which she thinks is a warning of coming disaster. The Princess Mary and the ladies-in-waiting fail to reassure her. The King enters and repudiates both mother and daughter on the ground that he ought not to have married his brother's widow. Catherine says he merely wishes to marry Anne Boleyn (Bolena).

Cromwell approves of Henry's plan and they resolve to win over Anne's father—not a very difficult task.

I reprint the whole scene to illustrate the standard of excellence attained by the German dramatists of the seventeenth century.

Bolen. Hier ist / Durchlauchtigster / sein unterthän'ger Knecht /
        Zu hören / was der Fürst genädigst wil befehlen.
Henr.   Mein Freund / demnach das heil'ge Recht
        Zertrennt mein Ersteres Vermählen /
        Und meine Liebe nun
        Wil auf Bolenen ruhn /
        Bolenen / die Ich mir zum Eh-Schatz ausserkohren /
        Als wird dein Vater Hertz der Heyrath stimmen bey /
        Und wünschen / dass dieselbe glücklich sey.
Bolen. Grossmächtigster Monarch / was mit entzückten Ohren
        Sein Diener angehört / kan meine Zunge nicht
        Nach Würden sprechen auss !
        Kurtz : Meine Seel / Gutt / Blut / und gantzes Hauss
        Ist Eurer Majestät auf ewig fest verpflicht.
        Bolene sol des Fürsten Sclavin bleiben /
        Biss man Sie wird ins Leich-Register schreiben. (!!)
Henr.   Wir nehmen gnädigst an
        Dein höffliches Entschlüssen /
        Es müss' uns stracks auf dieser Rosenbahn
        Bolenens Göttlichkeit begrüssen.
        Indessen sol zum Zeichen Unsrer Gunst
        Und wahren Liebes-Brunst
        Bolenus itzt Graff von Wilschire werden.
        Nim an von Unsrer Hand
        Diss göldne Gnaden-Pfand /
        Und lebe stets glückselig auf der Erden !
        Trag / Essex / heute noch dem Parlamente für /
        Dass Ihm geschenket ist die Graffschafft von Wilschir.
Bolen. Ich werde diese Gnad' auch in dem Sarch bedienen.
        Es müsse für und für der grosse Heinrich grünen.

(Act I. Sc. VI.)

In the last scene of the act Henry and Anne declare their affections in flawless stichomythia.

ACT II. The Pope's Nuncio and the Ambassador of Charles V join with Sir Thomas More and Fisher, Bishop of Rochester, in condemning Henry. Catherine enters, disguised as a fisher-woman, reveals herself and pleads for help, which is promised. Left alone, she laments her fate and decides to stab Anne. The latter conveniently appears at this moment and, refusing Catherine an alms, is about to be stabbed when Henry enters, disarms Catherine and has her imprisoned.

ACT III. Arthur's ghost appears to Henry and reproaches him. Boleyn and Cromwell allay his fears. The nuncio and the imperial ambassador convey their masters' displeasure to Henry, who defies both Pope and Emperor. More and Fisher plead for Catherine and lose their heads.

ACT IV. The ghosts of More and Fisher appear to Catherine and prophesy a peaceful death for her. The nuncio and the ambassador condole with Catherine and abuse Henry. Catherine dies.

ACT V. Boleyn tells Anne of Catherine's death. Anne vows to persecute the Catholics. Henry, meanwhile, is stricken with remorse and Anne has difficulty in getting him to consent to her schemes. Finally, the ghost of Catherine appears and prophesies disaster. She reveals the future in twelve visions, the last being the execution of Charles I. Henry is overwhelmed with distress.

There is a ballet after each act, in which Venus, Juno and other immortals take part.

All other references to English history in German literature of the period deal with the members of the House of Stuart, of whom Mary, Queen of Scots, and Charles I naturally receive the greatest share of attention. Georg Greflinger gives a short account of the whole dynasty in *Der zwölff gekröhnten Häupter von dem Hause Stuart unglückselige Herrschafft*, 1652[1]. I pass over Robert I, Robert II, James I, James II, James III, James IV, and James V and begin with

"Henry (Darnley). Blown up at the instigation of Mary, his wife, and the Earl of Bothwell, and then, being still alive, strangled by other hired ruffians with his own shirt-sleeve.

Mary. Beheaded at Fodringham (*sic*).

James VI. After being delivered several times by God from wonderful conspiracies, died in his bed, although some say he was poisoned.

Charles I. Beheaded at London, 1649.

Charles II. Escaped after the battle of Worcester and is now living in France."

Then comes a poem entitled *König Carls II. Danck-Lied/ Als er mit noch einem Herrn Nahmens Willmuht* (Wilmot) *aus seiner Feinde Hände nach Franckreich kam*. There is a reference to the oak-tree in verses 3–7. The poem is signed Seladon, i.e. Greflinger. The pamphlet concludes (Zur Ausfüllung des übrigen Raums!) with a quotation from the famous passage in H. Boethius: "Erant simul, Machabaeus (Macbeth) amitinus Regis Scotiae Duncani & Banco Stuart Forres vir strenuus, per Sylvas profiscentes (*sic*) ad Regem, heic (*sic*) obviam habuere, tres mulieres insolita facie, quarum una inquit: Salve Machabaee Thane Glammis...."

The numerous dramas in which Mary Stuart is the principal figure have been fully discussed by Kipka[2]. Some half-dozen call for attention here. The first in order of date is entitled *Königliche Tragödie. Oder Maria Stuarta, Königin von Schottland*, and was performed by the students of the Jesuit College at Prague on September 29th, 1644. The heroine is depicted as a fugitive, bereaved of her second husband by treason and murder, forced again into marriage and finally betrayed and

[1] Bibl. 153.
[2] Karl Kipka: *Maria Stuart im Drama der Weltliteratur*, 1907. Bibl. 159.

persecuted by heretics and rebels. She seeks the protection of
Elizabeth at the invitation of the latter and is cruelly imprisoned. Great emphasis is laid on her incomparable beauty
and virtue and her lively and versatile nature.

On July 31st, 1651, a play called *Maria Stuart* was given
before visitors at the Jesuit College of Krems but is now lost.
A third play of this nature, *Maria Stuarta Scotiae Regina*, was
acted at the College of Neuburg on the Danube on September
4th and 5th, 1702, and revised for the College of Eichstätt
in 1709.

Leaving these College plays let us now turn to Mary Stuart
as she appears in the Renaissance drama. The best known of
this type is *Maria Stuart of gemartelde Majesteit* (1646), by
the Dutch dramatist, Joost van den Vondel. Its importance
for us lies in its influence on German writers. Vondel remarks
in his preface : "The Aristotelian canon scarcely admits of such
an innocent and perfect figure (i.e. Mary) assuming the tragic
rôle ; it requires rather one who stands midway between virtue
and sin, who is guilty of some crime or has some fault or
other or is forced by violent passion or imprudence to some
terrible deed. With the object, therefore, of making good this
defect, we have shrouded Mary's innocence and the justice of
her cause in the mist of evil report, calumny, and malice of the
time, so that her Christian and queenly virtue might appear
doubly resplendent for its temporary eclipse." Vondel's drama
was twice adapted for the German stage. The first version,
by Christophorus Kormart[1], appeared at Halle in 1673 with
the title *Maria Stuart Oder Gemarterte Majestät, Nach dem
Holländischen Jost van Vondels.* This play had been previously
performed before some society in Leipzig. Kipka points out
that the second Abhandlung or act (there are four) is independent of Vondel.

Another adaptation of Vondel's drama appeared in 1681 in
a collection of three plays by Johann Riemer entitled *Der
Regenten Bester Hoff-Meister Oder Lustiger Hoff-Parnassus.*
It takes the form of a sequel to an original drama on the same

[1] Born *c.* 1642, Leipzig. Mag. Jur. 1665. Died at Dresden between 1718–
1722.

subject, entitled *Von hohen Vermählungen*. This latter play had been published separately at Weissenfels in 1679 with the fuller title *Der Ertz-Verleumder Und Ehe-Teuffel Von Schottland*.... Both Kormart and Riemer are dry and didactic, and impartial as far as the religious aspects of the theme are concerned. In *Von hohen Vermählungen* Riemer treats the story as a family tragedy and not from a political or historical point of view. Both his plays apparently passed into the repertoire of travelling players.

The last drama on the subject is the work of Count August Adolf von Haugwitz (1645–1706) and bears the title *Schuldige Unschuld, Oder Maria Stuarda, Königin von Schottland*. It was published at Dresden in 1683. Haugwitz had visited England in the course of his travels and seems to have acquired some knowledge of life at the English court. He tells us, on the occasion of a discussion with Boeclerus at Strassburg as to the reliability of the authorities he had consulted for his *Maria*, that the drama was completed several years before publication. From the fact that Haugwitz' travelling library included the works of Gryphius, Kipka thinks he must have been influenced by *Carolus Stuardus*, in the second act of which the ghost of Mary appears to Charles and utters a long monologue. Haugwitz' attitude towards Mary's guilt or innocence is one of utter indecision, as we may indeed gather from the title.

As the death of Mary is the only event of Elizabeth's reign which finds reflection in German literature, we must now turn to the references to current events which begin with the accession of James I.

The marriage of the Princess Elizabeth to Friedrich V, Elector of the Palatinate, is the first event of interest. In a letter dated 20 September, 1614, quoted by Reifferscheid[1], Jan Gruter writes to A. de Bibran: "Nuptias illas cur admirarer? ne mirabor quidem, cum omnia coibunt in corpus Britannicum. Utinam tamen ille dies ante meos obitus!" Surprise at James' lukewarm support of Friedrich is expressed by Lingelsheim in a letter to Grotius written from Heidelberg on July 17th, 1621. G. Remus, writing from Nuremberg to P. Brederodius on

---

[1] Bibl. 51.

the "V Eid. Apr. 1624," compares James unfavourably with Elizabeth: "Sane quod viriles animos gesserit Elisabeth femina, Jacobus vero vir muliebriter valde hactenus egerit, accidit, ut poeta festive notarit hoc versu:

> Rex erat Elisabeth, nunc est regina Jacobus."

This is possibly the epigram referred to by Gruter in a letter to Zincgref of May 3rd, 1623: "Epigramma in Anglum nimis est mordax."

Charles' vain wooing of the Spanish Infanta evidently amused Gruter, for he writes four times to Lingelsheim from Tübingen on the subject: "Britannicae nuptiae cum Hispana iam iterum redeunt in theatro, quae ipsae diserte evertunt doron eius basilicon" (29. 1. 1622). "Anglum Hispanus pergit naso ducere, tanquam si esset buculus" (2. 2. 1623). "At Valliae princeps quam indigne se gerit in ducenda Hispana" (24. 3. 1623). "Quod si etiam sponsus Anglus ex Hispania revertitur sine sponsa, numquid restat, quam ut indignationis bilem tota navigatione collectam evomat in Hispanum et Infantem?" (30. 4. 1623). Nor was Charles' betrothal to Henrietta Maria of France viewed with much favour. In April, 1624, Remus, in a letter already quoted, thinks a marriage between persons of different religions unfortunate: "De connubio inter Cornwalliae principem et Ludovici XIII sororem tibi, vir sapientissime, adstipulor omnino. Vix bene concordans erit matrimonium inter diversae religionis principes." Finally, Gruter, in a letter to Lingelsheim, expresses his doubts as to whether Charles will prove a better king than James: "Sed et plura nobis expectanda ab Carolo quam Jacobo, nisi et ille in sinu patris didicit simulationum falsa."

Buckingham's assassination in 1626 also attracted attention, for in 1631 Bernegger composed and printed at his own press an epitaph, which he sent on May 8th to Robert Mason, "nobili Anglo," at Padua. Mason disapproved of it and Bernegger therefore destroyed all copies.

The execution of King Charles roused a storm of indignation in Germany, as elsewhere on the continent, and numerous pamphlets were written in protest. One of the most curious has been described by Powell[1]. It was written by a lady and apparently addressed to Fairfax in particular. It has the following quaint title:

> *Ein Schreiben über Meer gesand*
> *an die Gemeine in Engeland*
> *auss einer alten Frawenhandt*
> *die ungenandt | Gott ist bekandt.*
> *Anno 1649.*

```
        B
        D
        B
B D B V B D B
        B
        D
        B
```

Bekenne deine bossheit und besser dich bald
Fairfax dein bossheit und gewald
Am König begangen
wirst nun Lohn empfangen.
wie du hast verdienet
dan dein Unglück grünet
Zweiffel nicht daran
Du Gottloser Man.

The authoress upbraids the nation and Parliament for permitting the execution.

Buchner wrote a defence of Charles in Latin, entitled *Quid Carolus I. Britanniarum Rex, Loqui potuerit lata in se ferali sententia, Oratio, Seu Declamatio Gemina*[2]. This was translated into German by Zesen as *Was Karl der erste| König in Engelland| bei dem über Ihn gefälltem todesuhrteil hette fürbringen können. Zwei-fache Rede*[3]. The date of both treatises is apparently 1649. Zesen remarks in his dedication to Dietrich von dem Werder: "England has sinned against the sanctity, nay, the divinity, of kingship. It seems as though the nation were expressly born to imprisonment and slaughter, inasmuch as in its perverseness it did not hesitate shamefully to despise His Majesty and, what is still more scandalous, to stain by public condemnation its unjust hands with holy, royal blood."

The greatest tribute to Charles is the tragedy of Gryphius, *Ermordete Majestät oder Carolus Stuardus König von Gross*

[1] G. H. Powell: *Anti-English Germany* (1649), 1903. Bibl. 158.
[2] Bibl. 151.   [3] Bibl. 152.

Britanien[1], first published in 1657 in *Andreae Gryphii Deutscher Gedichte, Erster Theil.*　In the preface to the second edition (1663) Gryphius says the tragedy, which was written shortly after the event and subsequently revised, had a mixed reception:

"Carolum Tragoediam, postquam nuper ultimum recognovi, ac quod dudum publico pollicitus, uberiore facinoris atrocissimi adumbratione insignem theatro reddidi; Tu maxime occurebas VIR NOBILISSIME, cujus fidei atq; Tutelae permitterem scriptum ambigua huc usque judiciorum statera libratum.　Ut ut (*sic*) enim, quibus cordi fas decorque rerum atque integritas recti ingente encomio exornarint Poema, quod paucos intra dies attonito, atque vix condito in hypogaeum REGIS cadavere, sceleris horror expressit: fuere tamen qui censerent imprudentem me, haud tantum nimis ex propinquo, sed quasi ipso parricidii momento Sontes arguere.　Alii stilo nimis acri, signum quasi ultionis dare contendebat, absit enim illos ut morer queis flagitii aestimium inerat.　Absolvit tandem Germania ferme universa insons carmen, quae Tertium Tragoediam hancce flagitabat.　Itaque ne spernere judicium Serenissimorum, atque Illustrissimorum, denique Eorundem videret, qui omne in hisce studiis aevum trivere, opus REGIO CRUORE horridum, denuo aggressus, addidi quae & longior dies, & nonnulli qua scriptis in publicum, qua monitis calamoque sollicito rerum earundem detexere...

Glogov. Idib. Januar.
A. 1663.　　　　　　　　　　　　　　　　　　　　　　A. Gryphius."

After the preface comes an "Epitaphium Cromwellii" (not flattering!) by C.H.A.H.S.

The play, which, needless to say, is written in alexandrines, is too tedious to be worth reading for its own sake.　The following is a summary of the plot:

ACT I.　Lady Fairfax determines to persuade her husband to save Charles from death.　Fairfax, after a long argument, agrees to try to change the sentence to banishment.　Lady F. knows on whom she may count but does not tell her husband.

Hugo Peter, a fanatical "Independent," Colonel William Hewlett and Daniel Axtel determine to make the execution as shameful as possible.

A chorus of murdered English kings laments Charles' fate and England's doom.

ACT II.　The ghosts of Strafford and Laud lament the state of affairs. Mary Stuart's ghost appears to Charles and laments his fate, prophesying revenge.

Charles prepares for execution and takes leave of his younger children, Elizabeth and Henry.

A chorus of Sirens laments the state of affairs generally.

ACT III.　Fairfax tells his wife that the king's rescue is assured.

Hugo Peter suspects Fairfax and gloats over the king's approaching death.

Two colonels (the men on whom Lady F. counts) discuss the probable consequences of Charles' death and are inclined to save him, if possible.

[1] Bibl. 157.

Fairfax sounds them. They hesitate to commit themselves and Fairfax, not feeling sure of them, assumes indifference to Charles' fate and does not open his mind.

(This, the most critical scene of the drama, is puerile. Henceforth, there is no hope for Charles.)

Cromwell gloats over Charles' fate; Fairfax has qualms. They argue the point at length in stichomythia. Hugo Peter fears the populace. A long discussion on divine right follows.

Fairfax fears much of the responsibility for the king's death will attach to himself and decides to resign his command if the execution takes place.

The Scottish ambassador reproaches Cromwell and expresses his misgivings for the future. Long argument in stichomythia.

Peter informs Cromwell that everything is ready.

A chorus of English ladies laments the king's fate and apostrophizes the sun and moon.

ACT IV. Charles regards his fate as the penalty for sanctioning the execution of Strafford.

The escort comes for Charles, who declares his readiness to die and appeals to Strafford's ghost for pardon.

Lady F. can get no news of her husband and is in despair. She reproaches one of the colonels for not keeping his promise. He asks if she had succeeded in winning Fairfax over and, on being told that this had been done, wonders why Fairfax did not declare himself. Hastens to find the latter and remove the misunderstanding, but of course it is too late.

The figure of Religion appears, surrounded by a chorus of heretics, and laments the wickedness done in her name.

ACT V. Poleh, one of the king's judges, enters in a frenzy of remorse and has visions. He sees Peter and Hewlett being quartered; the corpses of Cromwell, Ireton and Bradshaw dangling from the gallows; the coronation of Charles II and the ghosts of Laud and Strafford.

The scene is now prepared for the execution. Charles harangues his enemies in a long speech, prophesies disaster and is then executed (on the stage). The ghosts of murdered kings appear and foretell great calamities.

Gryphius adds a number of notes, in which he quotes several historical documents and shows considerable knowledge of the facts. The tragedy may be regarded as an argument in favour of the divine right of kings.

In addition to this tragedy, numerous short poems and epigrams by Logau[1], Kongehl[2] and others refer to Charles I Schupp, in the preface to *Salomo*, 1658[3], mentions Cromwell with reference to the uselessness of academic disputations: " If the united Universities of Oxford and Cambridge were to come to London and bring all their Scalas Praedicamentales to bear and make an assault, they would not gain the mastery in

---

[1] Bibl. 144. [2] *Sieg-Prangender Lorbeer-Hayn*, 1700. Bibl. 133.
[3] Bibl. 177.

London nor shake the Protector's resolve, but he would say, Gentlemen, Magistri nostri, nostrique magistri, I have here fifty thousand scholars who bear muskets and have their mouths and pouches full of bullets and plenty of powder and burning matches. They will give you an adequate reply to your syllogisms in Barbara & Celarent, Darapti & Felapton."

Charles II is made the subject of two pamphlets by Zesen, *Die verschmähete/ doch wieder erhöhete Majestäht*[1] and *Die Gekröhnte Majestäht*[2]. Both appeared in 1662, the latter being merely an account of the coronation festivities. *Die verschmähete...Majestäht* contains a portrait of Charles II, dated 1662, and a Latin poem by Nicolaus Heinsius entitled *In Effigiem Serenissimi, ac Potentissimi Domini, Caroli Secundi, Angliae, Galliae, Scotiae, & Hiberniae Regis*. According to a letter at the end from Daniel Weidman, of London, to the author, the work, which is an account of Charles' exile and restoration, was to be submitted to the king himself.

The flight of James II and the accession of William and Mary are treated by Benjamin Neukirch[3] in a short poem beginning " Ein rechter König flieht, eh man ihn noch verjagt," printed in his edition (1697) of *Herrn von Hoffmannswaldau und andrer Deutschen auserlesener...Gedichte erster theil*[4]. He also contributes (p. 88) an epitaph on Monmouth and a few lines (p. 92) on the birth of the Prince of Wales (the Old Pretender). Part III of the same work contains epigrams on William III, Mary, the Prince of Wales, and Tyrconnell.

[1] Bibl. 154.   [2] Bibl. 155.
[3] Born 1665 at Reinke, Silesia. Educated at Bojanowo, Breslau, and Thorn. Wandered to Frankfort-on-Oder, Halle, Leipzig, and Berlin, where he lived twenty years in great poverty. Died at Ansbach in 1729. As a poet he imitated first Lohenstein, then Canitz.
[4] Bibl. 91.

CHAPTER VII

ENGLISH PHILOSOPHERS IN GERMANY

To Germany belongs the honour of having produced at Frankfort in 1665 the first complete edition of Bacon's works[1]. It is a folio volume, containing a portrait of the great philosopher, identical with the one in the London edition of 1638[2], and the undermentioned treatises in the order named:

Tractatus nempe de Dignitate & Augmentis Scientiarum.
Novum Organum Scientiarum, cum Parasceve ad Historiam Naturalem
    & Experimentalem.
Historia Ventorum.
Historia Vitae & Mortis.
Scripta de Naturali & Universali Philosophia.
Sylva Sylvarum, sive Historia Naturalis.
Nova Atlantis. ("*Novus Atlas*" in text.)
Historia Regni Henrici VII. Regis Angliae: Opus vere Politicum.
Sermones fideles, sive Interiora Rerum.
Tractatus de Sapientia Veterum.
Dialogus de Bello Sacro.
Opus illustre in felicem memoriam Elisabethae Reginae.
Imago Civilis Julii Caesaris.
Imago Civilis Augusti Caesaris.

The last four have no separate title-pages but go with *De Sap. Vet.*, which is dated 1668. The remaining treatises are all dated 1664 and have separate title-pages, except the *Atlantis*, which goes with *Sylva*. The index to the Essays (*Sermones*) contains 62 titles, but only 58 appear in the text, the last four being printed with *De Aug. Scient.* A portion of the editor's (J. B. Schönwetter) dedication to his patron, Johann Helwig Sinolt, runs:

" Est e Viris doctis, qui Angliam olim, eo ipso tempore, quo Franciscus Baconus Baro de Verulamio in culmine dignitatum suarum adhuc constitutus, postmodum vero, annon suo & rei litterariae commodo, dubitatur,

[1] Bibl. 174.   [2] Bibl. 171.

inde dejectus & vitam & Angliae Cancellarium egit, cum peragraret, ad Amicum suum in Germaniam literis perscripsit : Deum se testari, se in illo Europae angulo nullos invenisse homines, nullos inquam, sed profecto meras Gratias. Non invidebunt haec Anglorum, qualia qualia sint, Tempora, illis prioribus suam felicitatem vel ingeniorum subtilissimorum fertilitatem, quin potius illum, quicunque fuerit, vera scripsisse, calculum suum addent, & huic suae Nationis laudi non parum accessisse, pro Exemplo adducent Magnum illum Angliae Cancellarium Franciscum Baconum, Virum quod ingenii sui testantur monumenta juris, inprimis Anglicani, peritissimum Philosophum omni ex parte verum, Eloquentiae autem laude incomparabilem. Hujus ego opera omnia et singula, quae quidem illo vel in vivis existente, maxima ex parte in Anglia, vel post illius obitum apud Batavos passim divulgata fuerunt, uno comprehensa fasciculo & in unum congesta, imo conquisita volumen, cum typis describi curaverim, de Patrono, cujus nomini tanto operi condigno, illud inscriberem, dispiciendum existimavi... Dabantur Francofurti ad Moenum ipsis Nundinis Autumnalibus A.R.S. MDCLXIV."

Another complete edition appeared at Leipzig in 1694[1]. It contains the whole of the Frankfort edition with the addition of thirty short treatises and speeches : "Ultra triginta Tractatus Historico-politici ac morales antea nunquam editi, nunc ex Anglico sermone latine redditi, quos a folio operis hujus, 1324. usque ad 1584. legere est." The biographical notices, text, pages, and paragraphs of both editions are identical. The volume is dedicated by Simon Johann Arnold to Karl Philipp, Margrave of Brandenburg, in these terms :

"...Isthaec Francisci Baconi Verulamii opera, quae ex Anglicano in Latinum transtuli sermonem, ut REVERENDISSIMAE CELS : TUAE dedicarem, & eorum me movit argumentum, & praesens rerum facies. Exiguum est, quod in hoc opere meum nuncupare possum ; offero tamen illius Viri librum, qui JACOBO REGI Doctissimo, charus olim, nunc apud eruditos omnes magno est in pretio. Et habeant sibi eruditi Organon ejus, teneant Sylvarum Sylvam ; Principi certe debentur, quae hoc complexa volumine, de Uniendis, tractant, regnis, de formandis Legibus, de coloniis deducendis, de Ecclesia firmanda, de Regum vita tuenda, de populi salute, de judicibus instituendis, de tributorum integritate, & innumeris aliis ad rempublicam pertinentibus..."

The various treatises are grouped as in the Frankfort edition and the separate title-pages all bear the date 1693. The new matter begins with "Felix Scotiae cum Angliae Unio" and concludes with "Epistola & Discursus ad Henricum Savilium." This edition was published simultaneously at Copenhagen. It is not mentioned by Kuno Fischer[2].

---

[1] Bibl. 175.
[2] *Francis Bacon und seine Schule*, 1904[3]. Bibl. 183.

There is no evidence to show, nor do we expect it, that Bacon's works were known in Germany in their English form. Even the few selections which were translated into German were made from the Latin text. We possess two small volumes of this kind, both belonging to the same year, 1654, and by the same author, Johann Wilhelm von Stubenberg[1]. The first, *Getreue Reden: die Sitten-Regiments- und Hausslehre betreffend*[2] is a translation of 57 of the Essays. Bacon is referred to in the preface as "the Aristotle of our time." I give as a specimen the beginning of Stubenberg's translation of the first Essay, "Of Truth":

"What is truth? said jesting Pilate; and would not stay for an answer. Certainly there be that delight in giddiness; and count it a bondage to fix a belief; affecting free-will in thinking, as well as in acting. And though the sects of philosophers of that kind be gone, yet there remain certain discoursing wits, which are of the same veins, though there be not so much blood in them as was in those of the ancients. But it is not only the difficulty and labour which men take in finding out of truth; nor again, that when it is found, it imposeth upon men's thoughts; that doth bring lyes into favour: but a natural though corrupt love of the lye itself..."

Von der Wahrheit.

"Was ist die Warheit? sprach der Spötter Pilatus / wolte aber keiner Antwort erwarten. Es gibt in warheit Leute / die sich mit dem Gedankenschwindel belustigen / und die Einschränkung eines fästen Glaubens / und beständiger Hauptlehrsätze / vor eine Dienstbarkeit achten; dem gebrauche des freien Willens / sich nicht minder in Gedanken / als im Tuhn / nachsehnend. Und ob zwar dergleichen Vernunftlehrer-zunften abkommen / so finden sich doch noch theils aufgeblasene rollende überbliebene Gemühter / die gleichmässige / wiewol nicht so blutreiche Adern / wie die Alten / haben. Aber / es bringt den Lügen / weder die blosse Beschwerlichkeit und Mühe / so die Menschen bey erfindung der Warheit anstehen / noch die Gefangenschafft / so durch deren Fund denen Gedancken auferlegt wird / einige Gunst zuwegen / sondern bloss die Natürlich-doch verderbte Liebe zur Lügen..."

The other volume, which is entitled *Fürtreffliche Staats-Vernunfft- und Sitten-Lehr-Schrifften*[3], has three parts, the first of which, *Von der Alten Weissheit*, is a translation of *De Vet. Sap.* (1609). The others, *Etliche Einrahtungen aus den Sprüchen Salomonis* and *Die Farben (oder Kennzeichen) des Guten und Bösen*, I have not been able exactly to locate, but am inclined

---

[1] Freiherr von Kapfenberg und Mueregg, Herr von Schallenburg und Sichtenberg. Born 1631. Member of the Fruchtbringende Gesellschaft (Der Unglückselige) 1647. Died 1 May, 1688. He translated numerous Italian and French authors into German.
[2] Bibl. 173.　　　　　　　　[3] Bibl. 172.

to think they are translations of portions of *De Aug. Scient.*
(1605; Latin, 1623)[1].   Stubenberg remarks in the preface:
" The present work is just as little in need of a recommendation
as good wine of a sign; especially as the learned world has
thought so highly of it as to translate it most carefully from
the original English into the principal European languages,
Latin, French, and others.   For the benefit, therefore, of
Germans who are ignorant of these languages, I was induced to
translate it into our beloved and magnificent mother-tongue...
Schallenburg, 1 March, 1654."

That Bacon was held in the highest esteem in Germany
during the seventeenth century is clear from the nature of the
numerous references to him in almost every branch of literature.
Harsdoerfer quotes from *De Dig. et Aug. Scient.* in the third
part of his *Poetischer Trichter*[2], 1653 (*Prob und Lob der Teutschen Wolredenheit,* IV. 32), and again in a note to the dedication
of *Heraclitus und Democritus,* 1661.   A quotation from *De Sap.
Vet.* occurs in *Trichter,* x. 94, and in *Nathan und Jotham*[3],
1659, p. 140, Harsdoerfer describes Bacon's costly laboratories.
Kongehl, in his *Sieg-Prangender Lorbeer-Hayn*[4], 1700 (a sort
of biographical dictionary in verse), has the following lines on
Bacon :

> Baco / der verdekte Ding' Entdekkende.
> Wie Baco Verulam / der Britten Cancellar /
> ein hochgelahrter Kopff / und kluger Staatsmann war /
> so dient er auch der Welt mit tief-ersinnten Schrifften ;
> Was in der Wissenschafft seither verdekt gestekt /
> das hat Er angezeigt / und theils der Welt entdekt ;
> Dies' und dergleichen Schrifften mehr
> vermehren seines Nahmens Ehr ;
> Durch Schrifften kanst du dir das beste Denkmal stifften.

Then follow a short biography of Bacon in Latin and an
anecdote in German.

But the two men who, above all others, felt the influence of
the English statesman were Johann Balthasar Schupp[5] and
Daniel Georg Morhof.

---

[1] Bibl. 170.   It has since occurred to me that these may not be translations
of Bacon at all, but of portions of Joseph Hall's *Solomon's Divine Arts* (1609),
and *Characters of Vertues and Vices* (1608).   Owing to the rarity of Stubenberg's
work I have had no opportunity of verifying this conjecture.
[2] Bibl. 179.   [3] Bibl. 129.   [4] Bibl. 133.
[5] Born Giessen, 1610.   Studied at Marburg, Königsberg and Rostock.

The parallel passages in the works of Schupp and Bacon (some sixty in number) have been quoted and discussed by Zschau[1], who concludes: "Schupp's attitude towards a whole series of economic questions, towards agriculture, handicraft, traffic, commerce and colonization is determined by Bacon, whom he follows in thought and in word." With this opinion Carl Vogt[2] agrees: "It would be difficult to overestimate Bacon's importance for Schupp...His influence is strongest at the beginning of Schupp's career—in *Orator Ineptus* (1638). Then come *De Opinione* (1639), *Proteus* (1642) and *Aurora* (1642). Quotations are most frequent in *Ars Ditescendi* (1648)[3], but it contains old material. The passage in *Florian* (1667) is a repetition; *Salomo* (1657)[4] contains more, and *Der Teutsche Lehrmeister* (1667) and *Vom Schulwesen* (1667) are strongly reminiscent of *Salomo*. In the interval Bacon's influence is more latent, but present nevertheless." Schupp read Bacon almost certainly in Latin and seems to have been most familiar with *De Dig. et Aug. Scient.*, *Novum Organum*, *Sermones fideles* (the Essays), *De Sap. Vet.* and *Historia regni Henrici VII*. Historical allusions from the latter work appear in *Salomo*, I. 16 (the extortions of Empson and Dudley), *Eylfertiges Sendschreiben* (1659), I. 570 (Lambert Simnel), *Der geplagte Hiob* (1659), I. 137, and *Der rachgierige Lucidor* (1657), I. 283 (Henry VII and the Pope). Many of Bacon's pedagogic views find a reflection in *De arte Ditescendi* (1648), e.g. a good school training is necessary for subsequent study at the university (*De Dig. et Aug.* Lib. II. Praef.), public instruction is preferable to private (*De Dig. et Aug.* VI. 4), teachers must be well paid (*De Dig. et Aug.* II. Praef.). The essay on *Parents and Children* is also quoted in this connection. *De arte Ditescendi* is interesting, moreover, for the fact that Schupp lets Bacon appear in person to address the oppressed German nation. He suggests the colonization of an island (cf. New Atlantis) and after explaining his own proposals, listens to those of Barclay and others.

Lectured in Marburg. Professor of History and Eloquence, 1635. Pastor of St Jacob, Hamburg, 1649. Died Hamburg, 26 Oct. 1661.
[1] Bibl. 184.   [2] Bibl. 185.   [3] Bibl. 176.
[4] Bibl. 177. For Schupp's other works I have used the Hanau edition of 1663, Bibl. 178.

Schupp introduces Bacon as follows: "Heri inter has & similes meditationes altior somnus me opprimebat. Neque enim mihi semper vigilare libet. Per somnium mihi apparebat Franciscus Baconus Baro de Verulamio, Vice Comes Sancti Albani, Vir magnae prudentiae, rarissimaeque eruditionis." Like Bacon, Schupp laments the separation of the universities from the world around them and shares his dislike of Aristotle. Like Bacon, he praises agriculture (cf. *De Opinione*, p. 55, and *De arte Dit.* p. 133, with *De Dig. et Aug.* VIII. 3). He quotes from the essay, *De hortis* (Of Gardens), with reference to handicrafts, and shares (*De arte Dit.* p. 173) Bacon's appreciation of mechanical inventions, e.g. gunpowder, the compass, etc. (*Nov. Org.* I. 129). Schupp's ethical theories are supported by many quotations from the Essays, but as these passages have been fully discussed by Zschau, it is scarcely necessary to enumerate them here.

Morhof[1] is concerned with Bacon chiefly as the founder of the study of literary history. In *Polyhistor, sive de Notitia Auctorum et rerum commentarii...*1688[2], Lib. I. Caput II, "De Historia literaria," he remarks: "...Majus animo opus conceperat maximi vir ingenii Baco Verulamius, qui inter consilia de ampliandis scientiarum terminis, hujus quoque operis ideam proposuit lib. 2. de Augm. Sc. cap. 4. Absque hac Historiam mundi statuae Polyphemi eruto oculo non absimilem facit, cum ea pars imaginis desit, quae ingenium & indolem personae maxime referat..." The authority of Bacon is again cited both in this and later chapters of the book, e.g. XIV, "De aliis eruditorum societatibus" (Cap. XIII is entitled "De collegiis secretis"), and XV, "De conversatione erudita." These are all references to *De Dig. et Aug.*, but in Cap. XIX Morhof praises *Historia regni Henrici VII*. There are further allusions to *De Dig. et Aug.* in Liber II, e.g. in Cap. IV, "De subsidiis dirigendi judicii": "Recte quidem Verulamius libr. de Augm. Scientiarum V cap. 1. Rationales scientiae reliquarum omnium

---

[1] Born 6 Feb. 1639, Weimar. Studied at Rostock. Professor of Poetry, 1660. Professor at Kiel, 1665 (taught Wernicke). Visited England and Holland in 1660 and 1670. Friend of Isaac Voss and Robert Boyle, translated some of the latter's works into Latin. Died 30 July, 1691.
[2] Bibl. 254.

claves sunt. Et quemadmodum manus instrumentum instrumentorum, anima forma formarum; ita et illae artes artium ponendae sunt. Neque solum dirigunt, sed ut arcum tendat fortiorem..." Chapters v, vii, and viii of this Book and ix of Liber iii (i.e. Part II) also contain references to Bacon.

The collected works of James I[1] were published at Frankfort and Leipzig in 1689, uniformly with those of Sir Thomas More[2], but earlier allusions to single works are not wanting. Reifferscheid[3] speaks of a translation of *Donum regium sive de institutione principis ad Henricum filium* by Petrus Denaisius[4] (1604), and quotes a letter from Lingelsheim to J. Bongarsius (No. 9): "Denaisius noster multum debet tibi de tam amico et aequo iudicio de suo libello, vides non vane me antea tibi hominis virtutes praedicasse." G. Remus, writing to P. Brederodius in 1624 (V. Eid. Apr.), mentions one of the king's speeches: "Orationem regis Jacobi ad comitia Britann., ordines inquam congregatos, habitam legi, pro cuius communicatione gratias tibi debeo maximas." Another of James' pamphlets, *Apology for the Oath of Allegiance*, first published anonymously, was acknowledged in 1609 and dedicated to "Rodolph II, Emperor of Germany, Hungary, etc., and to all other right high & mighty Princes and States of Christendome." A copy seems to have been conveyed to the Emperor by Sir Robert Aytoun.

We may note in passing one or two works of a miscellaneous nature. Reference has already been made (see Chapter i) to Barclay's *Icon animorum*[5], a series of moral-psychological sketches. In 1601 Lingelsheim published at Heidelberg a work entitled *Henrici Savilis commentarius de militia Romana ex Anglico Latinus factus*, with reference to which O. Giphanius writes from Prague on April 20th, 1603: "Libellum, quem de Gallico Germanicum fecisti, de fatali illa societate libenter legi; Saviliana sive potius tua a te plura expecto."

The last Englishman of note with whom we have to deal in this chapter is Sir Thomas Browne, the first (unauthorized)

---

[1] Bibl. 186. [2] Bibl. 113. [3] Bibl. 51.
[4] Born at Strassburg, 1561. Visited England before 1590. Died at Heidelberg, 1610.
[5] Bibl. 63, 64, 65.

edition of whose *Religio Medici*[1] appeared in 1642. It was translated into Latin (apparently without Browne's knowledge) by John Merryweather in 1644 and in this form attracted considerable attention on the continent. In 1652 it appeared in Latin at Strassburg with voluminous notes by Levinus Nicolaus Moltkenius. This edition was reprinted in 1665 and 1692[2]. Moltkenius says he turned to literature on his retirement from court and, chancing upon the *Religio*, became deeply interested and wrote a number of notes: " Inter alios autores incidi tunc in librum, cui titulus Religio Medici...Edi haec (annotata) amicorum impulsu, permisi, ut liber, qui multorum in manibus versatur, multorum commodo inserviat....Auctor noster est Thomas Browne, ut testatur praefatio in Editione Leidensi; natione Anglus; arte medicus, ut manifestum faciunt sectio 1. & 5 l. 1. & sect. 9 l. 2. Quod attinet hominis religionem; non fuit Puritanismo addictus, aut turpitudine independentium errorum foedatus...Scripsit hunc tractatum lingua vernacula. Quidem Anglus nomine Johan Merryweather, latinum reddidit illum: nec in sermone aliquid reprehendendum existimo....Tu, benevole Lector, ea, quibus tibi prodesse volui, aequi bonique consulas obsecro, si quid vero inveneris, quod satis non arrideat, ne id in sinistrum sensum rapias iterum atque iterum rogo; aliud praemium non ambio. Vale. Argentinae Anno MDCLII." The date of the preface remains unchanged in the edition of 1665 but is altered to 1691 in the edition of 1692.

These notes attracted the attention of Thomas Keck, who edited the fourth English edition of 1656[3]. In his preface, dated March 24th, 1654, he remarks:

"...Since the time he (i.e. Kenelm Digby) Published his Observations upon it, one Mr. Jo. Merryweather, a Mr of Arts of the University of Cambridge, hath deem'd it worthy to be put into the universall Language, which about the yeare 1644 he performed : and that hath carryed the Author's name not only into the Low-Countreys and France (in both which places the Book in Latine hath since been printed) but into Italy and Germany; and in Germany it hath since fallen into the hands of a Gentleman of that Nation (of his name he hath given us no more than L. N. M. E. M.[4]), who hath written learned Annotations upon it in Latine, which were printed together with the book at Strasbourg in 1652... (Keck

[1] Bibl. 187.   [2] Bibl. 188, 189.   [3] Bibl. 187.
[4] Wrongly printed L.N.M.E.N. in Sayle's modern edition (1904), Bibl. 191.

here quotes a portion of Moltkenius' preface to show in what repute the *Religio* stood abroad)... But for the worth of the Booke it is so well knowne to every English-man that is fit to read it, that this attestation of a Forrainer may seem superfluous.

The German, to doe him right, hath in his Annotations given a fair specimen of his learning, shewing his skill in the Languages, as well antient as moderne; as also his acquaintance with all manner of Authors, both sacred and profane, out of which he hath amass'd a world of Quotations: but yet, not to mention that he hath not observed some Errors of the Press, and one or two main ones of the Latin Translation, whereby the Author is much injured, it cannot be denyed but he hath pass'd over many hard places untouch'd, that might deserve a Note; that he hath made Annotations on some, where no need was; in the Explication of others hath gone besides the true sense.

And were he free from all these, yet one great Fault there is he may be justly charg'd with, that is, that he cannot *manum de Tabula* even in matters the most obvious : which is an affectation ill becoming a scholar; witness the most learned Annotator, Claud. Minos. Divion. in praefat. commentar: Alciat: Emblemat. praefix: Praestat (saith he) brevius omnia persequi, et leviter attingere quae nemini esse ignota suspicari possint, quam quasi ῥαψωδεῖν, perq; locos communes identidem expatiari... I go not about by finding fault with his, obliquely to commend mine owne, I am as far from that, as 'tis possible others will be; All I seek by this preface, next to acquainting the Reader with the various entertainment of the Book, is that he would be advertiz'd that these Notes were collected ten yeares since, long before the German's were written, so that I am no Plagiary (as who peruseth his Notes and mine will easily perceive :) and in the second place that I made this Recueil merely for mine own entertainment, and not with any intention to evulge it,... I say further that the German's is not full and that... my Explications do in many things illustrate the text of my Author."

In spite of the three Strassburg editions references to the *Religio Medici* are not really numerous in German literature of the seventeenth century. Schupp speaks of it in *Salomo*[1], Chap. x. Browne himself, I believe, mentions that it had been translated into German, but I have discovered no trace of such a version[2].

There does exist, however, a translation of *Pseudodoxia Epidemica, or Enquiries into very many received Tenents and commonly presumed Truths* (1646). It is the work of one Christian Rautner (Peganius) and appeared in 1680. As may be gathered from the title-page[3], the volume is altogether a curious compilation. It begins with Browne's preface to the reader, followed by Book I, of which Chapters x and xi are

---

[1] Bibl. 177.
[2] Watt (Bibl. 3) mentions a German translation published at Leipzig in 1680 by Chr. Knorr. I have not seen a copy.
[3] Bibl. 190.

wrongly numbered XI and XII. Then follow two treatises, the
first (pp. 70–200) on Natural Science by an anonymous writer,
who signs himself "Spes mea est in Agno," the second (pp.
201–253) entitled *Ein ander vortrefflicher Tractat wider die
gemeinen Irrthümer / Von der Bewegung natürlicher Dinge* by
a certain G. G. L. L. Then we have (pp. 254–444) a translation of Chapters VI–XXVI of Henry More's *Enchiridion
Metaphysicum*, a treatise on the incorporeal, directed against
Descartes, and finally the remaining books of the *Pseudodoxia*
with notes inserted in the text. This work is discussed by
Morhof in *Polyhistor*[1].

[1] Bibl. 254.

CHAPTER VIII

THE THEOLOGIANS

(a) *German Theologians in England.*

THE study of Luther's influence in England belongs more properly to the realm of theology than literature and would, moreover, fill a volume. Many of his hymns[1] and several of his commentaries[2] were translated into English long before the close of the sixteenth century. Consequently, I shall confine my attention solely to the *Colloquia Mensalia* or *Table Talk*, which appeared in 1652, the original having escaped destruction, if we are to believe the translator, Captain Henry Bell, in a most romantic manner. The *Tischreden*[3] are said to have been set down by Dr Anton Lauterbach and were first published in 1566. Bell's translation[4] appeared nearly a century later, in 1652. The book is dedicated to the Lord Mayor and Corporation of London and contains a preface by Thomas Thorowgood, who has much to say in praise of Luther:

"The lazie Monks were wilde against Luther when hee awaken'd them out of their errors, idleness, and ignorance....

Scultetus names several learned men of that age in divers nations...But the fame of Martin Luther did soon arise to the clouding of many other lights and Ulenbergius (none of his friend) reports, that when Mellerstadius saw him, and heard his disputations, hee said, This Monk hath deep eies, marvelous phantasies, and hee will trouble all the Doctors....

But I have somewhat to speak concerning this Book of his that is now first commended to the English world: It hath been of a long time well known and approved of in other Nations, 'tis the same which Ulenbergius, before-named, mentions once and again, *Magnum Colloquium mensalium volumen*: of his Table-discourses saith Fabritius, I need not saie much, for they are in all men's hands...."

[1] See Herford, Bibl. 59.
[2] E.g. *Upon the Epistle to the Galatians.*   London, 1577.
[3] Bibl. 192.   [4] Bibl. 193.

I did not intend to exceed the bounds of an Epistle, give mee leave then I praie to add som few words of the Translator, his Work, and the Dedication....

I was not unwilling, upon request, to premise these lines in memorie of the noble Captain (unknown to mee, yet) my countrie man both by birth and education, of Norfolk and at Elie ; His familie is of great note and nobilitie in the former : his father was Dean of the later : hee had been a militarie man it seemeth in Hungarie and Germanie, but was afterwards emploied in State-affairs by the two last Kings ; which with the success is related by himself, as also the manner how hee came by the Original Copie...."

Then follows "Captain Henrie Bell's Narrative, or Relation of the miraculous preserving of Dr. Martin Luther's Book, entituled *Colloquia Mensalia*...." It appears that the Protestant towns and princes had decreed that a copy should be kept on a chain in every church in their dominions. Pope Gregory XIII, however, induced Rudolph II to order all copies of the *Mensalia* to be burned throughout the empire. In consequence of this edict 4000 copies were destroyed and it was thought none had escaped. "Yet it pleased God," says Bell, "that Anno 1626 a Germane Gentleman, named Casparus van Sparr, with whom, in the time of my staying in Germanie about King James's business, I became very familiarly known and acquainted, having occasion to build upon the old foundation of an hous, wherein his Grand-father dwelt at that time, when the said Edict was published in Germanie, for the burning of the foresaid Books, and digging deep into the ground under the said old foundation, one of the said original printed Books was there happily found, lying in a deep obscure hole, beeing wrapped in a strong linnein cloth, which was waxed all over with Bee's wax within and without; whereby the Book was preserved fair without any blemish." The finder, fearing for the safety of the book, Ferdinand II being then Emperor, sent it to Bell with a request that he might translate it into English. Bell began the task several times, but was continually interrupted and eventually laid the book aside for a considerable period. One night an old man appeared to him in a vision, reproached him for neglecting the work and said he would shortly have an opportunity of completing the task. Within a fortnight Bell was arrested for some reason which he never learnt, and imprisoned in the Gate-House at Westminster, where he remained ten years, five of which he spent in translating the *Mensalia*. Eventually this came to the ears of Laud, who sent for the book, read it and on two occasions made Bell presents of £10 and £40. A year later Bell received his translation again, together with the original, and was set at liberty. Laud had promised to see to the printing but was shortly afterwards (Dec. 1640) thrown into prison himself.

The House of Commons then appointed a committee to examine Bell's version:

"And Sir Edward Dearing beeing Chair-man said unto mee, that hee was acquainted with a learned Minister benefic'd in Essex, who had lived long in England, but was born in high Germanie, in the Palatinate, named Mr Paul Amiraut, whom the Committee sending for, desired him to take both the Original, and my Translation into his custodie, and diligently to compare them together, and to make report unto the said Committee, whether hee found that I had rightly and truly translated it according to the original : which report he made accordingly, and they beeing satisfied therein, referred it to two of the Assemblie, Mr. Charls Herle, and Mr. Edward Corbet, desiring them diligently to peruse the same, and to make report unto them, if they thought it fitting to bee printed and published.

Whereupon they made report dated the 10. of November. 1646. that they found it to bee an excellent Divine Work, worthie the light & publishing, especially in regard Luther, in the said Discourses, did revoke his opinion, which hee formerly held, touching Consubstantiation in the Sacrament. Whereupon the Hous of Commons the 24. of Februarie 1646. did give Order for the Printing thereof...

Given under my hand the third daie of Julie 1650.
Henrie Bell."

Then come two business documents relating to the printing, a short extract from Joannes Aurifaber's[1] preface, three contemporary opinions (1650) of the book and finally Aurifaber's complete preface, dated 7th July, 1569. This is a misprint; the original[2] has 1566. The translation, like the original, contains 80 discourses, with the difference that whereas the English index contains 80 entries, the German has 82, although Nos. 23 and 32 do not appear in the text. Nos. 1 (*Of God's Word, or the Holie Scriptures*) to 22 (*Of Preachers and Church Officers*) appear in the translation in the same order as in the original, but Bell's subsequent arrangement is capricious. I give as a sample of the translation a paragraph from No. 1, p. 13:

[1] Luther's *famulus* or private secretary. Born 1519, probably at Weimar. Educated at Wittenberg, where he heard Luther's lectures. Edited many of Luther's works. Died 1575 at Erfurt.
[2] Bibl. 192.

" Gottes wort ist ein fewriger Schild allen so darauff vertrawen.

Ein fewriger Schild ist Gottes Wort / darumb das es bewerter vnd
einer ist denn Golt das in fewer probiret / welches Golt im fewer nichts
verleuret / vnd gehet jme nichts abe / sondern es bestehet / bleibet vnd
vberwindet alles. Also wer dem Wort Gottes glaubet / der vberwindet alles /
vnd bleibet ewig sicher wider alles vnglück. Deñ dieser Schild fürchtet
sich nichts weder fur den pforten der Hellen / noch fur dem Teufel / sünde
oder tod / sondern die pforten der Hellen fürchten sich fur jme / denn
Gottes Wort bleibet ewiglich / es erhelt vnd beschirmet auch alle die
darauff vertrawen. Sonst one Gottes Wort hat der Teufel gewonnen spiel /
denn es kan jme niemand wider stehen / noch sich seiner erwehren / on
allein Gottes Wort / wer das ergreifft / vnd daran festiglich gleubet / der
hat gewonnen. Darumb sollen wir des Göttlichen Worts nicht vergessen /
noch viel weniger es verachten / wie solches denn der Teufel suchet."

" That God's Word is a shield of fire to all that trust therein.

A Firie shield is God's Word : therefore (said Luther) it is of more
substance and purer than gold, which in the fire is tried ; and as gold
looseth nothing of its substance in the fire, neither decreaseth, but resisteth
and overcometh all the furie of the firie heat and flame ; even so, hee that
believeth God's Word overcometh all, and remains sure everlastingly
against all mishaps : for this shield feareth nothing, neither hell-gates,
nor the Divel ; but the gates of hell must stand in fear of it : for God's
Word remains for ever, and defendeth and protecteth all those that trust
therein."

If we may judge from this sample, Bell's translation, although
it omits much, is certainly not inferior to the original in vigour.

Leaving Luther we can now turn to Jacob Boehme the
theosophist. He was born at Alt-Seidenberg, near Görlitz, in
1575 and followed the trade of a shoe-maker from 1589 until
about 1612. In that year he wrote his first treatise, *Morgenröthe
im Aufgang,* which, though unfinished, was copied and circulated
in MS by Karl von Ender. He was denounced as a heretic from
the pulpit by Gregor Richter. He was examined in July, 1613,
by the town council of Görlitz and dismissed with the injunction,
which he obeyed for five years, not to write any more. His
chief crime was apparently that his examiners failed to understand him. From 1619 onwards he wrote voluminously but
published only one volume, *Der Weg zu Christo,* Görlitz, 1624.
Clerical hostility was again aroused and he was summoned
before the Upper Consistorial Court at Dresden in May, 1624.
He won fresh admirers but died the same year on the 17th of
November, still pursued by the ill-will of the clergy. His
works appeared singly at Amsterdam between 1631 and 1682.
Boehme enjoyed an extraordinary popularity in England during

the Commonwealth and regular societies of "Behmenists" were formed. His works were translated into English between 1645 and 1662 by John Sparrow[1], with the assistance of John Ellistone (died Aug. 22nd, 1652) and Humphrey Blunden. The undertaking was financed by Blunden and Durand Hotham, who published a life of Boehme[2] in 1654. C. J. Barker, in his reprint (1909) of *The High and Deep Searching out of the Threefold Life of Man*[3], gives a complete list of the English translations of Boehme writings in the seventeenth century, comprising 32 volumes. Of these, 23 are by Sparrow, 2 by Sparrow and Blunden, 1 by Sparrow and Ellistone and 2 by Ellistone alone. The remainder bear no name. Sparrow is probably the author of *Mercurius Teutonicus ; or a Christian Information concerning the last Times. Gathered out of the Mysticall writings of Jacob Behmen* (1649)[4]. He observes in the preface: "Thou hast here divers Predictions, or Propheticall Passages, taken out of the Letters and Writings of J(acob) B(oehme) of high and worthy Consideration in these distractive and destructive times....What this Author was (called by the Learned, Teutonicus Phylosophus) and what ground he had to write as well Prophetically, as Philosophically, and Theosophically, his Writings do testifie.... What thou hast here by peecemeals, thou maist more at large and fully finde in his Writings: some of which are printed already in English, viz. The 40 Questions of the soule, wherein is a Catalogue of his Bookes: the way to Christ, and the Three Principles. Also the Threefold Life (which is now preparing for the Presse); and his Mysterium Magnum (a Commentary upon the first Book of Moses called Genesis) are desired, expected, and intended to be published." Ellistone also has something to say of Boehme in the preface to the *Epistles*[5], 1649:

"As there is no Booke or Treatise which this Author hath written, but the footsteps and Characters of Divine Light, and knowledge are therein Imprinted & discerned, and may be of speciall use and improvement to the Christian, impartiall, Reader ; so likewise these his Epistles, written at sundry times, and occasions to severall Friends ; and thus gathered &

---

[1] Born 12 May, 1615, at Stambourne(?), Essex. Member of Inner Temple, 1633. Died 1665(?).
[2] Bibl. 198. [3] Bibl. 201. [4] Bibl. 197.
[5] Bibl. 195.

compast together, may of right be reckoned as one Booke, not of the smallest benefit and direction to the Reader, Lover & Practitioner of that Divine Light, and knowledge, which his Writings doe containe, and hold forth...

These Epistles are not fraught with fine complementall straines, and pleasing Notions of humane Art; or with the learned Quotations of ancient Authors, or with the witty glances of accute Reason, trimmed up in the Scholastique pompe, and pride of words, to tickle and delight the fansie of the Reader...but he hath written (according to the Divine Gift which he received) of the greatest and deepest Mysteries, concerning God and Nature...   In a word, Courteous and Christian Reader, these Epistles will serve as an Introduction, and right information to shew thee what this Author was, & whence hee had his great knowledge; and upon what ground and centre it was founded; and likewise how thou mayest come really to understand the drift and meaning of his Writings, and effectually find the excellent use thereof...

J. E."

This volume contains thirty-five letters, after the last of which is a note: "Translated into the Nether-Dutch out of Jacob Behmens owne hand-writing: And out of the Nether-Dutch into English."

I quote a few more observations from Sparrow's preface to *Several Treatises*[1], 1661:

"Several of the Writings of this Author Jacob Behme have been published in his native Tongue the German, and were so loved and desired, at the first notice of them, about the year 1612, by some noble, vertuous and learned Persons, who procured Transcripts out of the Library at Gerlitz, where the Primate Gregory Rickter had commanded it to be kept, that it should no more come to the Authors hands again: that beyond his expectation they wrote to him, to know whether he were the Author of them; and upon his Answer in return, they ceased not to solicite him to further writing, according to his high knowledge in the deepest Mysteries; which he performed from the year, 1619. to, 1624. in which year he departed this mortal life...

John Sparrow."

Another noteworthy criticism of Boehme, although by no means as eulogistic as the preceding, is that of Henry More entitled *Philosophiae Teutonicae censura, sive epistola privata*[2]. More thinks the number of errors in Boehme's work precludes the idea that he had divine revelations. Nevertheless, he regards him as a great man.

The last book we have to notice in connection with the influence of Boehme in England during the seventeenth century appeared in 1691 under the title of *Jacob Behmen's Theosophick*

---

[1] Bibl. 196.   [2] Bibl. 199.

Philosophy unfolded[1]. Of the author, a certain Edward Taylor, little seems to be known. The publisher states in his preface:

"We can give but a very short account of the Author, but hope this Publication may produce a fuller, from some of his Personal Acquaintance. As we are informed, it was one Mr. Edward Taylor an English Gentleman, the latter part of his time he lived in Dublin, in much Privacy and Retirement, where he made this his Work and Business. He died at Dublin about the year 1684. His Manuscripts were preserved by the care of a Friend, and brought over hither, where they have lain for some time in Private...

The Writings of the Divinely inspired Jacob Behmen, called the Teutonick Philosopher, have been by many received with great Satisfaction, and have contributed towards the Extricating their Minds out of those Labyrinths and Difficulties, wherein Evil Practice and Opinions (kept up by Custom) had involved them. The greatest Objection raised against the said Writings have been their Abstruseness, and Uncouth Expressions, making them almost impossible to be understood ; which now is answered & removed..."

(b) *English Theologians in Germany.*

The popularity of English divines in Germany during the seventeenth century is most extraordinary. In 1613 the Dutch scholar Grotius writes to Lingelsheim in the following terms: "In Britanniam missus fui...Theologos quoque ibi inveni complures, non rigidos, praefractos, duricervices, sed lenes, aequos, faciles, in quibus scientiae est plurimum, charitatis non minus[2]." Lingelsheim remarks in his reply from Heidelberg on July 24th : "De theologis Britannicis paria retulit Scultetus noster...." No less than forty-eight treatises and pamphlets, the work of eight different authors, were translated into German and many ran through five or six editions. To quote in full the numerous flattering references to Joseph Hall, Richard Baxter and others in the prefaces with which the various translators have thought fit to introduce their authors, would be tedious. I shall therefore merely give one or two selections to bear witness to the esteem in which each writer was held in Germany, and content myself beyond that with a simple enumeration of the various translations.

The first writer to engage our attention is William Perkins (1558–1602).

1602. *Der Catholische Reformierte Christ* (Bibl. 202).

---

[1] Bibl. 200. [2] See Reifferscheid, Bibl. 51.

Translation by Johann Heidfelt of *A Reformed Catholike; or, a Declaration, shewing how neere we may come to the present Church of Rome in sundrie Points of Religion; and wherein we must for euer depart from them.* Cambridge. 1597. The translator contributes a lengthy eulogy of Perkins in the preface and mentions Spanish and Latin translations of the work.

1604. *Christliche Erklärung der zehen Gebotte* (Bibl. 203). By Johann Heupel. The title of the corresponding English original is uncertain.

From a letter from Koeler to Opitz (March, 1631) we gather that Nüssler intended to translate a work of Perkins: "Adiunget aliquod Perkinsi opusculum Nüslerus, serius mihi amicus." This plan was never carried out.

1667? *Tractätlein Von des Menschen natürlichen Gedancken* (Bibl. 204). By Georg Heinius. Apparently a translation of *Of Man's Imagination.* Appended is a treatise *Von gottslästerlichen Gedancken,* by John Dounam (died 1644). I cannot discover the English original.

1688. In this year Perkins' *Foundation of Christian Religion* was published in English at Hamburg in one volume with John Wallis' *Grammatica Linguae Anglicanae* (Bibl. 205).

1690. *Gewissens-Spiegel* (Bibl. 206). A translation by T. D. of *The whole Treatise of the Cases of Conscience.* 1611. Contains a portrait of Perkins and the usual long-winded appreciation in the preface.

Joseph Hall (1574–1656).

Joseph Hall is by far the most popular of the English theologians. There exist no less than three[1] independent German translations of *Characters of Vertues and Vices* (1608), all published within a period of fifty years. His *Balme of Gilead* (1646) was twice translated and of another work we possess three editions in German. To quote fully all the passages in which he is appreciated would fill a volume.

1628. *Vorbildungen der Tugenden und Vntugenden* (Bibl. 207). A translation, like the next two, of *Characters of Vertues and Vices* (1608), by W. H. N. N.

[1] Perhaps even four. See p. 88, note.

1652. *Kenn-Zeichen Der Tugend und Laster* (Bibl. 209). By Georg Philipp Harsdoerfer[1]. The translator says he has occasionally taken the liberty of adapting the text to the character of the German nation. He also takes the opportunity of publishing the following sonnet:

> Der Tugend Wieder hall / ist bey dem Hall zu hören
> Den weiland Engeland pflegt über hoch zu ehren.
> Es reimet sich der Nam zu seiner Schriften Zier /
> und dringt sein wahrer Ruhm in diesem Werck herfür,
> Er könt in seiner Sprach ein kleines Völcklein lehren /
> und wird auff diese Weiss die Teutschen Künste mehren /
> nachdem ihm offen steht die vor-verschlossene Thür /
> erschallet hier und dar der Wissenschaft Begier
> nechst hohem Tugend-preiss. Allhier ist nichts verblümet
> das rechte Wesen-bild / der angebohrne Thon
> erschallet in dem Ohr / auss diesem Tugend thron
> Der Laster / List und Lust erweist sich missgestimmet
> Der Hall / beduncket mich ist nechst der Wahrheit Quell /
> in der des Lesers Hertz sich weist Chrystallen-hell.

1685. *Merckzeichen der Tugenden und Laster* (Bibl. 208). By Balthasar Gernard Koch. For the sake of comparison I quote a short passage with the three different German renderings. There is nothing to show that Harsdoerfer and Koch were acquainted with the earlier translation.

Of the True Friend.

"His affections are both united and divided ; united to him he loveth ; divided betwixt another and himselfe ; and his owne heart is so parted, that whiles he hath some, his friend hath all. His choice is led by vertue, or by the best of vertues, Religion ; not by gaine, not by pleasure ; yet not without respect of equall condition, if disposition not unlike ; which once made, admits of no change, except hee whom he loveth, be changed quite from himselfe ; nor that suddenly, but after long expectation."

Der Trewe Freund.

"Seine zuneigungen seind zugleich vereiniget und zertheilet / nemlich also / dass / gleich wie er sie gegen den / welchen er liebet / zusammen helt / und einiget / also zerstücket er sie gegen alle andere. Sein Hertz ist also abgetheilet / dass zwar er etwas davon vor sich behelt / das übrige aber gantz und gar seinem Freunde gibt zu besitzen. Nach der Tugend oder nach dem Gottesdienst und Religion, welches die beste unter allen Tugenden ist / pflegt Er seine Freunde / nicht aber nach gunst / gewinn oder wollust zu erwehlen. Dabey aber gibt er fleissig acht auff die gleichheit des zustandes und gemüts / auff dass die wahl / so einmahl mit gutem bedacht / und nach langer prüfung geschehen / unverandert bleibe / es sey denn dass der / so zum Freund angenommen / sich ganzlich verändere..." (W. H. N. N. 1628.)

---

[1] According to Herdegen (Bibl. 43), the second part of Harsdoerfer's *Nathan, Jotham und Simson*, 1650–1 (Bibl. 129), contains further translations from Hall. I have not had an opportunity of verifying this.

Der getreue Freund.

"Seine Gemühts-Neigungen sind getheilt und gesammt: getheilet unter ihn und seinen Freund; gesamt mit dem / den er liebet: Sein Hertz ist so zertheilt / dass sein Freund das gantze für seinen Antheil empfanget. Seine Wahl wird geleitet durch die Tugend und durch die Furcht Gottes / die Königin aller Tugenden; Keines weges durch Gewinn oder Belusten / noch Ansehen der ungleichen Personen.

Die einmahl ergriffene Wahl / ist keiner Reue fähig / wann sich der / so sie betrifft nicht verändert und gantz umwendet; alsdann kan sich die Freundschafft in etwas mindern / doch nach langer Nachwart der Besserung / und vielfältigen Ermahnungen." (Harsdoerfer, 1652.)

Der Freund.

"Seine Zuneigungen sind zugleich vereiniget und zertheilet: vereiniget mit dem / den er liebet / zertheilet aber zwischen ihn und einen andern / und sein Hertz ist also getheilet / dass in dem er einen theil hat / sein Freund es dennoch gantz besitzet / seine Wahl ist allezeit auff Tugend gerichtet / oder auff Frömmigkeit / welche besser ist denn alle Tugend / niemahls aber auff Gewinn oder Lust / und dennoch nicht ohne Absehen auff gleichen Stand / und auff nicht gar ungleichen Sinn und Gemühte. Die Wahl die er einmahl gethan / lässet keine Verenderunge zu / wenn nicht derselbe / den er liebet / sich gantz und gar verendert..." (B. G. Koch. 1685.)

1632. *Himmel auf Erden* (Bibl. 210). A translation, by Kristof Koeler (Colerus), of *Heaven upon Earth, or of true Peace and Tranquillitie of Minde* (1606). This work, which was translated from a Latin version, is mentioned by the translator in a letter to Opitz, "a. d. V Martii, 1631." The publisher, David Müller of Breslau, contributes the usual puffing preface.

1662. *Die alte Religion*...(Bibl. 211). A translation of *The Old Religion; or, The Difference betwixt the Reformed and Roman Church* (1628), by Theophilus Grossgebauer, Pastor in Rostock. In the preface the translator mentions, in addition to Hall, William Perkins, James Ussher, and Thomas Morton.

1663. *Baalsam aus Gilead*....A translation, by Heinrich Schmettau, chaplain to the Duke of Liegnitz, of *The Balme of Gilead; or comforts for the distressed both morall and divine* (1646). Schmettau, in a more than usually fulsome preface, commends Hall for his learning and the blamelessness of his life. The date is "Liegnitz, 24 Feb., 1662." (Bibl. 212.)

1663. *Balsam auss Gilead* (Bibl. 213). This is Johann Jacob Schädler's version of the same work. The preface is dated "Zürich, 7 March, 1663." For the sake of comparison I quote a passage from the first page of the book.

Comforts for the sick bed.

"What should we do in this Vale of Tears, but bemoan each others miseries? Every man hath his load, and well is he whose burthen is so easie that he may help his neighbours. Hear me, my son : my age hath waded through a world of sorrows ; the Angel that hath hitherto redeemed my soul from all evill, and hath led me within few paces of the shore, offers to lend thee his hand to guide thee in this dangerous foard, wherein every error is death ; Let us follow him with an humble confidence, and be safe in the view and pity of the wofull miscarriages of others."

Trost aufs Siechbette.

"Was können wir anders thun / in diesem Thranenthal / als einer des andern Elend beweinen? Ein ieder hat seine Last / und wohl ist dehme / dessen Bürde so leichte ist / dass Er seinem Nechsten die seine tragen helffen kan. Höre mich mein Sohn / Ich habe in meinem Leben eine Welt voll Trubsal durchgewatet ; Der Engel der mich bisshero erlöset hat von allem Ubel / und mich einige wenige Schritte aufs Ufer treten lassen / recket auch dir die Hand / dich zu leiten in diesem gefährlichen Furth / da ein ieder Fehltritt der Todt ist ; Lass uns ihm folgen mit demütigem Vertrauen / und bleibe also du selbst sicher / in dehm du andere mit mitleidendem Anschauen sihest sich aufs jämmerlichste verirren." (Schmettau.)

Hertz-sterckende Erquickungen / in langwierigen Kranckheiten dess Leibs.

"Was liget vns allen in diesem jamerhafften Thränenthal anders ob zuthun / als dass je einer des anderen Elend beklage? Dann ob zwar ein jeder seinen eigenen last empfangen hat / so ist jedoch der jenige noch für glückselig zu schätzen / welchem ein so ertragenliche burde auffgelegt worden / dass er jnzwischen auch seinem Nebenmenschen hülfflich kan beyspringen. Höre mir hierüber zu Lieber Mensch : Mein gantzes Leben ist zwar gewatten durch ein welt voll Trübsalen / aber der Engel / der mich bissher erlöset hat von allem übel / vnd in wenig schritten mich geläitet an das erwünschte gestad / der erbeut sich nun dir darzuräichen sein Hand / vnd dich zu läiten in diesem gefährlichen furth / da ein jede verjrrung der tod selber ist : Lasset vns derowegen jhme mit demütiger zuversicht folgen / vnd vns selber in sicherheit bringen / in dem wir ob ander leuthen traurigem vndergang mit erbarmung vnd mitleyden vns erspieglen." (Schädler.)

1663. This volume (Bibl. 214) contains three further translations by Schmettau, viz., *Soliloquia...*, *Der gläubigen Seelen Irdisches Valet...*, and *Der Rechte Christ*. The originals are *Soliloquies; or Holy Self-Conferences of the Devout Soul*, *The Soul's Farewell to Earth* and *The Christian*.

1665–6. *Biblische Gesichter* (Bibl. 215, 216). A translation, by Schmettau, of *Contemplations upon the principall passages in the Holie storie* (1612–26). The title-page of Part I (Books I–XI) is dated 1666, but the illustrated title-page bears the date 1665 and the preface is dated 1 Aug. 1664. Part II is dated 1665. An edition de luxe was published in three volumes in 1672–4–9, the title being altered to *Biblische Geschichte* (Bibl. 217), as is also the case with the third edition of 1699 (Bibl. 219).

1683. This volume (Bibl. 220) contains three translations by Henning Koch (not B. G. Koch, see Bibl. 208) of Helmstädt. They are I. *Nacht-Lieder*. II. *Der heilige Orden*. III. *Die Klage und Thränen Sion*. The original is a single work entitled *The Holy Order, or Fraternity of the Mourners in Sion ; with Songs in the Night, or Cheerfulness under Affliction*. The book contains a portrait of Hall.

1684. *Gebrauch Der Heil. Schrifft* (Bibl. 221). By an anonymous translator. The Berlin copy is bound up with the last and contains the same portrait. The English original is unknown to me.

1684. *Salomons Regir-Hausshaltungs- und Sitten-Kunst* (Bibl. 223). A translation by Andreas Beyer, Pastor of St Nicholas, Freiberg, of *Solomon's Divine Arts of* 1. *Ethics*, 2. *Politics*, 3. *Economics* (1609). Beyer says his attention was drawn, after completing the translation, to a work entitled *Salomonis Tugend-Regiments und Hauslehre* by Dorotheus Eleutherus Meletephilus[1] (Bibl. 222). This is merely a series of extracts from Hall's work.

Daniel Dyke, a Puritan divine of great eminence and learning. Educated at Cambridge. Minister of Coggeshall, Essex. Suspended 1588. Died *c.* 1614.

1638. *Nosce Teipsum : Das grosse Geheimnis dess Selbbetrugs* (Bibl. 224). A translation, by D.H.P., of *The Mystery of Self-Deceiving ; or, A Discourse of the Deceitfulness of Man's Heart* (1614). The work was at first attributed in Germany to Jeremiah, Daniel's brother, who contributes a preface in which he expressly states that Daniel wrote the book and even prepared it for the press before his death. This first edition was published at Basel. The second edition was published at Frankfort in 1643 by Christian Klein and the heirs of Clement Schleich (Bibl. 225). The third edition (Bibl. 226), wrongly

[1] I.e. Georg Philipp Harsdoerfer (according to an entry in the Catalogue of the Göttingen University Library).

dated 1663[1], also appeared in 1643 at Frankfort, published by Johann Jacob and Philip Weiss. A fourth edition (Bibl. 227) appeared at Danzig in the same year. The title-page of this edition correctly states that the work was written by Daniel Dyke and published by Jeremiah. The fifth and sixth editions (Bibl. 228, 229) appeared at Frankfort in 1652 and 1691, the former being published by Johann Philip Weiss, the latter by Martin Hermsdorff. Schaible[2] states that Theodor Haake translated Dyke's work, as well as Henry Scudder's *The Christian's Daily Walk* and a book entitled *The old Pilgrim*, by an anonymous writer. The letters D.H.P. may therefore stand for " Dietrich Haake, Palatinus." I have discovered no trace of the other two translations.

1643. *Nützliche Betrachtung...der Wahren Busse* (Bibl. 230, also 226, 228, 229). By the same translator, and published with the second, third, fifth and sixth editions of *Nosce Teipsum.* Correctly assigned to Daniel Dyke in the third edition (1652), i.e. the fifth edition of *Nosce Teipsum.* The original is *A Treatise concerning Repentance*, published posthumously in 1631.

John Barclay. The only Catholic represented in this chapter. (See Chapter IV.)

1663. *Ermahnung An Die Vncatholische dieser Zeit* (Bibl. 231). This is a translation of *Paraenesis ad sectarios* (1617). The book is dedicated by the translator, H.E.V.R., to Elizabeth Amalia Magdalene, Electress of the Palatinate.

Sir Richard Baker. Born *c.* 1568 at Sissinghurst, Kent. Was a Commoner at Hart Hall, Oxford, from 1584–7. Knighted 1603. High Sheriff of Oxfordshire, 1620. Having engaged to stand surety for some of his wife's relations, he was reduced to poverty and had to spend many years in the Fleet prison, dying there on Feb. 18th, 1645. His devotional works were written in prison.

1663. *Frag-Stück und Betrachtungen über Das Gebett des*

---

[1] Corrected in pencil to 1643 in the Berlin copy.
[2] K. H. Schaible: *Geschichte der Deutschen in England*, 1885. Bibl. 77.

Herren (Bibl. 232). This is *Meditations and Disquisitions on the Lord's Prayer* (1637) and the translator is Andreas Gryphius, who is also responsible for the next volume.

1688. *Betrachtungen der I. Sieben Buss-Psalm* (Bibl. 233), i.e. *Meditations and Disquisitions on the Seven Penitential Psalms* (1639). The volume also contains translations of *Med. and Dis. on the Seven Consolatory Psalms* (1640) and *Meditations and Motives for Prayer on the Seven Days of the Week* (1640). This volume was published by Christian Gryphius, his father having died in 1664.

Richard Baxter was born at Rowton, Shropshire, in 1615. In 1638 he was ordained and in 1641 appointed Vicar of Kidderminster. During the war he became Chaplain to Colonel Whalley's regiment in the Parliamentary army. He endeavoured to counteract sectarian differences. The Ejectment Act of 1662 severed his connection with the Church. In 1680 and 1684 he was arrested under the Five-Mile Act. In 1685 he was tried by Jeffreys for sedition and imprisoned for nearly two years. From 1687 until his death in 1691 he was allowed to live in peace and continued to preach and publish almost to the end. He died in London on the 8th of December. His separate works are said to number 168 and his popularity in Germany was second only to that of Joseph Hall.

1663? *Der Quacker Catechismus* (Bibl. 235). A translation by an anonymous author of *The Quaker's Catechism or the Quakers questioned* (1655). The copy in the British Museum is bound up with several German works dealing with the Quakers, e.g. Johannes Lassenius: *Historische...Erörterung der...neuen Secte der Quacker* (Jena, 1661) and Christianus Pauli: *Augensalbe/Vor die/welche sagen; Wir sind reich und dörffen nichts... sonst Quacker genandt* (Danzig, 1663).

1665... *Von der Verläugnung Unser Selbst* (Bibl. 236, 237, 238). *A Treatise of Self Denyall* (1660). This translation was reprinted in 1675 and 1697. Translated by J.F.L.

1673. *Die Wahre Bekehrung* (Bibl. 239). *Directions and Persuasions to a Sound Conversion* (1658). The translator's preface is signed J.D., but the title-page runs: " übersetzet/

Durch J.D.B." The third letter perhaps stands for "Buch-händler," or for the name of some town.

1678. *Nun oder Niemahls* (Bibl. 240). *Now or Never; or the holy, serious and diligent Believer justified, &c.* (1669). There is no clue to the name of the translator.

1685. *Christliches Hauss-Buch* (Bibl. 241). A translation by Anton Brunsen of *The Poor-Man's Family-Book* (1674). Brunsen says his translation is based on the third English edition (1677) and was already completed in 1680. Publication was, however, delayed and another version appeared while his was in the press. Consequently, only a limited number of copies was published. I have seen no copy of the other version.

1684. In this year appeared *Der Heiligen Ewige Ruhe*, a translation of *The Saints' Everlasting Rest* (1650), at Cassel. I have not been able to discover a copy.

1685. *Ein Heiliger oder Ein Vieh* (Bibl. 242). A translation by J.D. of *Saint or Brute; a Sermon on Luke X.* 41, 42 (1662). The volume contains a portrait of Baxter dated 1683.

1697. *Theologische Politick* (Bibl. 243). *Christian Directory; or a Sum of Practical Theology, and Cases of Conscience* (1673). The translator is Johann Heinrich Ringier, who died before its publication. He says he omitted much for the sake of clearness and also because a large part of the work is applicable only to English conditions. He mentions translations of several other works, viz., *Von der Bekehrung* (*Treatise on Conversion*, 1657), *Von dem unvernünfftigen Unglauben* (*The Unreasonableness of Infidelity*, 1655),... *Von der Creutzigung der Welt* (*Crucifying the World by the Cross of Christ*, 1658),... and *Der geistliche Samariter*, the original of which I cannot discover. I have not seen any of these translations.

1697. *Ausgesonderte Schrifften* (Bibl. 244). This volume, translated by J.D., includes *Method for a Settled Peace of Conscience* (1653), *The Life of Faith* (1670), *Vain Religion of the formal Hypocrite* (1660), *The Fool's Prosperity, the Occasion of his Destruction?* (1660) and *Of Redemption of Time*. Each treatise has a separate title-page and the last three are dated 1697.

William Bates (1625–1699).

1701. *Richard Baxters...Ehren-Gedächtniss* (Bibl. 245). A translation by Johann Georg Pritius of *A Funeral Sermon for the reverend, holy and excellent divine Mr R. Baxter...with an account of his life* (1692). Pritius gives a list of Baxter's works, 57 in all, and mentions fourteen German translations, comprising most of those I have already enumerated and in addition *Stimme Gottes an die Menschen* (*A Call to the Unconverted from the Living God*, 1658), *Zeichen eines schwachen / starcken und heuchlerischen Christen* (*The Character of a sound confirmed Christian, as also, 2 of a weak Christian: and 3 of a seeming Christian*, 1669), *Das Gottliche Leben* (*The Divine Life*, 1664), *Mitleidender Rath an die Jugend* (*Compassionate Counsel to all Young Men*, 1682), *Sterbens-Gedancken* (*Dying Thoughts*, 1668), *Geistlicher Wachstum in der Gnade Gottes* (*Directions for Weak Christians to grow up in Grace*, 1669). I have met with no trace of these translations.

James Ussher (?) (1581–1656), Archbishop of Armagh.

1672. *Harmonica Evangeliorum* (Bibl. 246, 247). This is simply a harmony of the Gospels with a treatise on the chronology of the New Testament. The translator's name is not given, but the second edition (1699) has a preface by August Hermann Francke, the pietist, who, with Jacob Philipp Spener, acquired a considerable following in England and America at the beginning of the eighteenth century. It is by no means certain whether this harmony is the work of Ussher. The manuscript was found in his library.

Isaac Barrow. Born 1630. Educated at the Charterhouse school, Peterhouse, and Trinity College, Cambridge. Professor of Greek, 1660. Fellow of the Royal Society, 1663. Professor of Mathematics at Cambridge, 1664. Renounced mathematics for divinity, 1669. D.D. 1670. Master of Trinity, 1672. Vice-chancellor, 1675. Died May 4th, 1677.

1678. *Nutz der Gottesfurcht* (Bibl. 248). A translation by David Rupert Erythropel of *The Profitableness of Godliness*. Erythropel declares his intention of translating *The art of Contentment*, but I am not aware that it was ever carried out.

Samuel Slater, died 1704. Ejected for nonconformity from the living of St Mary's, Bury St Edmunds, in 1662. Subsequently Pastor of a congregation in Crosby Square, London.

1706. *Ausführliches Gespräch zwischen dem Glauben und der Seele*...This translation of *A Dialogue between Faith and a Doubting Soul* (1679) by Johann Burchard Menke (Philander) is printed with his *Ernsthaffte Gedichte*, 1706 and 1713 (Bibl. 249).

(c) *Minor Translations and religious Lyrics, etc.*

There are a few translations from the *Enchiridion* (1640) of Francis Quarles in the *Teutsche Gedichte* of Daniel Georg Morhof (1682). A second edition appeared in 1702 (Bibl. 255). The following is a complete list of the extracts, one of which I quote in full as a specimen:

III. Theil, XV. Zusagen und Halten. ("A promise is a child of the understanding," Cent. 2, Cap. 1.)

III. XVI. Gefallen und Misfallen. ("If thou hope to please all thy hopes are vain," 2. 6.)

III. LXXXI. Die Ehre. ("Take heed of that honour, which thy wealth hath purchased thee," 2. 82.)

III. LXXXII. Gebet Gott/ was Gottes ist/ und dem Kayser/ was des Kaysers ist. ("Gold is Caesar's Treasure, Man is Gods," 2. 77.)

III. LXXXVIII. Gebrauch und Missbrauch des Geldes.

> Herrsch' über Geld und Gut / wenn du begütert bist /
> Dieweil es sonsten nur dein Herr uñ Herrscher ist /
> Und bietet dir den Kopff. Denn / branchestu es recht /
> So bleibestu sein Herr / wo nicht / so bistu Knecht.

("If thou art rich, strive to command thy money, lest she command thee, if thou know how to use her, she is thy Servant, if not, thou art her slave," 2. 55.)

III. LXXXIV. Freygebigkeit gegen die Armen. ("What thou givest to the poor thou securest from the thief," 2. 15.)

III. LXXXV. Sein selbst Herr seyn. ("The way to subject all things to thyself is to subject thyself to reason," 2. 19.)

The *Teutsche Apothegmata* of Julius Wilhelm Zincgref, in the enlarged edition of Johann Leonhard Weidner, 1693, contain two quotations from John Knox (Cnoxius!) and others from

George Buchanan, Thomas More, John Hooper, Lawrence Sanders, Nicholas Ridley, Thomas Cranmer, Sir Walter Raleigh and Sir John Mandeville.

Johann Burchard Menke has a few translations from the religious poems of Edward Sherburne and Richard Flecknoe in his *Ernsthaffte Gedichte*[1]. They are included among the *Andächtige Gedancken* and number eight in all, six from Flecknoe and two from Sherburne.

X. Und sie legten ihn in eine Krippe. ("And they laid him in a manger," Sherburne[2].)

XVI. Auf die Worte: O Weib, dein Glaube ist gross. ("On these Words of our B.S. O Woman, great is thy Faith!" Flecknoe[3].)

XVII. Auf die Beschneidung unsers Heylandes. ("On the Circumcision of our B.S.," Flecknoe.)

XVIII. Auf die Worte des Heylandes: Seyd vollkommen. ("On these Words of our B.S. Be perfect, etc.," Flecknoe.)

XIX. Über das Bild der weinenden Magdalenen. ("On the Picture of a Weeping Magdalen," Flecknoe.)

XX. Die Weisen aus Morgenland. ("On the Magiis following the Star," Flecknoe.)

XXI. Von dem Vergnügen, das wir haben, etwas gutes zu thun. ("The Pleasure of doing Good," Flecknoe.)

XXII. Die weinende Maria Magdalena unter dem Creutze Christi. ("Mary Magdalena weeping under the Cross," Sherburne.)

With reference to the Psalms we may mention Opitz and Kongehl. The former, in the preface to his own version, mentions two English translations, one by an anonymous writer and the other by George Wither. Kongehl, in his *Lorbeerhayn* (1700)[4], eulogizes George Buchanan and especially commends his Psalms.

The magnificent German hymns of the century remained unknown in England until about 1720 and did not receive adequate attention until the middle of the nineteenth century.

[1] Bibl. 249.
[2] *Salmacis...With Severall other poems*, 1651. Bibl. 87.
[3] *A Collection of the choicest Epigrams...*1673. Bibl. 258.
[4] Michael Kongehl, Bibl. 133.

CHAPTER IX

LATER TRAVELLERS

As far as English travellers in Germany are concerned there is again little to record. James Howell's *Instructions for Forreine Travell*[1] (1642) refer more to Holland and France than to Germany. Of the language he says, "There is no language so full of Monosyllables and knotted so with Consonants as the German, howsoever she is a full mouthed, masculine speech." The *Travels*[2] of Edward Browne, a son of Sir Thomas, though interesting enough in their way, have no bearing on literature. He gives an account of the University of Altorf, where he made the acquaintance of Hoffmann, Professor of Botany and Anatomy, and Wagenseyl, Professor of Law. The latter's library roused Browne's admiration. These *Travels* were translated into German in 1676 (Nuremberg) from a Dutch version. The *Letters* of Sir George Etheredge[3] from Ratisbon, where he lived as English Resident from 1685 to 1689, are sometimes of a severely official nature, sometimes petulant outbursts occasioned by the unexciting character of his post. He mentions the arrival of a company of actors from Nuremberg in November, 1685, but has on the whole very little to say of German life, beyond the usual reference to the consumption of beer, to which he adds a few disparaging observations on German women.

A full account of the principal German travellers in England has been given by Schaible[4] in his *Geschichte der Deutschen in*

[1] Bibl. 76.   [2] Bibl. 74.
[3] In *The Works of Sir George Etheredge* (ed. Verity), 1888. Bibl. 78.
[4] Bibl. 77.

England (1885).   Many of them, like Matthias Pasor (M.A.
Oxford, 1624), Friedrich Spanheim, Andreas Müller, Johann
Michael Wansleb, Victorinus Rhythmer, Johann Andreas
Eisenmenger and Daniel Ernst Jablonski, were scholars of
repute and, curiously enough, all Orientalists.   The famous
Franz Junius, the pioneer of Germanic philology, was born at
Heidelberg in 1589 and came to England in 1620.   For thirty
years he lived in the house of Thomas, Earl of Arundel, and
paid frequent visits to Oxford.   After a sojourn of several years
in Friesland he returned to England in 1674 and settled at
Oxford in 1676, where he died the next year in the house
of his nephew, Isaac Voss.   The latter was the son of Johann
Gerhard Voss, who, after holding a professorship in Leyden,
became a Doctor of Law at Oxford in 1629.   He was held in
high esteem by Laud and made a prebendary of Canterbury
Cathedral.   Isaac was also made a Doctor of Law at Oxford in
1670 and became a canon of Windsor three years later.   He
died in the Castle in 1688 and left a famous library.   Of the
German Protestants who held office in England, although such
appointments grow rarer towards the end of the century, one of
the most important was Dr Anton Horneck.   Born at Bacharach
in 1641, he came to England in 1660 and was made M.A.
of Oxford.   In 1663 he became Vicar of All Hallows, Oxford,
and in 1665 tutor to Lord Torrington, the son of General Monk.
In 1671 he became Vicar of the Savoy Church in London, and
in 1696 Chaplain to William and Mary.   He was a famous
preacher of his day and wrote principally in English.

Still, these men played only a small part in the dissemina-
tion of English thought.   More important for our purpose are
Morhof, Ernst Gottlieb von Berge, Otto Menke and his son,
Johann Burchard, and Theodor Haake.   The last-named was born
at Neuhausen, near Worms, but was forced, after Tilly's invasion
of the Palatinate and its subjection by the Catholic Maximilian
of Bavaria, to take refuge in England.   He was in Oxford as
early as 1625 and had a large share in the establishment of the
Philosophical Society, 1645.   By 1649 the Society had two
branches, one in Oxford and the other in London, but the
Oxford branch did not long survive and the other became the

Royal Society in 1662. Prior to this Haake had been a deacon under Bishop Hall and translated several theological works from Dutch into English and from English into German. Reference has already been made to the latter (Chapter VIII). To him we owe the first, though unpublished, translation of *Paradise Lost,* and he also prepared for the press English translations of some 3000 German proverbs. Some of his letters and observations were published in *Philosophical Collections* for May, 1682. He died in 1690 and was buried in St Andrew's Church, Holborn. The second translator of Milton, Von Berge, spent only two years in England (1678–80), but seems to have moved in the best literary circles. He was a friend of Lloyd, Bishop of St Asaph, and contributed information about Russia, of which country he had considerable experience, to Moses Pitt's *English Atlas.* He returned to Berlin about 1680 and became interpreter to the Elector of Brandenburg in 1682. He died in 1722.

Otto Menke was the general editor of the *Acta eruditorum,* to which reference will be made in the next chapter. He was seven times Dean of the Philosophical Faculty at Leipzig and five times Rektor of the University. His son, Johann Burchard, published several translations from the English between 1705 and 1713 and was elected a Fellow of the Royal Society in 1732. Another well-known Fellow of the Royal Society was the scientist Samuel Hartlib, who came to England about 1628. He was the friend of Milton and Cromwell.

The Pegnitzorden of Nuremberg is remarkable for the number of its members who visited England. The fifth President, Christoph Fürer, made the acquaintance of Elias Ashmole and Theodor Haake in 1683. The sixth President, Joachim Negelein, travelled extensively in England in 1701 and met Gilbert Burnet, Bentley, Archbp. Tenison and many other scholars and divines. Christoph Arnold studied in the Cambridge University Library and obtained the autograph of Milton. Christoph Wegleiter visited London, Oxford, and Cambridge between 1685 and 1688, met several scholars and consulted the principal libraries. Johann Friedrich Riederer arrived in 1698 and stayed eighteen months. He wrote verses in English.

One of the best accounts of England is that of Martin Kempe[1], also a member of the Pegnitzorden and of several other societies as well.   He reached London from Holland in July, 1670, and proceeded to Oxford, where he worked for six hours each day in the Bodleian, occasionally making himself useful to the librarian, Thomas Hyde.   He also met Thomas Barlow, John Wallis, Edward Pocock, Thomas Tully, Nicholas Lloyd, Robert Boyle, Isaac Voss and many more.   The Royal Society requested him to make inquiries of the Fruchtbringende Gesellschaft concerning a complete *Lexicon Linguae Germanicae* which had been begun by G. H. Henisch[2] and which the Society was anxious to see. On July 10th, 1671, Kempe sent an account of his travels to Sigmund von Birken and the Pegnitzorden in the form of a poem in alexandrine verse[3].

This list does not exhaust the number of German visitors to these islands, but I can add no name, with the possible exception of Christian Hofmann von Hofmannswaldau, of importance for the establishment of firm literary relations between the two countries.   To Hofmannswaldau, who visited this country with the Count de Fremonville about 1640, is due the first attempt at an appreciation of English literature.

On the whole, therefore, the second half of the century, more particularly the period subsequent to the Restoration, is a period of direct personal intercourse between English and German scholars.   What the results of that intercourse were, will be seen in the next chapter.

---

[1] Quoted by Herdegen, Bibl. 43.
[2] *Thesaurus linguae et sapientiae germanicae*, Augsburg, 1616.
[3] The following lines are a fair sample:

> Aus London kehrt ich mich was fürter, ohn verweilen,
> Und reiste Landwärts ein fest bey die funfzig Meilen.
> Die Lufft ist angenehm, das Land mit Frucht erfüllt,
> Die Fluth hat Schuppen-Brut, der dicke Wald sein Wild.
> Bald nahet ich der Stadt, die Vieler Thürne Spitzen,
> Von Steinen sehen läst, mit achtzehn Musen-Sitzen,
> Nebst seinen Hallen prangt. Ja so viel weise Leut
> In ihren Mauren hegt, dass ihrer Treflichkeit,
> Kein ein'ge hohe Schul der Europäer Erden,
> Wie man aus Büchern weiss, kan vorgezogen werden :
> Oxonien mein ich, des Lands Athen und Rom,
> Der freyen Künste Burg, dabei der Isis Strom,
> Läst sein Crystallen-Nass mit sanftem Sausen fliessen,
> Biss dass es sich zuletzt muss in die Tems ergiessen,
> Du Oxfurt! bist der Ort, der mein Gemüth erlabt,
> Auch meinen Durst gestillt, den ich vorhin gehabt.

CHAPTER X

THE AWAKENING OF GERMANY AND THE GROWTH OF ENGLISH INFLUENCE

SCHAIBLE[1] remarks that the study of Upper German in England dates from the time of the Reformation. Prior to this, and for purely commercial reasons, more attention had been paid to Dutch; but our relations with the German Protestant party and the settlement of English refugees in Frankfort, Basel and elsewhere caused German to be more generally studied. Many of the great divines of the sixteenth century, e.g. Archbishop Grindal of Canterbury, Bishops Hooper, Coverdale and others, were diligent students of the language, as also were Robert Sidney, Earl of Leicester, and Philip, his brother. Passing to the next century we learn that John Evelyn, the author of the *Diary*, studied High German in Paris in 1646. The somewhat superficial observations of Moryson and Howell have already been quoted. In 1635 a sort of Academy called Musaeum Minervae was founded in London, and German figured in the curriculum. At first native German grammars were used, e.g. Schottel's, but grammars written for Englishmen soon appeared. The first of these is by a certain Aedler and bears the title *The High Dutch Minerva a la Mode*, 1680. The second, *Zweyfache Gründliche Sprach-Lehr, für Hochteutsch englisch, und für Engländer hochteutsch zu lernen*, by Heinrich Offelen, "Professor of the French, Spanish, Italian, Latin, English, High and Low German languages" (!), appeared in 1687. Nearly twenty years elapsed, however, before the

---

[1] *Geschichte der Deutschen in England*, 1885. Bibl. 77.

third book of this kind, John King's *English and High-German Grammar* (1706), was published. This meagre list compares very unfavourably with the great collection of French grammars enumerated by Upham[1]. We may add one or two phrase-books, e.g. Michael Sparkes' *Colloquia et Dictionariolum*, in which German figures in company with other European languages. The earliest German-English dictionary is apparently that of Ludwig, which appeared in Leipzig in 1706. It is advertised as *Ludwig's englisch-teutsch-französisches lexicon* at the end of Part IV (1709) of *Herrn von Hoffmannswaldau und andrer Deutschen...Gedichte*[2]. For the study of English in Germany the best book would be Offelen's *Sprachbuch*, although a reprint of John Wallis' *Grammatica Linguae Anglicanae* appeared at Hamburg in 1688.

There are some references to the English language and literature in K. G. von Hille's *Teutscher Palmenbaum*, 1647[3]. He quotes the Lord's Prayer in Old and Modern English to show that German is not the only language which has undergone change in the course of centuries. He then goes on to say: "Although English is regarded as a language clumsily compounded of many others, yet it is indeed by no means so insignificant and paltry as the ignorant imagine. It possesses rather such elegance and fulness of meaning that we may read books, both sacred and profane, of the greatest merit, written by Englishmen, not in Latin, but in their own mother-tongue. It is therefore heartily to be desired that we Germans should study this language more diligently than is unfortunately the case, so that we might translate likewise into our High German tongue the other excellent religious books they have written; not to mention various other magnificent works, especially the *Arcadia* of Sir Philip Sidney..." The whole of this passage, indeed practically the whole of Hille's book, is reprinted without the slightest acknowledgement by Georg Neumark in a similar work, *Der...Teutsche Palmenbaum*, 1668[4]. He also refers (p. 98) to the excellence of books written in English and observes: "They are all written in the language of Middlesex, such as is

[1] *The French Influence in English Literature*, 1908.   Bibl. 55.
[2] Bibl. 91.   [3] Bibl. 41.   [4] Bibl. 42.

spoken in the neighbourhood of the capital, London, and not in the language of Argyle, Cumberland, Pembroke and similar ruder dialects..."

Hofmannswaldau discusses, in the preface to his *Deutsche Übersetzungen und Gedichte*, 1679[1], not only Old and Middle High German, but also English literature. "The English have at all times shown themselves to be lovers of poetry, though not always with equal felicity, for the poems of merit are mostly by modern writers. In Chaucer, the English Homer, as his countrymen call him, and Robert of Glocester we do not meet with the same learning, art and elegance as in Edmond Spenser's fearie Queene and Michael Draiton's Poly-Olbion, Johnson's (i.e. Ben Jonson's) comedies and tragedies and the religious poems of Quarles and Don (i.e. John Donne)." This judgment is hotly contested by Christian Wernicke, who also spent several years in England, in a note to one of his epigrams (1697), *Auf die Schlesische Poeten*[2]. He says: "Of the English writers he (Hofmannswaldau) mentions with admiration Donn and Quarles, whom no Englishman ever reads, and has not a word for Milton, Cowley, Denham and Waller, whom they justly regard as their best poets." In another note (II. 48), Wernicke praises Cowley's *Brutus*.

The two works of Daniel Georg Morhof which claim our attention in this chapter are his *Unterricht von der deutschen Sprache*, 1682, and *Polyhistor*, 1692. The first[3] is an encyclopaedic work dealing with language and literature in general and German in particular. The philological portions of the work are occasionally amusing. Morhof discusses, for example, with perfect seriousness a theory of a certain Joannes Webbe to the effect that Chinese is the oldest language because the Chinese settled in their country immediately after the Flood and before the erection of the Tower of Babel, "in which they presumably had no share." He is, however, inclined to contest the assertion of Rodornus Schickius that German and Hebrew are only to be distinguished as dialects. In Part II, "Von der

[1] Bibl. 252.
[2] Reprinted in Pechel's modern edition, 1909. Bibl. 264.
[3] Bibl. 255.

Engelländer Poeterey," he indicates the affinity of Old English
and German and explains the mixed nature of contemporary
English.   He notes its terseness but refuses to admit the
inferiority of German.   The disparaging references to German
in the preface to an English version of Rapin's *Reflections on
Aristoteles Treatise of Poetry,* 1674[1], rouse Morhof to fury...
"The German (says Thomas Rymer, the translator) still con-
tinues rude and unpolisht, not yet filed and civiliz'd by the
commerce and intermixture with strangers to that smoothness
and humanity which the English may boast of."   "German,"
retorts Morhof, "is altogether more suited to epic poetry
than any other language, much more so than English, which is
a bastard German and so corrupted by intermixture and effemi-
nate pronunciation that there is absolutely nothing manly
about it.   Its only good points must be ascribed simply and
solely to German, which is its mother."   He ridicules the
opinion current in England that English combines the merits
of all other languages and quotes Milton's treatise *Of Education*
to the effect that English is obscure.   Thomas Sprat and
Rymer place Cowley above the Italians.   "It seems to me,"
says Morhof, "it would be a sufficient honour for Cowley to place
him on an equality with them, a position he justly deserves."

     Morhof then proceeds to give a short sketch of English
literature, beginning with the poems of King Alfred.   His chief
authority for this period is Sir John Spelman's (1594–1643)
Life of King Alfred the Great, though he quotes from the Latin
version of Christopher Ware (1678).   He quotes Rymer's
opinion of Chaucer, Spenser, D'Avenant and Cowley, and
thinks, as already mentioned, that Cowley's merits have been
over-estimated.   He seems to have a personal knowledge of his
poems and accuses him of pedantry.   He has praise for John
Donne and George Herbert's *Divine Poems* and mentions Cleveland, Waller and Denham.   Dryden's cool appropriation of the
drama ("The drama is wholly ours") is received with indignation.   "The Germans are not mentioned," complains Morhof,
"as though they had no share in it or were incapable of such a
work."   He then reverts to Rymer's condemnation of German.

[1] Bibl. 251.

"Just as though the whole world must recognize the English as its teachers, whose enlightened sagacity is held up to the ignorant, foolish, unpolished Germans as a model to which they must conform. I hope, if it please God, to have the opportunity, in a special work, of showing not only them but all other nations who speak of the Germans with similar contempt, that our merits in all sciences are greater than can ever be recognized or requited by them, nay more, that in many arts we have been their masters." Then he again quotes Dryden in a passage remarkable for the fact that in it Shakespeare's name is mentioned for the first time by a German writer: "John Dryden has written very learnedly concerning Dramatic Poetry. The Englishmen he mentions are Shakespeare, Fletcher, and Beaumont, of whose work I have seen nothing. Ben Johnson has written much and, in my opinion, deserves no small praise. He was well read in Greek and Latin authors..." Morhof quotes further admiring references to Jonson from Dryden, Selden, and Anthony Wood, and mentions, still drawing from Dryden, Suckling, Waller, Denham and Cowley. He adds: "There are many more, mentioned neither by the translator (i.e. Rymer) nor Dryden, who yet deserve to be remembered. Among them we may justly include John Milton. In his poems, although they were written in his youth, his genius is already apparent, and they are esteemed equally with the best. With his Heroic Poem, *The Paradis Lost*, we shall deal in the next chapter. We respect this intelligent nation and esteem them very highly, but we should like them to add to all their perfections modesty in their opinion of themselves and others." There are a few more words of censure for English poets in par. 13 of Part III, "Von den Erfindungen." "We must also discuss under this head the English practice of employing technical terms as metaphors, as we see in Donne, in whose works we find Atomos, Influentias, Ecstates and finicking conceits enough to make one sick." With reference to the proper place of description in poetry, Rymer[1], in the preface already mentioned, censures all

---

[1] Born 1641 at Yafforth, Yorks. Entered Sidney Sussex Coll., 1658; Gray's Inn, 1666. Wrote many critical works and a tragedy *Edgar* (1677). Died Dec. 14th, 1713.

poets except his own countrymen and quotes the following description of night, which he thinks superior to those of Vergil, Apollonius, Tasso, Marini, Chapelain, and Le Moyne:

> All things are hushed, as Nature's self lay dead.
> The Mountains seem to nod their drowsie head,
> The little birds in dreams their Songs repeat,
> And sleeping flowers beneath the Night-dew sweat.

Morhof, on the contrary, considers the metaphors extravagant and prefers the passage in the *Aeneid*, IV ("Placidum carpebant fessa soporem corpora per terras").

The scope of *Polyhistor, Sive de Notitia Auctorum et rerum commentarii*, 1692[1], including as it does a discussion of writers in almost all branches of science, is even wider than that of the *Unterricht*.... In Chapters III–VII, which deal principally with libraries, their foundation and importance, the Bodleian is frequently mentioned and occasionally criticized, e.g. "Bodleiana Oxoniensis singulis diebus patet. Quae tamen secretiores sunt, commendatione Patronorum expugnari possunt. Manuscriptorum non adeo facile copia dari solet. Est ubi invidia illam negat; est ubi furti metus peregrinos arcet. Nullos ea in re praeter Anglos difficiliores se sensisse queritur in praefatione ad Polybium Gronovius" (Chap. III). In the next chapter he extols the example of Richard de Bury, "Is cum fuerit Cancellarius & Thesaurus Angliae, brevi temporis spatio rarissimos sibi libros collegit." He also draws largely on Anthony Wood's *Historia et Antiquitates Universitatis Oxoniensis* (1674) and refers to Thomas Bodley and Gilbert Sheldon. In Chapter VII he quotes a letter from Christoph Arnold to Georg Richter in which the Cambridge University Library and the College libraries of Peterhouse, Queens' and St John's are mentioned with admiration: "In Academia Cantabrigiensi Abr. Whelocus Arab. atq. Anglo Saxon. linguae. Professor & Bibliothecarius publicus codices Manuscriptos cumprimis Graecos, perlubenter mihi impertit, ex eadem Bibliotheca publica aliquot Episcoporum Bibliothecis mirifice aucta. Hujus commendatione gratiam adeptus sum inspiciendi illustres in domo Petri, Collegio Reginae, & Collegio Joannitico,

---

[1] Bibl. 254. N.B. Books I–III were published in 1688. There is a reference to Morhof and his *Polyhistor* in the *Gentleman's Journal* for April, 1694.

Bibliothecas, thesauris Manuscriptorum refertissimas. Obstupui in Johannitica, cum mihi magnam sacrorum librorum Graeco barbarorum copiam ostenderent, a benefactore quodam Anonymo suasione Richardi Sybhes[1] S. Theol. Professoris & hujus Collegii quondam Socii Senioris A.D. 1628 dono oblatorum..." Henry More ("Philosophus Anglus") is mentioned in Chapter XII (De eo, quod in disciplinis divinum est, excursus) and the *Mathematical Magic* (1648) of John Wilkins in Chapter XIII (De collegiis secretis). The next chapter deals largely with the foundation of the Royal Society. "...Quare aliter rem in Physiologiae & Matheseos studiis instituerunt Angli, qui novam Societatem pro excolenda philosophia naturali instituerunt auspiciis Regiis, certis quibusdam rationibus & legibus, quae apud Thomam Spraat in Historia ejus societatis Regiae habentur, Anglica & Gallica lingua edita. Jamdudum talis Collegii ideam aliquam dederat Baco Verulamius, in elegantissima illa fabula novi Atlantis...Origo societatis ejus ex eo est, quod in Academia Oxoniensi primum viri quidam ingeniosi privatum aliquod experimentale studium susceperunt; inter quos fuere Sethus Wardus, Boylius, Wilkins, Christophorus & Matthaeus Wrenii, Wallisius, Willisius &c viri ingenio & scriptis omnes celebres. Illa cum perveniret ad Gallos fama, ipsi Academiam Parisiensem, quae in linguae Gallicae culturam instituta erat, ad studium rerum naturalium transtulerat..." The same chapter contains a reference to Abraham Cowley, " poeta insignis, & in caeteris philosophiae & medicinae partibus insigniter eruditus..." Anthony Wood's *Hist. et Ant. Univ. Ox.* is discussed in Chapter XVI and again, with Richard de Bury's *Philobiblion*, in Chapter XVII, where the catalogues of Thomas James (1620) and Thomas Hyde (1674) are also mentioned in connection with the Bodleian. In the next five chapters we meet with the names of Baleus (John Bale?), John Pitseus, Edward Leigh, Burton, George and William Lily (Lilly?), Thomas Dempster, Camden, James Howell and John Langston. Chapters XXIII and XXIV provide discussions of the letters of Roger Ascham, James Howell, John Milton and John Donne. Of Ascham Morhof says: "Pene unus e gente Anglica est,

---

[1] Also spelt Sibbes, Sibbs and Sibs.

cujus stylus veterem latinitatem sapit.   Cum Joh. Sturmio singularem coluit amicitiam ; cujus exemplo erectus, elegans dicendi genus sectatus est.   Ac fuit ipse Sturmius vir eruditissimus, non Rhetor tantum optimus, sed & qui feliciter stylo exprimeret veteres autores minime fucato, ac puro, cujus & epistolae in pretio haberi merentur.   Epistolae ejus prodierunt Hanoviae in 12°. ann. 1610.   Idem & Anglica lingua libellum de informanda juventute scripsit." Howell is criticized for condemning French literature in general and the letters of Balzac in particular, but Morhof is astonished at the ground covered by Howell's own letters and admires his erudition. He singles out some half-dozen as deserving especial praise. The letters of Milton and of Jane Weston[1] are only briefly mentioned.   Of Donne Morhof says : "In Anglicis Johannes Donne, Decanus Ecclesiae Paulinae, Poëmatibus Anglicis & Sermonibus factis celebris, Epistolas Anglica lingua scripsit, Londini editas 1651. in 4to, quae elegantissimae & argutissimae sunt."   The last English book mentioned in Book I is Thomas Sprat's reply[2] to Sorbière's *Voyage en Angleterre* (1664).

Book II includes the names of Roger Bacon, who is also mentioned in Book I, Chap. II, John Wilkins, Robert Fludd, and Sir Thomas Browne.   "Ut sunt, qui de corruptis artibus, quemadmodum Vives, egerunt; aut de erroribus vulgi scripserunt, ut Thomas Broun in sua Pseudodoxia Epidemica, quo titulo ille librum Anglica lingua scripsit, in Belgicam linguam conversam...sed nunc ille auctior Anglica lingua prodiit." The numerous references to Francis Bacon throughout the work have, of course, been discussed in a previous chapter.

In 1682 appeared the first volume of the *Acta eruditorum*[3], a Latin periodical edited by Otto Menke and devoted to the review of new works in all branches of science and literature. The following is a list of the English writers mentioned in the first nineteen volumes under the six heads of "Theologica et ad Historiam Ecclesiasticam spectantia, Juridica, Medica & Physica,

[1] A copy of her poems (*Parthenicon...*) at Göttingen (P. lat. rec. II. 6352) contains the following MS note : "Elisabeth Johanna, Vxor Joannis Leonis, in Aula Imp[li]. Agentis ex familia Westoniorum Angla. Pragae 16 Augusti, Ao 1610." See p. 36 n.
[2] *Observations on Monsieur de Sorbier's Voyage into England.* 1665.
[3] Bibl. 18.

Mathematica, Historia et Geographica, and Philosophia & Philologica Miscellanea."

Theo. 1682. Thomas Burnet, "Scriptor Anglus; qui supra vulgus hominum philosophaturus, &, quantum in ornando argumento, ut ut paradoxo valeat," Samuel Gardiner.

1683. Joseph Glanvill (*Saducismus Triumphatus, Or ful and plain evidence concerning witches & apparitions*, 1681).

1684. Samuel Parker.

1685. Roger Boyle (Bp. of Cloghere), Gilbert Burnet, William Cave, William Lloyd, Thomas Spark, John Turner.

1686. William Cave, Henry Dodwell, Humphry Hody, John Lightfoot, Edward Pocock, John Spencer, Thomas Tanner.

1687. William Cave, Henry Hammond, Thomas Smith.

1688. Henry Dodwell, Samuel Parker, John Pearson, Edward Stillingfleet, Gabriel Towerson, James Usher.

1689. Edward Stillingfleet.

1690. Gilbert Burnet, William Cave, Henry Dodwell, John Pearson.

1691. Edward Brown, Thomas Burnet, Thomas Comber, Edward Gee, Thomas Godwin, John Overall, Robert Pearson, Francis Porter, William Sherlock, Thomas Smith, James Usher, Erasmus Warren, Henry Wharton.

1692. Thomas Barlow, William Cave, Samuel Hill, Humphrey Hody, Bryan Turner, Daniel Whitby.

1693. Richard Bentley, Robert Burscough, John Edwards, Luke Milbourne, Henry More, John Quick, William Sherlock.

1694. John Doughty, Jonathan Edwards.

1695. William Sherlock, Edward Stillingfleet.

1696. John Edwards, Francis Gregory, William Nichols, Robert Sheringham, Henry Wharton.

1697. Thomas Bray, George Bull, Gilbert Burnet, Edward Leigh, William Nichols, John Norris, Simon Patrick, William Whiston.

1698. John Locke, Edward Stillingfleet, Edward Thwaites.

1699. William Cave, Henry Hammond, Richard Kidder (Bp. of Bath and Wells), John Lightfoot, Faithful Teate[1].

1700. Richard Blackmore, Gilbert Burnet, Richard Kidder, William Nichols.

Jur. 1684. John Selden (*Tracts*, 1683).

1685. Francis Clarke, Thomas (?) Mocket, Richard Zouch.

Med. and Phys. 1682. Robert Boyle, Nehemiah Grew, Thomas Sydenham, Edward Tyson.

1683. William Briggs, E. Mainwaring, Edward Tyson.

1684. Robert Boyle, Walter Charleton, Daniel Duncan, Nehemiah Grew, John Jones, M. Lister, Robert Plot, Thomas Sydenham, Edward Tyson.

1685. David Abercromby, Robert Boyle, William Gould, Nehemiah Grew, Griffith Hatley, Martin Lister, Robert Plot, Robert Sibbald, Edward Tyson.

1686. David Abercromby, George Ash, Robert Boyle, William Briggs, Walter Charleton, William Cole, Samuel Derham, William Molyneux, D. Pierce, Robert Plot, Nathaniel Sprye, Thomas Sydenham, Richard Wiseman.

---

[1] Not mentioned in the *Dictionary of National Biography* and *Encyclopaedia Britannica*. Some particulars are given in the *Universal-Lexicon aller Wissenschafften und Künste*, Leipzig and Halle, 1732–46. His principal work, *Tertria*, a treatise on the Trinity, was translated into German by Gottfried Wagner in 1698.

1687.   David Abercromby, Robert Boyle, John Brown, Edmund Halley, Francis Willoughby.

1688.   Robert Boyle, John Goad, Edmund King, John Shipton, Edward Tyson.

1690.   Walter Harris.

1691.   Robert Boyle, John Locke (review, pp. 501–5, of *An Essay concerning Humane understanding*, 1690); Leonard Plunket.

1692.   Robert Boyle, Richard Carr, Nehemiah Grew, Edmund Halley, John Shipton, Edward Tyson.

1693.   Robert Boyle, Bulstrode Whitelocke, William Cole, Richard Morton.

1694.   Robert Boyle, Samuel Dale, Thomas Gibson.

1695.   Gideon Harvey, Charles Leigh, Martin Lister, Thomas Sydenham.

1696.   Bernard Connor, Thomas Creech, Nehemiah Grew, H. Ridley.

1697.   W. Cockburn, John Colbatch, Martin Lister, W. Whiston.

1698.   Robert St. Clair, William Cockburn, John Colbatch, Bernard Connor, John Pechey, Robert Pierce, Edward Tyson.

1699.   William Cowper, George Dampier, Christopher Pitt.

1700.   William Cowper, Edward Tyson, John Woodward.

Math.   1682.   John Flamsted, Jonas Moore.

1683.   — Heathcot, John Wallis.

1684.   Isaac Barrow, Gilbert Clark, Edmund Halley.

1685.   Thomas Baker, Thomas Everard.

1686.   John Craig, John Flamsted, William Molyneux, Samuel Morland, John Wallis, Maurice Wheeler.

1687.   William Molyneux, William Petty.

1688.   Francis Jessop, Isaac Newton.

1690.   John Scarlett.

1691.   Henry Coggeshall, William Leybourn.

1692.   Edmund Halley.

1693.   Edmund Halley.

1696.   David Gregory, John Wallis.

1697.   Isaac Newton.

1698.   David Gregory.

1700.   David Gregory, Thomas Savery, John Wallis.

Hist. and Geog.   1684.   Gilbert Burnet, Samuel Clark, Francis Sandford.

1686.   Edward Herbert of Cherbury, Francis Mackenzie, Roderick O'Flaherty.

1687.   Gilbert Burnet, William Dugdale, Richard Parr, William Winstanley.

1688.   Gilbert Burnet.

1689.   Richard Blome, George Mackenzie, George Wheeler.

1691.   Thomas Hyde.

1692.   Richard Bentley, Edmund Chilmead, John Fordun, Thomas Gale, Ranulf Higden, Humphrey Hody, Anthony Wood.

1693.   William Acton, Henry Dodwell, Edmund Gibson, Sir William Temple.

1694.   James Melville, Francis Bacon (review of Leipzig edition, 1694), George Dawson.

1695.   Gilbert Burnet, Henry Dodwell, Robert Nanton.

1696.   Richard Blackmore, William Camden, Edmund Gibson, William Temple, Henry Wharton.

1697.   Ezekiel Burridge, W. Nicholson, James Tyrrel.

1698.   Edward Thwaites.

1699.   Henry Dodwell, Charles Gildon, John Hudson, Martin Lister.

1700. Bernard Connor, William Lloyd, William Nicholson, Thomas Smith, John Toland (review of edition and *Life* of Milton, 1698).

Phil. et Phil. Misc. 1683. Martin Lister.
1684. William Dugdale, John Gibbon.
1686. — Herbert, Bp. of Hereford, George Mackenzie, James Turner.
1687. Nicholas Lloyd, William Robertson.
1689. Robert Sanderson.
1691. Thomas Pope Blount, William Fleetwood, William Petty.
1692. John Selden.
1693. Thomas Burnet.
1695. Joshua Barnes, John Potter.
1696. Richard Blackmore, Charles Boyle, William Dryden, John Milton (review of *Poetical Works*, London, 1695), Thomas Smith.
1697. John Selden.
1698. John Evelyn, William Lloyd, John Potter.
1699. John Locke, Edward Stillingfleet.
1700. John Dryden (review of *Fables*, 1700), Thomas Johnson, Sir William Temple.

Of Dryden the reviewer says (p. 322): "...Certe inter Anglos hactenus praecipue eminuit, seu cetera spectes poëmatum genera, seu, quod difficillimum est, Tragoediam, in qua neque Gallorum Cornelio cessit, neque Anglorum Shakespario, atque hoc tanto praestantior fuit, quanto magis litteras calluit. Commendatur ejus tragoedia, cujus titulus: *All for Love, or the World well lost...*, celebratur *Œdipus*...Memorantur plura illius dramata, quorum catalogum exhibent Langbainius[1] ejusque continuator Gildonus in Vitis & Characteribus Poëtorum Dramaticorum Anglorum p. 41 seq. neque vulgaris eruditionis est, quam *de Dramatica Poësi* Anglice scripsit, dissertatio, quamlibet haud multarum plagularum..." This comparison of Dryden with Corneille and Shakespeare is interesting, inasmuch as Shakespeare is here, for the first time in Germany, recognized as the greatest English dramatist.

Another writer who was very familiar with English writers is the historian, Hermann Dietrich Meibohm. In his *Programma...in notitiam Regnorum...Europae*, 1702[2], he mentions Henry Savile, William Camden, John Selden, Thomas Gale, Robert Sheringham, John Spelman, Thomas More, Francis Bacon, Edward Herbert, Gilbert Burnet, Robert Johnston, William Sanderson, Milton, Thomas Smith, Edward Chamberlain, Thomas Wood and James Ware.

[1] Gerard Langbaine: *Account of the English Dramatic Poets*, 1691.
[2] Bibl. 256.

CHAPTER XI

LATER LYRICS

THE volume of poems entitled *Herrn von Hofmannswaldau und andrer Deutschen auserlesener und bissher ungedruckter Gedichte erster theil*[1], edited by Benjamin Neukirch in 1697, contains a poem, *Auf ihre schwartze und sauersehende augen*, translated from the English by C.E. It consists of five verses, of which I quote the first:

> Ihr schwartzen augen ihr, eur schatten-voller grund
>   Macht mein verhängniss mir im glück und unglück kund,
> Wann ihr in liebe last die strahlen auf mich schiessen,
>   So seh ich vor mir nichts denn güldne berge stehn ;
> Ach! aber, wenn ihr mich verächtlich wolt begrüssen,
>   So heist ihr mich so fort zum finstern grabe gehn.
> Ihr schwartzen augen ihr, in euren dunckeln gründen
> Kan ich itzt glück und tod, itzt höll und himmel finden...

The English original is unknown to me. According to Johann Ulrich von König[2], "C.E." was a certain Eltester, who was still alive in 1732. As Dorn[3] points out, this Eltester cannot be the Christian Eltester, architect and engineer to the court of Brandenburg, who died in 1700.

We now come to two volumes of poetry, which, although not published until the end of the first decade of the eighteenth century, contain a number of translations from the English made several years before. Nicolai von Bostel (1670–1704), a native of the town of Stade, left a number of poems which were published posthumously in 1708. The majority, so we are told in the preface, were written by the author in his youth.

---

[1] Bibl. 91.
[2] *Des Herrn von Besser Schriften*, Teil I. Neuer Vorbericht, p. xxiii. Leipzig, 1732. Bibl. 268.
[3] Bibl. 84.

On page 157[1] is a drinking-song ("Erquickender Wein / Dein lieblicher Schein Kan keinem Vernünfftigen wiederlich sein ") to be sung to the melody, *How strange is the fate of a poor English state.* The poem, *Es ist die Liebe bloss ein Schatten unsrer Sinnen,* is a translation of *Love's but a Shadow by Reflection made,* written by "J.G." and published in the *Gentleman's Journal*[2] for March, 1693. In the same journal (Oct., 1693) is a poem entitled *On Love,* by "A Lady of Quality." It begins *Love! thou'rt the best of human joys* and is translated by Bostel as *Liebe! schönster Schatz auf Erden....* Another translation is the poem beginning *Wenn ich die Lieblichkeit erwege,* the original being the Earl of Rochester's *While on those lovely looks I gaze*[3]. Finally we have a translation of a poem beginning *If love's a sweet passion why does it torment,* which is quite unknown to me. I give the first verses of two of these poems and the whole of another as samples of Bostel's skill.

On Love, by Mr J. G.
Love's but a Shadow by Reflection made
  Of some imagin'd Beauty in our Mind,
Why shoud it then our peaceful soul invade,
  And with delusive Joys deceive Mankind?
To Women all as to Earth's Center tend,
  But 'tis from thence removing we to Heav'n ascend....
                            (2 verses.)

Es ist die Liebe bloss ein Schatten unsrer Sinnen /
Den in der Phantasie der Schönheit Irlicht macht /
Drum muss der blaue Dunst verstieben und zerrinnen /
So bald der reine Glantz der Seelen nur erwacht.
Ihr Blend-Werck sucht allein sein Centrum auff der Erden /
Das Frauen-Zimmer ist das Ziel der falschen Lust /
Wer nun vom Irdischen nicht kan entwehnet werden /
Dem bleibt die Süssigkeit des Himmels unbewust....

On Love. By a Lady of Quality.
Love! Thou'rt the best of human Joys,
  Our chiefest Happiness below;
All other pleasures are but Toys,
  Music, without thee is but Noise,
  And Beauty but an empty Show.

Heav'n, who knew what Man could move
  And raise his Thoughts above the Brute,
Said, let him live and let him love;
  'Tis this alone that can his Soul improve,
  What e're Philosophers dispute.

[1] *Poetische Neben-Werke.* Bibl. 92.   [2] Bibl. 88.   [3] Bibl. 89.

Liebe ! schönster Schatz auf Erden /
Gröstes Glücke dieser Welt /
Alles muss zur Thorheit werden /
Was man dir entgegen hält /
Schönheit und Music sind Gaben
Die ohn dich kein Leben haben.

Der des Menschen edle Triebe
Höher als die Tiere schätzt /
Sprach : Er lebe / sprach : Er liebe ;
Dis ist was sein Hertz ergötzt ;
Ob gleich die Sophistschen Lehren
Sich bemühn es zu verkehren.

A Song.
While on those lovely Looks I gaze
To see a Wretch pursuing ;
In Raptures of a blest Amaze,
His pleasing happy Ruin :
'Tis not for pity that I move ;
His Fate is too aspiring,
Whose Heart, broke with a Load of Love
Dies wishing and admiring.... (2 verses.)

Wenn ich die Lieblichkeit erwege /
So aus den holden Augen blickt /
Und die Entzückung überlege /
Wo durch ein schwacher Geist erstickt /
So kan ich ihn gar nicht beklagen /
Ein Hertz / so an der Liebes-Last /
Sich aus dem Athem hat getragen /
Und unter dieser Müh erblast /
Stirbt in der süssen Lust und angenehmsten Ruh /
Ein traurigs Beyleyd kommt denselben gar nicht zu.

The other writer who demands our attention in this chapter is Johann Burchard Menke, whose familiarity with Flecknoe and Sherburne has already been mentioned in Chapter VIII. In his preface to the *Galante Gedichte*[1] he says : " Finally I must not forget those English writers who were just as little insensible to the emotion of love as unable to express themselves to perfection in verse. I will not dwell on the notorious Earl of Rochester...and I hope that the pieces I have translated from his works will give no offence. The celebrated Afara Behn, known in England under the name of ' Astraea,' could never have inspired the other poets of her time with so many love-themes nor described the voyage to the Island of Love in such delightful verse, had she not possessed, in addition to her

[1] Bibl. 93.

uncommon beauty, an uncommon sensibility as well. Of the famous Edward Sherburne and the unfortunate epigrammatist, Richard Flecknoe, I can only say that their greatest beauty lies in their love-poems." The first edition of Menke's *Galante Gedichte* appeared in 1705, but the following list of translations from the English is taken from the second edition of 1710.

1. Die Violen in der Cloris Busen. (*Violets in Thaumantia's Bosome*, Sherburne[1].)

> Twice happy Violets! that first had Birth
> In the warm Spring, when no frosts nip the Earth ;
> Thrice happy now ; since you transplanted are
> Unto the sweeter Bosome of my Fair.
> And yet poor Flowers! I pitty your hard Fate,
> You have but chang'd, not better'd your Estate :
> What boots it you t' have scap'd cold Winters breath,
> To find, like me, by Flames a sudden death ?

> Wie glücklich seyd ihr doch, ihr niedrigen Violen,
> Die ihr im Frühling schon die harten Felder schmückt,
> Jetzt aber da ihr euch der Chloris Brust befohlen,
> So schätzet jedermann euch noch weit mehr beglückt.
> Doch arme Blumen ihr, ihr seyd dennoch betrogen,
> Weil euer Sitz vertauscht, doch nicht verbessert ist ;
> Was hilft es, dass ihr euch habt Wind und Frost entzogen,
> Wenn ihr, so wol als ich, bey Flammen sterben müst ?

15. Das willige Frauenzimmer. (*The Willing Mistress*, Afra Behn[2].)
17. Der Theure Schwur. (*The Vow*, Sherburne.)
35. Chloris läst sich zwingen. (Sir Thomas More, *Epigrams.*)
56. Die kostbare Chloris. (A Song : *Caelia weeps*, Flecknoe[3].)
67. Treuhertzige Ermahnung an die Phyllis. (A Song : *Phillis be gentler I advise*, Rochester[4].)
68. Liebe und Eifersucht. (A Song : *My dear Mistress has a Heart Soft as those kind Looks she gave me*, Rochester.)
69. Die Liebes-Schule. (?   , Rochester.)
78. Das Dilemma. (*The Dilemma*, Sherburne.)
102. Gespräch zwischen Strephon und Daphne. (*A Dialogue between Strephon and Daphne*, Rochester.)
116. Auf ihr Pater noster. (From an English MS.)

---

[1] Bibl. 87.
[2] *Poems upon several occasions.* Bibl. 90.
[3] *A Collection of the choicest Epigrams and Characters.* Bibl. 258.
[4] *Poems, (&c,) On Several Occasions.* Bibl. 89.

CHAPTER XII

LATER SATIRE

THAT the works of John Dryden were not unknown in Germany is clear from the criticisms quoted in Chapter x. Of his satirical poems the only one that concerns us is *Mac Flecknoe*.

It will be remembered that on November 24th, 1681, Shaftesbury was acquitted of a charge of high treason. The Whigs had a medal struck to celebrate the event and so Dryden attacked Shaftesbury in *The Medal, a Satire against sedition*. This was in March, 1682. The challenge was answered by Dryden's rival, Shadwell, in a scurrilous poem entitled *The Medal of John Bayes*, "John Bayes" having been Dryden's nickname since the appearance in 1672 of a farce, *The Rehearsal*, the joint work of Buckingham, Samuel Butler, Thomes Sprat, and Martin Clifford. Dryden retaliated with *Mac Flecknoe, or a Satire on the true blue Protestant Poet, T.S.*, October, 1682[1]. The original bone of contention between Dryden and Shadwell had been the merits of Ben Jonson, which Dryden refused to acknowledge. In 1668 Shadwell criticized Dryden's taste in the preface to *The Sullen Lovers*, but even in 1676 their relations were still friendly. In that year, however, Shadwell produced his *Virtuoso* and made several offensive references in the Prologue, Epilogue and Preface of that play to Dryden's *Aureng-Zebe*. In *Mac Flecknoe* Shadwell is represented as the adopted son of Flecknoe and his

---

[1] See K. Kuchenbäcker: *Dryden as a Satirist*, 1889. Bibl. 262. Also Introduction to *Works* (ed. Saintsbury), 1882. Bibl. 261.

heir in the realm of Nonsense. Flecknoe[1], whose name had become proverbial as that of a wretched poet, determines to lay down the sceptre he has so long wielded and solemnly prepares to invest Shadwell with the insignia of office. Dryden, of course, turns this mock ceremony into a scorching criticism of Shadwell's poetical aspirations.

This altercation has a parallel in the history of German literature, although in this case the causes were purely literary, not political. In 1678 the first German opera appeared in Hamburg. One of its principal admirers was Christian Heinrich Postel (1658–1705), a lawyer and poet of that town. He was an imitator of Marino and Hofmannswaldau. The extravagances of the Silesian poets were attacked by Christian Wernicke, who settled in Hamburg in 1700 after a stay of several years in England. Towards the end of 1701 Postel published a sonnet in which he compared Wernicke to a hare skipping round a dead lion. The next year Wernicke replied with *Ein Heldengedicht, Hans Sachs genannt, aus dem Englischen übersetzet*[2]. This poem is an imitation of Dryden's *Mac Flecknoe*. Hans Sachs, the king of harlequins, chooses Stelpo (Postel) to be his successor. The latter's qualifications are enumerated and his claim to absolute stupidity established beyond doubt. How closely Wernicke follows Dryden may be seen from a comparison of the beginnings of the two poems:

> All human things are subject to decay,
> And when fate summons, monarchs must obey.
> This Flecknoe found, who, like Augustus, young
> Was called to empire, and had govern'd long ;
> In prose and verse, was own'd, without dispute ;
> Through all the realms of Nonsense, absolute....

Was Irrdisch ist, vergeht ; was Menschlich ist nimmt ab :
Und ein Monarche selbst fällt mit der Zeit ins Grab.
Diss ward Hans Sachs gewahr, der lang' in Deutschland herrschte,
Und nach der Füsse Maass' hier Schuhe macht und verschte :
Der in der Dummheit Reich' und Haubstat Lobesan
Den ersten Preiss durch Reim' ohn' allen Streit gewann....

Wernicke's satire is more comprehensive than Dryden's and

---

[1] An Irish priest and insignificant poet and dramatist, though Dryden's satire is unfair in its application to him. Travelled widely in South America and elsewhere and died in 1670.

[2] See R. Pechel: *Christian Wernicke's Epigramme*, 1909, Bibl. 264; and especially A. Eichler's article (Bibl. 263), to which I am much indebted.

the scene is localized in Hamburg, the coronation taking place in the theatre. Stelpo takes a solemn oath to combat reason and purity of speech and is anointed with pitch and tallow. One detail of Stelpo's career is taken, as Eichler[1] points out, not from *Mac Flecknoe*, but from the second part of *Absalom and Achitophel* (457, 458). This is contained in lines 17, 18:

> Selbst seine Amme fasst nach der Geburt ihn um
> Weissagt' und segnet' ihn mit diesem Wunsch : Sey dumm....

The original lines are:

> The midwife laid her hand on his thick skull,
> With this prophetic blessing—Be thou dull!

Like Flecknoe, Hans Sachs gives his successor much advice ("Lern' aber du von mir arbeiten ohne Nutzen"). As he finishes speaking, a trap-door opens and he vanishes, leaving his cobbler's apron to Stelpo. This corresponds exactly to the conclusion of Dryden's poem:

> He said ; but his last words were scarcely heard:
> For Bruce and Longvil[2] had a trap prepar'd,
> And down they sent the yet declaiming bard.
> Sinking he left his drugget robe behind,
> Borne upwards by a subterranean wind.
> The mantle fell to the young prophet's part,
> With double portion of his father's art.

Other English satirists are mentioned by Menke in his *Anhang einer Unterredung von der Deutschen Poesie*, which is appended to his *Galante Gedichte*[3]. After referring to Rochester, he turns to Butler. "The English *Hudibras*," he says, "a very long but uncommonly spicy satire, is written throughout in short lines." In the preface to his *Schertzhaffte Gedichte*, 1706, he tells us that his seventh satire is an imitation of one by John Hall[4], of whom he says "it is to be regretted that this is the only satire he wrote." The theme of Hall's satire is the debasement of poetry and it begins:

> Pray let m'alone, what do you think can I
> Be still, while Pamphlets thus like hailstons fly
> About mine eares[5]?

---

[1] Bibl. 263.
[2] Two characters in Shadwell's *Virtuoso*, 1676.
[3] Bibl. 93.
[4] 1627–1656. Native of Durham. Studied at St John's, Cambridge, and at Gray's Inn.
[5] John Hall: *Poems*, 1646. Bibl. 257.

Menke's version is entitled *Wider die Menge unnützer Schrifften und Gedichte, Wie auch wider die böse Erziehung der Jugend*[1]. The epigrams of More are also commended in this passage, and two of them are included in the following list of translations from English poets in the *Schertzhaffte Gedichte*:

27. Ein Antiquarius. (From More : *Epigrammata.*)
28. Der Geplagte. (Flecknoe.)
29. An die Chloris, die Herr im Hause ist. (Flecknoe.)
30. An einen unschuldigen Soldaten. (Flecknoe.)
31. An einen, der sich nicht kund geben wolte. (Flecknoe.)
32. An einen, der alle Leute censirte. (Flecknoe.)
33. Ein Verläumder. (Flecknoe.)
34. Capitain Mops, ein verzagter Soldate. (*On Captain Ansa, a bragging Run-away*, Flecknoe[2].)
36. Die beschwerliche Nase. (More.)

[1] *Schertzhaffte Gedichte*, 1706. Bibl. 260.
[2] In *A Collection of the choicest Epigrams and Characters*, 1673. Bibl. 258.

CHAPTER XIII

MILTON IN GERMANY

WE have been wandering hitherto through the dreary by-ways of literature but are now at last on the broad high-road which leads by easy stages from *Paradise Lost* to Klopstock's *Messias*.

The earliest references to Milton's poetical works occur about the year 1680. One quotation from Morhof's *Unterricht*, 1682, has already been given (see Chapter x), and I now give, from the same work (II. 7, "Von den Reimen, ob sie nothwendig sind in der gemeinen Poesie"), a passage in which the nature of blank verse is discussed : "Not only English writers of comedies, like Johnston (*sic*) and others, but also writers of Heroic Poems, have used rhymeless verse. The famous John Milton has written a complete poem, called *The Paradise lost*, entirely without rhymes. In the preface he advocates this style of versification, particularly for the reason that the poet is often obliged for the sake of the rhyme, to insert, against his will, words and even whole phrases, which, but for this obstacle, might be better and more properly expressed." There is also an allusion to Milton's masques in a later chapter which deals with the Drama[1].

The earliest printed attempt to introduce blank verse into Germany, viz. Ernst Gottlieb von Berge's translation of *Paradise Lost*, likewise belongs to the year 1682, but before proceeding to discuss this version I must deal with Haake's fragment, which was probably written about 1680 and is now

[1] Bibl. 255.

preserved in MS in the Landesbibliothek at Cassel[1]. It consists of 56 leaves, comprising Books I–III and 50 lines of Book IV. The translation, like von Berge's, is in the metre of the original. As the latter refers to Haake's fragment in the preface to his own version and makes, moreover, the most liberal use of it, it is clear he must have seen a copy before 1682. Another, Bolte[2] tells us was sent to Johann Sebald Fabricius, Professor of Logic and Greek at Heidelberg, but resident in Oxford after 1675. Schaible[3] quotes the opinion of Fabricius as expressed in a letter to the translator: "incredibile est quantum nos omnes afficerit gravitas styli et copia lectissimorum verborum." Both these copies are now lost, and the only one known to be in existence, therefore, is the one at Cassel. It is written in a fairly legible hand and bears the title, *Das Ver-Lustigte Paradeiss auss und nach dem Englischen I.Mᵉ. durch T.H. Zu übersetzen angefangen—voluisse sat.*

Von Berge's translation, *Das Verlustigte Paradeis*[4], appeared at Zerbst. He tells us in the preface that no sooner had he read the poem than he felt impelled to translate it into German " in a style similar to that employed not long ago by the famous Theodor Haake, an eminent member of the Royal Society, in his unfinished translation....If this version be well received (says Berge) a translation of *Paradise Regained* will follow."

This intention was never carried out, probably owing to the small impression *Das Verlustigte Paradeis* produced in Germany. Even as early as 1732 the book seems to have been almost forgotten. In that year appeared Johann Ulrich von König's edition of Johann von Besser's works[5], and on p. 891 König quotes a line from Berge's Milton to illustrate the use of monosyllables in versification. In a note he adds: " Ernst Gottlieb von Berge was interpreter to the Elector of Brandenburg and King of Prussia and council-chamberlain in Berlin. He spoke at least seven languages perfectly. In addition to other English books, he translated this Heroic Poem of Milton's

---

[1] Bibl. 265.
[2] Johannes Bolte: *Die beiden ältesten Verdeutschungen von Milton's Verlorenem Paradies*, 1888. Bibl. 271.
[3] Bibl. 77. [4] Bibl. 266.
[5] *Des Herrn von Besser Schriften*, 1732. Bibl. 268.

in rhymeless verses of five feet. The present rarity of the book is in proportion to the difficulty of the undertaking, and I shall therefore deal with both him and his translation at greater length in another place." This promise was never kept, but in a letter to Bodmer[1] which was accompanied by an extract from Berge's translation, König says: "But I must tell you that Berge, especially as he bound himself too closely to the English style of versification, was so unsuccessful that the book is quite unknown, nor does anyone, except me, condescend to read it. Nor is it at all possible to obtain a copy, in spite of the pains I have taken to try to procure one for you. Your translation in prose is far more natural, but of this more later." This unfavourable opinion of Berge's work is shared by a modern critic, Bolte[2], who considers that his style is more strained than Haake's and exaggerates the latter's defects. He compares the verse-technique of both versions and quotes a lengthy passage from the beginning of the first book. The following extract from the famous debate in Hell (Book II) will allow the reader to see to what extent Berge borrowed from Haake:

> ...On the other side up rose
> Belial, in act more graceful and humane:
> A fairer person lost not heaven; he seem'd
> For dignity composed and high exploit:
> But all was false and hollow: though his tongue
> Dropt manna, and could make the worse appear
> The better reason, to perplex and dash
> Maturest counsels: for his thoughts were low:
> To vice industrious, but to noble deeds
> Timorous and slothful; yet he pleased the ear,
> And with persuasive accent thus began.
> "I should be much for open war, O peers,
> As not behind in hate; if what was urged
> Main reason to persuade immediate war,
> Did not dissuade me most, and seem to cast
> Ominous conjecture on the whole success;
> When he, who most excels in fact of arms,
> In what he counsels, and in what excels,
> Mistrustful grounds his courage on despair
> And utter dissolution, as the scope
> Of all his aim, after some dire revenge.

---

[1] See A. Brandl: *Zur ersten Verdeutschung von Miltons Verlorenem Paradies,* 1878. Bibl. 270.
[2] Bibl. 271.

First, what revenge? The towers of heaven are fill'd
With armed watch, that render all access
Impregnable: oft on the bordering deep
Encamp their legions: or, with obscure wing,
Scout far and wide into the realm of night,
Scorning surprise. Or could we break our way
By force, and at our heels all hell should rise
With blackest insurrection, to confound
Heaven's purest light; yet our great enemy,
All incorruptible, would on his throne
Sit unpolluted: and the ethereal mould,
Incapable of stain, would soon expel
Her mischief, and purge off the baser fire,
Victorious...."

...Jndessen regt sich Belial dort herfür,
11 mit angemasster mild- u. sitt-samkeit,
als weyland der gefallnen Schönster Engel
der nicht alss Glimpf u. Heyl noch für thut wenden;
dess falsche Zung tropft eytel Honigseim
am schein, kein Gift in that kan bittrer sein
des Molochs Räht behagt ihm nicht, dieweil
Er Mañlich schien, u. keine Tück noch Arglist
im Schilt fürhielt, auf Belials weis u. art,
dem redlich sein ein Greuel; drum, lieb-kosend,
fieng er also dar an zu haranguiren.
12 Eür Durchläucht haben zu gross Raht u. Fug
den Krieg zu fürdern, u. so grossen Feind
nicht ferner Raum zu lassen; aber mich
bedunckt es ungereimt, dass man diss Heer
Soll muhtig halten durch Verzweiflungs Grund;
Soll der auf dessen Macht u. Stärck Sie all
So billich sich verlassen, Ihnen ietzt
Verlusts gefahr eingeisten (?) wo nicht gar
des ewigen undergangs; u. dass Sie sich
an blosser Rachgier, ohn den vollen Lust
13 darin zu büssen, wohl vergnügen möchten.
Was kan damit sein aussgereicht? ist nicht
der Himel allenthalben starck besetzt
gantz unbelagerlich, unundgrablich,
uns unersteiglich? reicht die Ausswacht nicht
biss an die Tief mit gantzen Regimenten?
Für deren Huht u. Stärck kein Trug, List, Blendung,
Macht, Sturm sich schützen oder bergen kan:
u. wan die Höll gleich alles dran wolt setzen,
u. ihr geläng der Aussbruch weit und breit.
14 u. hoch, biss Himel an, wird doch der Höchste
gantz unverwirrt in Seinem Thron, den Trotz
gar leicht zernichten, schrecklich rächen können
uns recht dañ erst in äusserste Verzweiflung
einstürzend, und der Sieg im ewig pleiben.... (HAAKE.)

   Indessen regt sich Belial dort herfür /
mit angemasster Mild- und Sittsamkeit /
als der gefallnen / weyland / schönster Engel:
Der nichts als Glimpf und Heyl / pflegt fürzuwenden
Dess falsche Zung ein lauter Honigseim /

im schein / die Werck sind eytel Ottergift.
des Molochs Raht steht ihm nicht an / dieweil
er Mannlich schien / und keine Tück noch List
im Schild enthielt / auf Belials Weys und Art /
dem Redlich seyn ein Grewl ; Darumb / liebkosend /
Er also anfieng da zu haranguiren.
Ewr Hochheit haben ja gross Recht und Fug /
den Krieg zu fördern / und so grossen Feind
nicht ferner Raum zu lassen ; Aber mich
bedüncket es frey was ungereimt / man wolle
diess Heer nu durch verzweiflung muhtig machen ;
und dass der / dessen Stärck und Macht so wohl
bekent / und hochberühmt / jetzunder ihnen
verlusts Gefahr einhauchet / wo nicht gar
des ewigen Undergangs ; Ja / dass sie sich
an blosser Rachgier / ohn den vollen Lust
daran zubüssen / wohl vergnügen möchten.
Was / lieber / frommet uns all diess ? Ist nicht
der Himmel starck ? Gantz rund umher besetzt ?
Uns unbelägerlich ? Unundergräblich /
und unersteiglich ? Reycht die Ausswacht nicht
biss an die Tief / in gantzen Regimenten ?
Für deren Huht und Wacht kein Trug / List / Bländung /
Behendigkeit / sich bergen oder schützen kan ;
Und wan die Höll gleich alles nun dran setzte /
der Aussbruch auch uns weit und breit gerieht /
biss himmelan / so wird der Höchste doch /
gantz ungestört / in Seinem Thron / den Trotz
sehr leicht zertrümmern und zerstäuben können /
und dann erst recht in äusserste Verzweyflung
uns stürtzen / und der Sieg Ihm ewig pleiben....

(VON BERGE.)

Paradise Lost was not the only work of Milton's to become known in Germany before the close of the century. In 1690 a volume of his official letters appeared under the title of *Literae nomine Senatus Anglicani, Cromwellii Richardique Ad diversos in Europa Principes & Respublicas exaratae...*[1]. The majority of these letters are addressed to the Senates of Hamburg, Lübeck, and Bremen. In the preface, the editor, Johann Georg Pritius, observes :

"...Agnoscunt autem illae pro auctore Jo. Miltonum, qui tanto in pretio apud eruditos est, ut nemo vile quippiam aut protritum vel insubidum ab ipsius expectaverit ingenio, quod tum quidem vel maxime inclaruisse constat, cum suscepta pro populo Anglicano Regem suum capitali supplicio afficiente, defensione, cum adversario, qui tum temporis non immerito principem intro doctos agebat, in arenam descenderet...(Pritius here quotes a eulogy of Milton from Morhof's *Polyhistor*)...Erat sane Miltonus purioris

---

[1] Bibl. 267. Milton succeeded G. R. Weckherlin as "Secretary for foreign tongues" in 1649. The latter's retirement was probably due to failing health.

dicendi generis vehementer studiosus, quod & ipse diligentissime sectabatur, & qui Salmasium solecismos aliquando admittentem, salse admodum perstringebat. Itaq; puras Tibi exhibemus epistolas, faciles, jucundas, & amoenissimas veneres ubique spirantes, ut Musas ipsas vix castiori dicendi genere usuras, nec alibi politiores orationis formulas, quibus elegantissimum maxime delectatur seculum, perinde addisci posse aut facilius opinemur."

The following is an extract from Morhof's appreciation of Milton (*Polyhistor,* p. 304[1]) :

"Miltoni Epistolae Familiares extant libello exiguo. Non ignobilis fuit auctor Miltonus, quod e scripto Anti-Salmasiano constat...Quicquid tamen ejus sit, ostendunt Miltoni scripta virum vel in ipsa juventute : quae enim ille adolescens scripsit carmina Latina, una cum Anglicis edita, aetatem illam longe superant, qua ille vir scripsit poemata Anglica sed sine rhythmis, quos ut pestes carminum vernaculorum abesse volebat, quale illud 13. libris constans, *the paradise lost.* Plena ingeniis et acuminis sunt, sed insuavia tamen videntur ob rhythmi defectum, quem ego abesse a tali carminum genere non posse existimo, quicquid etiam illi, & Italis nonnullis, & nuper Isaaco Vossio in libro de poëmatum cantu, videatur. Epistolae ejus paucae sunt, in quibus tamen non pauca de autoribus veteribus, recentioribus, domesticis, exteris judicia, quae legere & nosse operae pretium est. Editae sunt Londini an. 1647. in 8."

An edition of Milton's *Poetical Works,* published by Jacob Tonson in 1695, was duly reviewed the next year in the *Acta eruditorum*[2] as follows :

"Quod novo vetustiorem paulo Poetam Anglicanum subjungamus, inter suos in heroico genere inveterata fama omnes facile superantem, apud nostri saltem orbis eruditos veniam facile inveniet, quibus omnibus divinum Miltono in hoc quoque scribendi genere ingenium fuisse, haud forte hactenus innotuit. Non tamen aegre ferent iidem, obiter solum ejus mentionem a nobis fieri, cum moris nostri non sit, libros tamdiu sub Sole versatos nostra quoque luce collustrare. Miltoni tamen interea famae, ejusque ingenii admiratoribus dandum id esse putavimus, ut praecipuorum ejus poematum catalogus hic quoque compareret. Primum inter ea locum, uti meretur, ita obtinet quoque in hac eorum collectione poema, quod de generis humani lapsu sub titulo *Paradisi amissi* concinnavit, sexta editione in hoc opere iteratum, de cujus sublimitate caeterisque virtutibus multa nunc essent commemoranda, nisi redditae jam a nobis rationes obsisterent. Id tamen praetereundum non esse existimavimus, censere plerosque, in quorum memoria adhuc viget temporum quibus floruit Miltonus conditio, eam poetice quidem, vivide tamen ab eo in hoc opere repraesentari. Notae quae huic poemati in nova hac editione accedunt, Anglicano imprimis Lectori inserviunt, cui obscura videri omnino poterant nonnulla, quae ex eruditionis paulo magis reconditae penu Miltonus illi adsperserat. Proximum autem huic poema restaurationem humani generis describit, titulo *Paradisi reparati* insignitum. Tertium *Simson agonistes* vocatum, Herois hujus, Palaestinorum ludibriis expositi, fata repraesentat : cui denique varii generis carmina, prout occasio tulit, elaborata & tertia vice nunc edita, succedunt. Id vero, antequam finem faciamus, monendum, tria illa heroica

[1] Bibl. 254.   [2] Bibl. 18.

poemata, priori loco a nobis commemorata, illo carminis genere a Miltono scripta fuisse, quod rhythmo destitutum metro solum gaudet, veterum Graecorum & Latinorum Poetarum exemplo : quod ante Miltonum inter Hispanos quidem & Italos nonnulli usurparunt, nemo vero Anglorum, apud quos tamen ejus exemplo excitatos, nihil hodie, in tragoedia imprimis, hoc carminis genere est frequentius."

In the volume of the same journal for 1700 is a long account (pp. 371 ff.) of Milton's life and works, the occasion being a review of John Toland's *Life of John Milton* (1690). Finally, I quote a sentence from Menke's *Unterredung von der deutschen Poesie*[1], as being the only disparaging allusion to Milton I have discovered. Referring to the esteem in which Milton was held in England, Menke proceeds to find fault with all epic poets and declares: "Milton afterwards forfeited by *Paradise Regained* all the renown he had won by *Paradise Lost.*"

[1] Bibl. 259.

CHAPTER XIV

CONCLUSION

THE literary relations of England and Germany are, as we have seen, merely spasmodic until about the year 1680. From this time onwards the figure of Milton assumes in German literature an importance which culminates in the *Messias* of Klopstock[1]. Still, we must not over-estimate the strength of the thread which leads from Haake's translation of *Paradise Lost* to the great epic of modern German literature. Haake's fragment was probably unknown, except to a few friends in England, until Berge mentioned it in the preface to his own version of 1682, which, in turn, was soon forgotten. When König wrote to Bodmer concerning it, the latter's prose translation was already in existence. Bodmer was the first to stimulate a real interest in the poem, although Milton's merits are constantly recognized in the pages of the *Acta eruditorum*[2], the last volume of which appeared in 1739.

This journal, moreover, throws considerable light on the scientific and philosophical relations of the two countries. Simultaneously with the growth of German interest in Milton, Prior[3], Thomson, Young, Richardson, etc., came the popularity of the English philosophers.

Locke's *Some thoughts concerning education* (1693) was translated into German in 1708[4] and a minor treatise, *A New Method of a Common Place Book* (1686), in 1711. The same

---

[1] See Franz Muncker: *Klopstock*, 1888. Bibl. 278.
[2] Bibl. 18.
[3] See Spiridion Wukadinović : *Prior in Deutschland*. Graz, 1895.
[4] Bibl. 273.

year saw the publication at Leipzig of a Latin translation of
Thomas Stanley's *History of Philosophy* (1655)[1].   In 1701 John
Toland, the author of *Christianity not mysterious* (1696), visited
Hanover as secretary to the embassy of the Earl of Macclesfield
and made the acquaintance of Leibniz, who had already praised
his *Life of Milton* (see Chapter XIII) in a letter to Burnet of
June 18th, 1701[2].   Leibniz himself had visited England between 1672 and 1676 and was well in touch with English
politics.   In 1703 Toland again visited Hanover and after a
stay of five or six weeks went on to Berlin.   His *Account of
Prussia and Hanover* (1705), which was translated into German[3] the next year, is full of extremely interesting observations
on those countries and was consulted by Carlyle for his *Life of
Frederick the Great.*

With Leibniz, Locke and Toland we are brought to a period
which lies beyond the scope of this volume.   The history of
the philosophical relations of England and Germany has been
fully discussed by Gustav Zart[4] and a short account of their
purely literary relations in the eighteenth century will be found
in the essay of Max Koch[5].

In conclusion, I repeat that whereas in the sixteenth
century England borrowed from Germany, in the eighteenth
the positions are reversed and the influence of English literature
and of English philosophy grows stronger as the years roll on.
The object of these studies has been to throw some light on the
course of events during the intervening period.

[1] Bibl. 275.
[2] See John Toland's *Christianity not mysterious*...(ed. Zscharnack), 1908.
Bibl. 279.
[3] Bibl. 75.
[4] *Der Einfluss der englischen Philosophie*, 1881.   Bibl. 276.
[5] Bibl. 277.

APPENDIX A

BIBLIOGRAPHY

The books and articles quoted in this list all contain information which I have been able to utilize. They are naturally very unequal in value and, with the exception of the more general works of reference, appear under the heading of the chapter to which they more particularly refer. Chronological order has been followed within the chapters, except where the insertion of an odd volume would have disturbed a sequence of books which refer to one author.

With very few exceptions the full wording of the title-page has been given and the spelling kept, although no attempt has been made to reproduce the typography of older books.

It should be remembered that the books quoted are the copies consulted by the author and not necessarily first editions, although the date of the latter has usually been added in small type. Particulars which have been ascertained from sources other than the book itself are given in brackets.

The letters and numbers quoted after the date refer to the various libraries and are to be interpreted as follows :

BM	British Museum.
KPB	Königlich-Preussische Bibliothek, Berlin.
LBC	Landesbibliothek, Cassel.
SBB	Stadtbibliothek, Breslau.
UBB	Universitätsbibliothek, Berlin.
UBG	,, ,, Göttingen.
LS	Lesesaal (Reading Room).
BZ	Beamtenzimmer (Librarian's Room).

Where no Cat. No. is given it is to be assumed that the book in question was consulted elsewhere.

The following abbreviations refer to the various periodical publications :

Archiv : *Archiv für das Studium der neueren Sprachen und Litteraturen.* 1846 onwards.

Atl. M : *Atlantic Monthly.* Boston. 1857 onwards.

Echo : *Das literarische Echo.* See Bibl. 23.

Euph : *Euphorion.* See Bibl. 22.

Grenzb : *Grenzboten.* 1842 onwards.

Mag : *Magazin für die Litteratur des In- und Auslandes.* 1830 onwards.

MLQ : *Modern Language Quarterly.* 1897–1904.

MLN : *Modern Language Notes.* 1886 onwards.

VLG : *Vierteljahrschrift für Litteraturgeschichte.* 1888–93.

Z. vgl. LG : *Zeitschrift für vergleichende Literaturgeschichte.* See Bibl. 20.

The other abbreviations require no explanation.

Bibliographies, Periodicals and General Works of Reference.

No.

1. (WILLIAM LONDON.) A Catalogue of The most vendible Books in England, Orderly and Alphabetically Digested; Under the Heads of Divinity, History, Physick, and Chyrurgery, Law, Arithmetic, Geometry, Astrologie, Dialling, Measuring Land & Timber, Gageing, Navigation, Architecture, Horsemanship, Faulconry, Merchandize, Limning, Military Discipline, Heraldry, Fortification and Fire-works, Husbandry, Gardening, Romances, Poems, Playes, &c. With Hebrew, Greek, and Latin Books, for Schools and Scholars. The like Work never yet performed by any. Varietas Delectat.
London. 1658.   KPB Am 8491.

2. (WILLIAM LONDON.) A Catalogue of New Books, By way of Sup-plement to the former, Being Such as have been printed from that time, till Easter-Term, 1660.
London. Luke Fawn & Francis Tyton. 1660.   BM E1025.

3. ROBERT WATT. Bibliotheca Britannica; or a General Index to British and Foreign Literature. 4 vols.
Edinburgh. Constable. 1824.   BM 820 l 45.

4. KARL W. L. HEYSE. Bücherschatz der deutschen National-Litteratur des XVI und XVII Jahrhunderts.
Berlin. J. A. Stargardt. 1854.   KPB(LS) 1. 143.

5. WILLIAM THOMAS LOWNDES. The Bibliographer's Manual of English Literature.
London. Henry G. Bohn. 1857–64.   KPB(LS) 1. 122.

6. W. CAREW HAZLITT. Hand Book to the Popular, Poetical, and Dramatic Literature of Great Britain, From the Invention of Printing to the Restoration.
London. John Russell Smith. 1867.   KPB(LS) 3. 288.

7. W. CAREW HAZLITT. Collections and Notes.
London. Reeves & Turner. 1876.   KPB(LS) 3. 289.
——   Second Series.
       B. Quaritch. 1882.
——   Third Series.   1887.
——   Third Series.   (Suppl. 1.)   1889.
——   Third Series.   (Suppl. 2.)   1892.
——   Fourth Series.   1903.

8. AUSTIN ALLIBONE. A Critical Dictionary of English Literature and British and American Authors.
London. J. B. Lippincott & Co. 1881.   KPB(LS) 1. 123.

9. KARL GEORG. Schlagwort-Katalog.
Hannover. 1889–1908.   UBB(BZ).

10. KARL BREUL. A Handy Bibliographical Guide to the Study of the German Language and Literature for the use of Students and Teachers of German.
London. Hachette & Co. 1895.

11. ARTHUR L. JELLINEK. Bibliographie der vergleichenden Literatur-geschichte.
Berlin. Alex. Duncker. 1903.   KPB Al 154.

No.

12. Louis P. Betz.   La littérature comparée.   Essai bibliographique.
Strasbourg.   Trübner.   (First ed. 1902.)   1904.

13. Clark S. Northrup.   A Bibliography of Comparative Literature.
(Supplement to 12.)
MLN.   XX.   1905.   KPB V 666/20.

14. F. Dietrich.   Bibliographie der deutschen Zeitschriften-Literatur.
Leipzig.   1907 onwards.   UBB(BZ).

15. Hinrichs Halbjahrs-Katalog.
Leipzig.   1907 onwards.   UBB Am 9690.

16. W. J. Harris.   The First Printed Translations into English of the
Great Foreign Classics.
London.   Routledge.   (1909.)   KPB Am 8703.

17. Robert F. Arnold.   Allgemeine Bücherkunde zur neueren deutschen Literaturgeschichte.
Strassburg.   Karl J. Trübner.   1910.   KPB(LS) 3. 252.

18. Acta Eruditorum Anno MDCLXXXII publicata, ac Serenissimo Fratrum
Pari, Dn. Johanni Georgio IV, Electoratus Saxonici Haeredi &
Dn. Friderico Augusto, Duobus Saxoniae &&&. Principibus
Juventutis dicata.   Cum S. Caesareae Majestatis & Potentissimi
Electoris Saxoniae Privilegiis.
Lipsiae.   J. Gross & J. F. Gletitsch.   (Vol. I.)   1682.
KPB Ac 5500.

19. Siegmund Jacob Baumgarten.   Nachrichten von merkwürdigen
Büchern.
Halle.   Joh. Justinus Gebauer.   1752–8.   KPB Ac 5880.

20. Zeitschrift für vergleichende Literaturgeschichte.
Berlin.   A. Haack.   (Vol. I.)   1886–7.   KPB(LS) 3. 150.
——   Neue Folge (Z. vgl. LG. u. Renaissance-Literatur).
Berlin.   A. Haack.   (Vols. I–IV.)   1887, 88–91.
——   (Z. vgl. LG.)   (Vol. v.)   1892.
„   Berlin.   E. Felber.   1893 onwards.

21. Jahresberichte für neuere deutsche Literaturgeschichte.
Stuttgart.   Göschen.   (Vols. I–III.)   1892–4.   KPB(LS) 3. 251.
Leipzig.   Göschen.   (Vols. IV–V.)   1895–7.
Berlin.   Behr.   (Vols. VI–XVIII.)   1899 onwards.

22. Euphorion.   Zeitschrift für Literaturgeschichte.
Bamberg.   C. C. Buchner.   (Vols. I–III.)   1894–6.   KPB(LS) 3. 54.
Leipzig u. Wien.   Carl Fromme.   1897 onwards.

23. Das literarische Echo.   Halbmonatsschrift für Literaturfreunde.
Berlin.   Egon Fleischel & Co.   1898 onwards.
KPB(LS) 3. 151a.

24. Germanisch-Romanische Monatsschrift.
Heidelberg.   C. Winter.   1909 onwards.

25. The Encyclopaedia Britannica, a Dictionary of Arts, Sciences and
General Literature.
Edinburgh.   Adam & Charles Black.   1875–1888.

No.

26. The New Volumes of the Encyclopaedia Britannica constituting in combination with the existing volumes of the Ninth Edition the Tenth Edition of that Work, and also supplying a New, Distinctive and Independent Library of Reference dealing with recent Events and Developments.
  Edinburgh & London. Adam & Charles Black. 1902–3.
  London. "The Times."

27. Dictionary of National Biography.
  London. 1885–1904.

Histories of Literature.

28. HERBERT J. C. GRIERSON. The First Half of the Seventeenth Century.
  Edinburgh & London. William Blackwood & Sons. 1906.
  BM 2308 d 7.

29. OLIVER ELTON. The Augustan Ages.
  Edinburgh & London. Blackwood. 1909. BM 2308 d 7.

30. HERMANN HETTNER. Geschichte der englischen Literatur von der Wiederherstellung des Königtums bis in die zweite Hälfte des 18. Jahrhunderts.
  Braunschweig. 1894[5].

31. RICHARD GARNETT and EDMUND GOSSE. English Literature. An illustrated Record. (4 vols.)
  Heinemann. 1903.

32. ARNOLD SCHRÖER. Grundzüge und Haupttypen der englischen Literaturgeschichte.
  Leipzig. Göschen. 1906.

33. The Cambridge History of English Literature edited by A. W. WARD and A. R. WALLER.
  Cambridge University Press. (Vols. I–VII.) 1908–11.

34. GUSTAV KÖRTING. Grundriss zur Geschichte der englischen Literatur von ihren Anfängen bis zur Gegenwart.
  Münster i/W. Heinr. Schöningh. 1910[5]. KPB(LS) 3. 293.

35. AUGUST KOBERSTEIN. Geschichte der deutschen Nationalliteratur.
  Leipzig. F. C. W. Vogel. 1872[5]. KPB(LS) 3. 259.

36. KARL GOEDEKE. Grundriss der deutschen Dichtung.
  Dresden. L. S. Ehlermann. (Vol. III.) 1887[2]. KPB(LS) 3. 260.

37. WILHELM WACKERNAGEL. Geschichte der deutschen Literatur (neu bearbeitet von Ernst Martin).
  Basel. Benno Schwabe. 1894[2]. KPB(LS) Yc 4917.

38. KUNO FRANCKE. A History of German Literature as determined by Social Forces.
  London. Bell. 1901. UBG H. lit. univ. 97g.

39. FRIEDRICH VOGT und MAX KOCH. Geschichte der deutschen Literatur von den ältesten Zeiten bis zur Gegenwart.
  Leipzig und Wien. Verlag des Bibliographischen Instituts. (Vol. I.) 1907[2]. (Vol. II.) 1904[2].

No.

40. Adolf Bartels. Handbuch zur Geschichte der deutschen Literatur. Leipzig. Eduard Avenarius. 1909². KPB(LS) 3. 264.

41. (K. G. v. Hille.) Der Teutsche Palmenbaum : Das ist / Lobschrift Von der Höchlöblichen / Fruchtbringenden Gesellschaft Anfang / Satzungen / Vorhaben / Namen / Sprüchen / Gemählen / Schriften und unverwelklichem Tugendruhm. Allen Liebhabern der Teutschen Sprache zu dienlicher Nachrichtung / verfasset / durch den Vnverdrossenen Diener derselben. Nürnberg. Wolffgang Endter. 1647. KPB Y 573.

42. (George Neumark.) Der Neu-Sprossende Teutsche Palmenbaum. Oder Ausführlicher Bericht / Von der Hochlöblichen Fruchtbringenden Gesellschaft Anfang / Absehen / Satzungen / Eigenschaft / und deroselben Fortpflantzung / mit schönen Kupfern ausgeziehret / samt einem vollkommenen Verzeichnüss / aller dieses Palmen-Ordens Mitglieder Derer Nahmen / Gewächsen und Worten / hervorgegeben Von dem Sprossenden. Nürnberg. Joh. Hoffman. 1668 (1673*). KPB Y 591.

43. (Johann Herdegen.) Historische Nachricht von dess löblichen Hirten- und Blumen-Ordens an der Pegnitz Anfang und Fortgang, bis auf das durch Göttl Güte erreichte Hundertste Jahr, Mit Kupfern geziert, und verfasset von dem Mitglied dieser Gesellschaft Amarantes. Nürnberg. Christoph Riegel. 1744. KPB Y 761.

44. O. Schulz. Die Sprachgesellschaften des siebzehnten Jahrhunderts. Berlin. 1824. KPB Y 500.

45. Leo Cholevius. Die bedeutendsten deutschen Romane des 17. Jahrhunderts. Leipzig. 1866. KPB Yt 91.

46. E. Höpfner. Reformbestrebungen auf dem Gebiete der deutschen Dichtung des 16. und 17. Jahrhunderts. Berlin (Progr.). 1867. KPB.

47. Carl Lemcke. Geschichte der deutschen Dichtung neuerer Zeit. I. Leipzig. E. A. Seemann. 1871. KPB Yc 5670.

48. Joseph Walter.. Über den Einfluss des 30-jährigen Krieges auf die deutsche Sprache und Literatur, dargestellt auf Grundlage der staatlichen und gesellschaftlichen Zustände der Zeit. Prag-Kleinseite (Progr.). 1871. KPB.

49. Hermann Palm. Beiträge zur Geschichte der deutschen Literatur des XVII und XVIII Jahrhunderts. Breslau. E. Morgenstern. 1877. KPB Yc 5694.

50. Karl Borinski. Die Poetik der Renaissance und die Anfänge der literarischen Kritik in Deutschland. Berlin. Weidemann. 1886. KPB Yb 6441.

* According to Herdegen (Bibl. 43), the book was not really published until 1673 owing to delay in the preparation of the copperplates.

No.

51. ALEXANDER REIFFERSCHEID. Quellen zur Geschichte des Geistigen
    Lebens in Deutschland während des siebzehnten Jahrhunderts. I.
    Heilbronn. Gebr. Henninger. 1889.   KPB At 741.

52. KARL BORINSKI. Die Hofdichtung des 17. Jahrhunderts.
    Z. vgl. LG. (N.F.) VII. p. 1 ff. 1894.   KPB(LS) 3. 150.

International literary relations.

53. THEODOR SÜPFLE. Geschichte des deutschen Kultureinflusses auf
    Frankreich.
    Gotha. E. F. Thienemann. 1886.

54. T. G. TUCKER. The Foreign Debt of English Literature.
    London. Bell. 1907.   KPB Aw 201.

55. ALFRED HORATIO UPHAM. The French Influence in English Litera-
    ture from the accession of Elizabeth to the Restoration.
    New York. Columbia Univ. Press. 1908.   KPB Ag 396.

56. SIDNEY LEE. The French Renaissance in England. An Account
    of the Literary Relations of England and France in the 16th
    Century.
    Oxford. Clarendon Press. 1910.

57. Anon. Die englische Litteratur in Deutschland.
    Grenzb. XXIII. 1864. Review of 58.   KPB Ac 7155.

58. KARL ELZE. Die englische Sprache und Litteratur in Deutschland.
    Dresden. 1864.   KPB Z 138.

59. CHARLES H. HERFORD. Studies in the Literary Relations of
    England and Germany in the Sixteenth Century.
    Cambridge. University Press. 1886.

60. G. HERZFELD. Zur Geschichte der deutschen Literatur in England.
    Archiv. CV. 1900.   KPB(LS) 3. 147.

61. SIDNEY WHITMAN. Former English Influence in Germany.
    N. Am. R. p. 221. 1901.   KPB. Ad 5215.

CHAPTERS I AND IX. *Travellers.*

62. (JACOB RATHGEB.) Kurtze vnd Warhaffte Beschreibung der Ba-
    denfahrt : Welche der Durchleuchtig Hochgeborn / Hertzog zu
    Württemberg vnnd Teckh / Grave zu Mümppelgart / Herr zu
    Heidenheim / Ritter der beeden Vhralten Königlichen Orden / in
    Franckreich S. Michaels / vnnd Hosenbands in Engellandt / &c.
    In negst abgeloffenem 1592. Jahr / Von Mümppelgart auss / In
    das weit-berümbte Königreich Engellandt / hernach im zurück
    ziehen durch die Niderland / biss widerumb gehn Mümppelgart /
    verrichtet hat. Auss J. F. G. gnedigem Bevelch / von dero mitrai-
    sendem Cammer-Secretarien / auffs kurtzist / von tag zu tag
    verzeichnet...
    Tübingen. Erhardus Cellius. 1602.   KPB Tv 1608.

No.

63. JOHN BARCLAY. Icon Animorum Oder Gründliche Beschreibung Menschlicher Gemüths Verwirrungen vnd Endrungen so guten als bösen an dem Menschen zusehen. I. In seiner Aufferziehung. II. Nach Vnterscheid der Nationen. III. Nach Vnterscheid der Complexionen. IV. Nach Vnterscheid der Professionen vnd Ständen dess gemeinen Lebens. Auss dem Lateinischen ins Teutsche aussgesetzet / Durch Johann Seyferten von Vlm Schwedischen Feldt Pastorn.
Bremen. Erhard Berger. 1649.   KPB Ya 7307.

64. —— Spiegel Menschlicher Gemüths Neigungen Auss dem Lateinischen ins Hoch Teutsche versetzt.
Bremen. (Pr. Frf. a/M.) Erhard Berger. 1660. KPB No 348.

65. —— Icon Animorum, Celeberrimi Viri, Augusti Buchneri, Notis, adjecto Rerum indice, illustrata. Cum Privilegio Electorali Saxonico.
Dresdae. Martin Gabr. Hübner. 1680.   KPB 6413.

66. WILLIAM BRENCHLEY RYE. England as seen by Foreigners in the days of Elizabeth and James the First. Comprising translations of the Journals of the Two Dukes of Würtemberg in 1592 and 1610, both illustrative of Shakespeare, with extracts from the travels of foreign princes and others, copious notes, an introduction, and etchings.
London. John Russell Smith. 1865.   KPB Tv 1612.

67. JOHANNES BOLTE. Schauspiele in Kassel und London 1602.
Z. vgl. LG. (Neue Folge) II. 1889.   KPB(LS) 3. 150.

68. H. HAGER. Diary of the Journey of Phil. Julius Duke of Stettin through England in the year 1602.
Engl. Stud. XVIII. 1893.   KPB(LS) 3. 281.

69. CHARLES HUGHES. Shakespeare's Europe. Unpublished Chapters of Fynes Moryson's Itinerary, Being a Survey of the Condition of Europe at the end of the 16th century...
London. Sherratt and Hughes. 1903.   KPB Pv 41.

70. KARL WITTE. Die Deutschen im Urteil eines Engländers vor 300 Jahren.
Nat. Zg. Nos. 462, 466. 1903.   KPB.
Review and summary of 69.

71. THOMAS CORYAT. Coryat's Crudities Hastily gobled up in five moneths travells in France, Savoy, Italy, Rhetia commonly called the Grisons country, Helvetia alias Switzerland, some parts of high Germany and the Netherlands; Newly digested in the hungry aire of Odcombe in the County of Somerset, and now dispersed to the nourishment of the travelling members of this Kingdome.
Glasgow. James MacLehose & Sons. 1905 (orig. 1611).
KPB Pw 15.

72. FYNES MORYSON. An Itinerary, Containing His Ten Yeeres Travell through the Twelve Dominions of Germany, Bohmerland, Sweizerland, Netherland, Denmarke, Poland, Italy, Turky, France, England, Scotland and Ireland.
Glasgow. James MacLehose & Sons. 1907–8 (orig. 1617).
KPB Pv 42.

No.

73. G. STEINHAUSEN. Die Deutschen in Urteil des Auslandes.
Deutsche Rs. 141, pp. 434–52. 1909.   UBB 119r.

74. EDWARD BROWN. An Account of Several Travels Through a great part of Germany : In Four Journeys. I. From Norwich to Colen. II. From Colen to Vienna, with a particular description of that Imperial City. III. From Vienna to Hamburg. IV. From Colen to London. Wherein the Mines, Baths, and other Curiosities of those parts are Treated of. Illustrated with Sculptures.
London. Benj. Tooke. 1677.   KPB S 15812.

75. JOHN TOLAND. Relation von den Königlichen Preussischen und Chur-Hannoverschen Höfen / an einen vornehmen Staats-Minister in Holland Überschrieben von Mr. Toland. Aus dem Englischen ins Teutsche übersetzet.
Franckfurt. 1706.   KPB Su 112.

76. JAMES HOWELL. Instructions for Forreine Travell. 1642 (ed. Arber).
London. 1869 (orig. 1642).   KPB Z 9540.

77. KARL HEINRICH SCHAIBLE. Geschichte der Deutschen in England von den ersten Germanischen Ansiedlungen in Britannien bis zum Ende des 18. Jahrhunderts.
Strassburg. Trübner. 1885.   KPB Tq 3412.

78. A. WILSON VERITY. The Works of Sir George Etheredge. Plays and Poems.
London. John C. Nimmo. 1888.   KPB Zc 10293.

CHAPTERS II AND XI. *Lyrical Poetry.*

79. ERNST HÖPFNER. Weckherlins Oden und Gesänge. Ein Beitrag zur Geschichte der deutschen Dichtung.
Berlin. Stilke u. van Muyden. 1865.   KPB Av 21666.

80. JULIUS WILHELM ZINKGREF. Auserlesene Gedichte deutscher Poeten.
Halle a/S. Max Niemeyer. 1879 (orig. 1624).   KPB Yc 7591.

81. JOHANNES BOLTE. Aus G. R. Weckherlins Leben.
VLG. V. 295 ff. 1892.   UBB.

82. W. BOHM. Englands Einfluss auf G. R. Weckherlin.
Göttingen. (Diss.) 1893.   KPB Ah 8663.

83. H. FISCHER. Georg Rudolf Weckherlins Gedichte.
Tübingen. I, II, 1893. III, 1907.   KPB Ag 308.

84. WILHELM DORN. Benjamin Neukirch, sein Leben und seine Werke.
Weimar. Felber. 1897.   UBB X 1471.

85. WILHELM BOLLE. Die gedruckten englischen Liederbücher bis 1600.
Berlin. Mayer u. Müller. Palaestra XXIX, 1903.

86. KURT FISCHER. Gabriel Vogtlaender, Ein Dichter und Musiker des 17 Jahrhunderts.
Berlin. (Diss.) 1910.   UBB Phil. Diss. 1910.

No.

87. EDWARD SHERBURNE. Salmacis, Lyrian and Sylvia, Forsaken Lydia, The Rape of Helen, A Comment thereon, With Severall other Poems and Translations.
London. Thomas Dring. 1651. BM 1076. d. 38.

88. The Gentleman's Journal : or the Monthly Miscellany. By way of Letter to a Gentleman in the Country. Consisting of News, History, Philosophy, Poetry, Music, Translations, &c.
London. R. Baldwin. 1692-3-4. BM P. P. 5255.

89. JOHN WILMOT, Earl of Rochester. Poems (&c.) On Several Occasions; With Valentinian ; A Tragedy.
London. Jacob Tonson. 1696. BM 79 a 30.

90. APHRA BEHN. Poems upon Several Occasions ; with a Voyage to the Island of Love. Also the Lover in Fashion, being an Account from Lycidus to Lysander, of His Voyage from the Island of Love. To which is added a Miscellany of New Poems and Songs, by Several Hands. The Second Edition.
London. Francis Saunders. 1697. BM 11626 bb 5.

91. HERRN VON HOFFMANNSWALDAU und andrer Deutschen auserlesener und bissher ungedruckter Gedichte erster theil nebenst einer vorrede von der deutschen poesie. Mit Churfl. Sächs. Gn. Privilegio.
Leipzig. Thomas Fritsch. 1697. UBB Yg 3121.

92. NICOLAI VON BOSTEL. Stad: Brem: Poetische Neben-Werke / bestehend In Deutschen und Lateinischen / Geistlichen / Moral-Trauer-Vermischten- und Uber-setzten Gedichten / Nach des Seel. Autoris Tode aus dessen hinterlassen Schrifften colligirt.
Hamburg. Samuel Heyl u. Johann Gottfried Liebezeit. 1708. KPB Yk 1071.

93. JOHANN BURCHARD MENKE. Philanders von der Linde Galante Gedichte Darinnen So wol eigene verliebte Erfindungen, als allerhand auswärtiger Poeten übersetzte Liebes-Gedichte, wie auch insonderheit des berühmten Grafen von Bussy-Rabutin Liebes-Maximen enthalten. Die andere Auflage, so mit Fleiss corrigiret.
Leipzig. Johann Friedrich Gleditsch und Sohn. 1710 (First ed. 1706). UBB Yp 37302².

CHAPTER III. *Sidney's Arcadia in Germany.*

94. SIR PHILIP SIDNEY. The Covntesse of Pembrokes Arcadia...Now the Fourth Time Published, With Svndry New Additions of the same Author.
London. Mathew Lownes. 1605. KPB Zd 980.

95. —— The Countess of Pembroke's Arcadia, with the additions of Sir William Alexander and Richard Beling, A Life of the Author and an Introduction by Ernest A. Baker, M.A.
London. Routledge. (1907.) KPB Zd 981.

96. —— Larcadie De La Comtesse De Pembrok Premiere Partie. Composee par Messire Philippes Sidney Cheualier Anglois. Tradvicte En Nostre Langve par vn Gentil-homme François. Auec enrichissement de Figures.

—— —— Seconde (Troisiesme) Partie...Tradvicte par D. Geneviefve Chappelain...
Paris. Robert Foüet. 1625. UBG Fab. Rom. IX. 385.

No.

97. —— Arcadia Der Gräffin von Pembrock. Das ist Ein sehr anmutige
Historische Beschreibung Arcadischer Gedicht vnd Geschichten /
mit eingemängten Schäffereyen vnd Poesien. Warinn nicht allein
von den wahren Eygenschafften keuscher vnnd beständiger Liebe
gehandelt / sondern auch ein lebendig Bildt dess gantzen menschlichen Wesens vnd Wandels / auffs zierlichst für Augen
gestellet wird: Allen Hoff-Raths-Kriegs- vnd Weltleuten / Edel vnd
Vnedel / Hohes vnd Niderstands Personen / die hin vnd wider /
sonderlich aber an Herrn Höfen / handeln vnd wandeln / lieblich /
nützlich vnd nöthig zulesen : Anfangs in Englischer Sprach beschrieben / durch den weyland Wolgebornen / Trefflich beredten
vnd Berümbten Englischen Graffen vnd Ritter H. Philipps Sidney:
Nachmalen von vnterschiedlichen vornehmen Personen ins Frantzösische ; Nun aber auss beyden in vnser Hochteutsche Sprach /
fleissig vnd trewlich übersetzt Durch Valentinum Theocritum
von Hirschberg. Mit schönen newen Kupfferstücken gezieret.
Frankfurt a/M.   Matthaeus Merian.   1629.   KPB Zd 988a.

98. —— Arcadia der Gräfin von Pembrock : Vom Herrn Graffen vnd
Rittern Herrn Philippsen von Sidney In Englischer Sprache
geschriebe / auss derselbigen Frantzösisch / vnd auss beyden
erstlich Teutsch gegeben Durch Valentinvm Theocritvm von
Hirschberg : Jetzo allenthalben vffs new vbersehen vnd gebessert :
die Gedichte aber vnd Reymen gantz anderst gemacht vnd
vbersetzt Von dem Edlen vnd Vesten M.O.V.B. (Martin Opitz
von Boberfeld) Auch mit schönen Kupfferstücken gezieret vnd
verlegt von Matthaeo Merian.
Frankfurt a/M.   Matthaeus Merian.   1638.   KPB Z 445.

99. ——   —— Hernach allenthalben auffs......Martin Opitz / V.B...
Leyden.   Frantz Heger.   1642.   KPB Zd 993.

100. ——   ——   —— 1646.   KPB Zd 995.

101. MARTIN OPITZ. Aristarchus, sive De Contemptu Linguae Teutonicae...
Bethaniae (Beuthen).   Johannes Dörfer.   (1617 ?)
                                              KPB Bk 6658.

102. —— Schäfferey Von der Nimfen Hercinie.
Breslau.   D. Müller.   1630.   KPB.

103. (GEORGE PHILIPP HARSDÖRFER.) Poetischen Trichters zweyter
Theil....Samt Einem Anhang von der Teutschen Sprache : durch
ein Mitglied Der Hochlöblichen Fruchtbringenden Gesellschafft.
Nürnberg.   Wolffgang Endter.   1648.   UBB Yb 11031.

104. (SIGMUND VON BIRKEN). Pegnesis : oder der Pegnitz Blumgenoss-
Schäfere Feld Gedichte in Neun Tagzeiten : meist verfasset /
vnd hervorgegeben / durch Floridan.
Nürnberg.   Wolf Eberhard Felsecker.   1673.   KPB Yi 3811.

105. —— Teutsche Redebind- und Dicht-Kunst / oder Kurtze Anweisung
zur Teutschen Poesy / mit Geistlichen Exempeln : verfasset durch
Ein Mitglied der höchstlöblichen Fruchtbringenden Gesellschaft
Den Erwachsenen. Samt dem Schauspiel Pysche und Einem
Hirten-Gedichte.
Nürnberg.   Christof Riegel.   1679.   KPB Yb 5461.

No.

106. GEORG WITKOWSKI. Martin Opitzens Aristarchus sive de contemptu linguae Teutonicae und Buch von der Deutschen Poeterei.
Leipzig. Veit & Comp. 1888. KPB Yb 5172.

107. K. BRUNHUBER. Sir Philip Sidney's Arcadia und ihre Nachläufer.
Nürnberg. M. Edelmann. 1903. BM 11853 g 44.

108. FRIEDRICH BRIE. Das Volksbuch vom "gehörnten Siegfried" und Sidney's "Arcadia."
Archiv. CXXI. p. 286 ff. 1908. KPB (LS) 3. 147.

CHAPTER IV. *The Latin Novel.*

109. SIR THOMAS MORE. Illustris Viri Thomae Mori Regni Britanniarum Cancellarii, De Optimo Reipublicae Statu, deque nova insula Vtopia, Libri Duo :...Nunc tandem bibliotaphis subreptum, & in gratiam Politicorum, concilio & cura Magnifici Domini Eberarti von Weihe / illustriss. ac potentiss. Principi ac Domino, Dn. Mauritio, Hessiae Landgrauio, &c. a conciliis, editum.
Francofurti. Peter Kopff. 1601. KPB Xf 11720.

110. —— (As above, omitting "Nunc tandem...editum.")
Hanoviae (Hanau). Peter Kopff. 1613. KPB Xf 11725.

111. —— De optimo Reipublicae Statu, Libellus vere aureus. Ordentliche vnd Ausführliche Beschreibung Der vberaus herrlichen vnd gantz wunderbarlichen / doch wenigen bisshero bekandten Insul Vtopia : Sampt vmbständlicher Erzehlung aller derselben Gelegenheiten / Städten / vnd der Einwohner des Lands Sitten / Gewohnheiten vnd Gebräuchen : Darinnen gleichsam in einem Muster vnd Model eigentlich fürgestellt vnd angezeigt wird / die beste weis vnd art einer löblichen vnd wolbestellten Policey vnd Regiments : zumahl fast kurtzweilig vnd auch nützlich zu lesen vnd zu betrachten : Erstlich durch den Hochgelährten vnd Weitberümpten Herrn Thomam Morum, des Königreichs Engelland Obristen Cantzler / in Lateinischer Sprach an tag gegeben : Nun aber mit sonderm fleiss in vnser Deutsche Sprach vbergesetzt : Durch[1] * * *
Leipzig. Henning Gross, Jnr. 1612. KPB Zf 11762.

112. —— —— ...überaus...und...wunderbahrlichen...Bisshero... Utopia : Sambt umbständlicher...deroselben...( )... / darinnen ...fürgestelt...angezeiget...Weiss und Art eines...wolbestelten ...(rest as above).
Frankfort o/M. Henning Gross. 1704. KPB Xf 11772.

113. —— Thomae Mori Angliae Quondam Cancellarii Opera omnia, Quotquot reperiri potuerunt ex Basileensi anni MDLXIII. et Lovaniensi anni MDLXVI. Editionibus deprompta, Diversa ab istis serie disposita, emendatioraque edita. Praefixa de Vita & Morte Thomae Mori, Erasmi et Nucerini Epistolae, ut et doctorum virorumque eo elogia.
Francofurti ad Moenum et Lipsiae. Christian Gensch. 1689.
KPB 907.

[1] Translator's name in Utopian characters reversed. The name is Gregorium Hyemsmensium (i.e. Wintermonat). See p. 40.

No.

114. —— The Utopia of Sir Thomas More, Ralph Robinson's Translation, with Roper's Life of More and some of his Letters, edited by George Sampson, with an introduction and bibliography by A. Gutkelch, to which is added the Latin text of the Utopia reprinted from the First Edition.
London. G. Bell & Sons. 1910. KPB.

115. (Joseph Hall.) Mundus Alter et Idem Sive Terra Australis ante hac semper incognita longis itineribus peregrini Academici nuperrime lustrata Auth: Mercurio Britannico.
Francofurti, apud haeredes Ascanij de Rinialme. (1605 ?).
KPB 5025.

116. —— ——
Hannoviae (Hanau) Sumptibus haeredum Ascanij de Renialme (per Gulielmum Antoniū). 1607. KPB Xf 12151.

117. —— Utopiae Pars II. Mundus alter et idem. Die heutige newe alte Welt. Darinnen aussfürlich vnd nach notturfft erzehlet wird / was die alte numehr bald sechstausenjährige Welt für ein newe Welt geboren / Aus derer man gleichsam in einem Spiegel jhrer Mutter vnd Gebärerin Art / Sitten / Wandel vnd Gebrauch augenscheinlich mag sehen vnd erkennen. Allen Liebhabern der Gottseligkeit / Tugenden vnd Künsten zu beharrlicher Fortsetzung vnd continuirung in jhrem loblichen vorhaben: Den Weltkindern aber zu getrewer Warnung von allem bösen / vnd denen hierinnen fürgebildeten Lastern abzustehen: Erstlich in Lateinischer Sprach gestellt / durch den Edlen vnd hochgelerten Herrn Albericum Gentilem in Engelland: Nun aber mit besonderm fleiss verteutscht / vnd mit newen Kupfferstücken vnd Landtaffeln gezieret / Durch Gregorium, Huemumer (?) ium[1].
Leipzig. Henning Gross, Jnr. 1613. KPB Xf 11762.

118. —— —— ...& idem...Newe-alte Welt / ...ausfürlich und... Nothturfft...Alte nunmehr...gebohren...gestellet...und hochgelehrten...Albericum Gentilem...Engeland...Fleiss verteusch / und...und LandTaffeln gezieret.
Leipzig. Henning Gross. 1704. KPB Xf 11772.

119. Jacob Wilhelm Blaufuss. Vermischte Beyträge zur Erweiterung der Kenntniss seltener und merkwürdiger Bücher.
Jena. Johann Adam Melchior's sel. Witwe. i, 1753. ii, 1756.
KPB 10,163.

120. Carl Friedrich Flögel. Geschichte der komischen Litteratur.
Liegnitz u. Leipzig. David Siegert. i, 1784. ii, 1785. iii, 1786. iv, 1787. KPB X 6130.

121. Henry Morley. Ideal Commonwealths, Plutarch's Lycurgus, More's Utopia, Bacon's New Atlantis, Campanella's City of the Sun and a fragment of Hall's Mundus Alter et Idem.
London. Routledge. 1885. BM 12204 gg 57.

122. Edward A. Petherick. On the Authorship and Translations of Mundus alter et idem (1605).
In "The Gentleman's Magazine," Vol. 281, pp. 66–87, July. 1896. BM 011851 i 5.

[1] See No 111.

No.

123. JOSEPH HALL. Mundus Alter et Idem (An old world and a new) edited for school use by H. J. Anderson.
London. G. Bell. 1908.   BM 012331 i 57.

124. JOHN BARCLAY. Joannis Barclaii Argenis. Editio Repetita, & Indice locupletior.
Augustae Trebocorum.   Eberhard Zetzner.   1622.
                                          KPB Xf 12242.

125. —— Ioannis...
Francofvrti. Sumptibus Danielis & Dauidis Aubriorum & Clementis Schleichij. 1623.   UBG Fab. rom. IX. 510.

126. —— Johann Barclaijens Argenis Deutsch gemacht durch Martin Opitzen, Mit schönen Kupffer Figuren Nach dem Frantzösischen Exemplar.
Breslau.   David Müller.   1626.   KPB Xf 12342.

127. —— Historie Von Poliarchus vnd Argenis / Fast nach Herrn B .layen Lateinischen Von F. N. Coeiffeteau Bischoffen zu Marsilien kürtzlich beschrieben. Auss dem Frantzösischen in das Hoch Teutsche.
Leipzig.   Elias Rehfeld.   1631.   SBB F 2146.

128. (GEORG PHILIPP HARSDOERFER.) XII. Andachtsgemähle gebildet durch den Spielenden.
(No place.)   (No year.)   KPB Yi 4801.

128a. —— —— Frauenzimmer Gesprechspiele so bey Ehr- und Tugendliebenden Gesellschaften, mit nutzlicher Ergetzlichkeit, beliebet und geübet werden mögen, Erster Theil. Aus Italiänischen, Frantzosischen und Spanischen Scribenten angewiesen, und jetzund ausführlicher auf sechs Personen gerichtet, und mit einer Zugabe gemehret, Durch Einen Mitgenossen der Hochlöblichen Fruchtbringenden Gesellschaft, Nürnberg.
Nürnberg.   Wolffgang Endter.   (Parts II–VIII, 1643–1649.) 1641.   KPB UBB.

129. —— Nathan und Jotham : Das ist Geistliche und Weltliche Lehrgedichte / zu sinnreicher Ausbildung der waaren Gottseligkeit / wie auch aller löblichen Sitten und Tugenden vorgestellet / und in diesem zweyten Druck vermehret Samt einer Zugabe / genennet Simson / Begreiffend hundert verzeilige Rähtsel / Durch ein Mitglied der Hochlöblichen Frucht Bringenden Gesellschaft.
Nürnberg.   Michael Endter.   1659.   KPB Yt 8594.

130. (BALTHASAR KINDERMANN.)   Kurandors Vnglückselige Nisette.
(Frankfort o/O. Melcher Klosemann.) (1669 ?)   BM 8010 a 10.

131. AUGUST BUCHNER. August Buchners Poet Aus dessen nachgelassener bibliothek heraus gegeben von Othone Prätorio / P. P.
Wittenberg.   Buchner's Erben.   1665.   KPB Yb 5361.

132. CHRISTIAN WEISE. Christian Weisens Neue Jugend-Lust / Das ist / Drey Schauspiele : Vom verfolgten David, I. Von der Sicil. Argenis, II. Von der verkehrten Welt.   Wie selbige Anno MDCLXXXIII. Von den gesamten Studierenden im Zittauischen Gymnasio aufgeführet worden.
Frankfort and Leipzig.   Christian Weidmann.   1684.
                                          KPB Yq 7181.

No.

133. MICHAEL KONGEHL. Michael Kongehls beygenahmt Prutenio Sieg-
Prangender Lorbeer-Häyn / Darinn das Ehren- und Preiss-Ge-
dächtniss Vieler / teils Lorbeer-Bekröhnten / teils anderwerts
Lorbeer- und Lobwürdigen Häubter / (Die Unwürdigen lauffen
mit unter.) Durch allerhand Ehren-Lehr- und Lust-Gedichte /
Nach den Buchstaben A.B.C. verunsterblichet wird. Nebst Einer
Fort Pflanzung des Immergrünenden Cypressen Häyns und Lust-
Quartiers.
Königsberg. 1700. 　　　　　　　　　　　KPB Yi 7466.

134. PAUL FLEMING. Deutsche Gedichte hrsg. J. M. Lappenberg.
Stuttgart. Litt. Verein. 1865. 　　　　　　　KPB Ag 308.

135. JULES DUKAS. Etude Bibliographique et Littéraire sur le Satyricon
de Jean Barclay.
Paris. Léon Techener. 1880. 　　　　　　　　BM 820 f 40.

136. KARL FRIEDRICH SCHMID. John Barclay Argenis. Eine literar-
historische Untersuchung. I. Ausgaben der Argenis, ihrer
Fortsetzungen und Übersetzungen.
Berlin and Leipzig. 1904. 　　　　　　　　UBB X 1471.

137. PHILIPP AUGUST BECKER. Johann Barclay 1582–1621.
In Z. vgl. LG. (N.F.) 15. 1904. 　　　　　KPB (LS) 3. 150.

138. CARL AUGUST V. BLOEDAU. Grimmelshausens Simplicissimus und
seine Vorgänger. Beiträge zur Romantechnik des siebzehnten
Jahrhunderts.
Berlin. Mayer u. Müller. (Palaestra LI.) 1908.
　　　　　　　　　　　　　　　　　　　　KPB X 8426.

CHAPTER V. *Epigrams.*

139. HEINRICH HUDEMANN. Henrici Hudemanni, F. Holsati, Divitiae
Poeticae.
Hamburg. Paul Lang. 1625. 　　　　　　　KPB Xe 4750.

140. BERNARDUS NICAEUS ANCUMANUS. Rosarium Das ist / Rosen Garten:
Auss des Hochgelarten und Kunstreichen Welsch-Englischen
Poeten Joannis Oweni Lateinischen Lusthoff ubergesetzet / und
auff den Teutschen Boden gebracht und gepflanzet / Durch Bern-
hardum Nicaeum Ancumanum, Dienern am Worte Gottes.
Emden. Helvig Kallenbach. 1641. 　　　　KPB Xe 1250.

141. JOHANN PETER TITZ. Florilegii Ovveniani centuria, colligente
Versibusque Germanicis exprimente Joh. Petro Titio.
Danzig. Andreas Hünefeld. 1643. 　　　　KPB Yb 5222.

142. SIMON SCHULTZ. Centuria Epigrammatum Martialis & Ovveni
Libris selectorum, Versibusque Germanicis redditorum a Simone
Schultzio Thoruneo.
Danzig. Andreas Hünefeld. 1644. 　　　　KPB Yb 5222.

143. VALENTIN LÖBER. Epigrammatum Ovveni Drey Bücher / ver-
deutscht / und In eben solche angenehme Kürtze gebracht durch
Valentin Löber / der Artzney Liebhabern.
(Hamburg.) Zacharias Hertel. 1651. 　　　KPB Xe 1258.
Contains *six* books, although the last three have separate
title-pages.

No.

144. (FRIEDRICH V. LOGAU.) Salomons von Golaw Deutscher Sinn-Getichte Drey Tausend. Cum Gratia & Privilegio Sac. Caes. Majestatis.
Breslau. Caspar Klossmann. (1654.) KPB Yi 1814.

145. DAVID SCHIRMER. David Schirmers Poetische Rosen-Gepüsche. Von Jhm selbsten aufs fleissigste ubersehen / mit einem gantz neuen Buche vermehret und in allem verbesserter heraus gegeben.
Dresden. Andreas Löfler. 1657. KPB Yi 3918.

146. JOHN OWEN. Epigrammatum Ioan Oweni Cambro Britanni Oxoniensis Editio Postrema, correctissima, & posthumis quibusdam adaucta.
Amstelodami. Ioannes Iansson. 1657. (First ed. 1606.)
KPB Xe 1180.

147. VALENTIN LÖBER. Teutschredender Owenus Oder; Eilf Bücher der Lateinischen Uberschriften des überaus sinnreichen Englischen Dichters Ovveni, in Teutsche gebundene Sprache / eben so kurtz / übersetzet / und mit etlichen Anmerckungen erläutert / Durch Valentinum Löbern / der Artzney-Kunst Ergebenen.
Hamburg. (Pr. Jena.) Zacharias Hertel. 1661. (First ed. 1653.) KPB Xe 1265.

148. ERICH URBAN. Owenus und die deutschen Epigrammatiker des 17 Jahrhunderts.
Berlin. E. Felber. 1900. KPB X 8145.

149. FRANZ SCHULTZ. Owenus und die deutschen Epigrammitiker des XVII Jahrhunderts von Erich Urban.
Archiv f. NS. 6, p. 178. 1908. KPB (LS).
Review of 148.

CHAPTER VI. *History in Literature.*

150. SAMUEL RAWSON GARDINER. Letters and other documents illustrating the relations between England and Germany at the commencement of the thirty years' war. 2 vols.
London. 1865. KPB Tq 680.

English History in German Literature.

151. (AUGUST BUCHNER.) Quid Carolus I. Britanniarum Rex, Loqui potuerit lata in se ferali sententia, Oratio, Seu Declamatio Gemina.
(1649?) BM 8122 bbb 2.

152. (PHILIPP VON ZESEN.) Was Karle der erste / König in Engalland / bei dem über Ihm gefälltem todesuhrteil hette für-bringen können. Zwei-fache Rede.
(1649?) BM 1326 e 2.

153. GEORG GREFFLINGER. Der zwölff gekröhnten Häupter von dem Hause Stuart unglückselige Herrschafft / In Kurtzem Aus glaubwürdigen Historien Schreibern zusammen getragen Von Georg Grefflinger Regenspurger / Keyserl. Notario.
1652. KPB Ts 82.

No.

154. PHILIP VON ZESEN. Die verschmähete / doch wieder erhöhete
Majestäht / das ist / Kurtzer Entwurf der Begäbnusse Karls des
Zweiten / Königs von Engelland / Frankreich / Schotland / und
Irland ; Darinnen sein gantzer Lebens-lauf bis auf diese Zeit /
sonderlich seine flucht / verbannung / und wieder-beruffung; wie
auch beiläuftig der Todt Karls des 1, und was sich mit den Hertzogen von Jork / und Glozester begeben / ausführlich beschrieben /
auch das vornehmste in unterschiedlichen kupferstükken ab-
gebildet wird : alles aus den wahrhaftigsten unterschiedlichen
Englischen Verzeichnungs-schriften gezogen / und in diese ver-
fassung gebracht durch Filip von Zesen.
Amsterdam. Joachim Noschen. 1662. KPB Tt 545.

155. —— Die Gekröhnte Majestäht : das ist / kurtz-bündiger Entwurf
der herrlich-prächtigen Kröhnung Karls des Zweiten / Königs von
Engelland / Schotland / und Irland / uam. Zu papiere getragen /
und H. Karl Friederich Schmieden / zugewiedmet durch Filip
von Zesen.
Amsterdam. Joachim Noschen. 1662. KPB Tt 545.

156. JOHANN CHRISTIAN HALLMANNS Von Bresslau / Jur. Utr. Candi-
dati und Practici beym Kaiser- und Königlichen Ober-Ambte
daselbst &c. &c. Trawer-Freuden- und Schäffer-Spiele / nebst Einer
Beschreibung Aller Obristen Hertzoge über das gantze Land
Schlesien.
Breslau. Jesaias Fellgiebel. (1684.) UBB Yp 8004.

157. ANDREAS GRYPHIUS. Andreae Gryphii um ein merckliches vermehrte Teutsche Gedichte. Mit Käyserl. und Churfl. Sächsischen
allergnädigsten Privilegio.
Breslau und Leipzig. Die Fellgiebelschen Erben. 1698.
KPB 8371.

158. G. H. POWELL. Anti-English Germany (1649).
In "Connoisseur" V. 207. 1903. BM R.P.P. 1931 pcx.

159. KARL KIPKA. Maria Stuart im Drama der Weltliteratur vornehm-
lich des 17. und 18. Jahrhunderts.
Leipzig. Max Hesse. 1907. UBB X 1509.

German History in English Literature.

160. KARL ELZE. George Chapman's The Tragedy of Alphonsus, Emperor
of Germany.
Leipzig. F. A. Brockhaus. 1867. KPB Zc 3504.

161. HENRY GLAPTHORNE. The Tragedy of Albertus Wallenstein, Late
Duke of Fridland, and Generall to the Emperor Ferdinand the
second. Written by Henry Glapthorne. Cedant carminibus
reges Regumque triumphi. The Scene Egers. And Acted with
good Allowance at the Globe on the Banke-side, by his Majesties
Servants.
In "The Plays and Poems of Henry Glapthorne..."
London. John Pearson. 1874. (First ed. 1639.)
KPB Zc 9978.

162. GEORG SCHMID. Die Wallenstein-Literatur. (1626–1878.)
In "Mitteilungen des Vereins für Geschichte der Deutschen
in Böhmen," Jahrgang XVII, Beilage zum 1. Heft.
Prag. 1879. KPB Sd 3406.

No.

163. VICTOR LOEWE. Ditto.
Dritte (Ergänzung) do. XXXIV. 1890.
Vierte   „   „ XL. pp. 514 ff. 1902.   KPB Sd 3406.

164. JOHANNES BOLTE. Eine englische Wallensteintragödie in Deutschland.
In Zs. f. d. Phil. XIX. 93–7. 1887.   KPB (LS) 3. 230.

165. THEODOR VETTER. Wallenstein in der dramatischen Dichtung des Jahrzehnts seines Todes: Micraelius—Glapthorne—Fulvio Testi.
Frauenfeld. J. Huber. 1894.   KPB Ry 6871.

166. RICHARD ACKERMANN. The Tragedy of Hoffman or, A Reuenge for a Father von Henry Chettle. Nach dem Quarto von 1631 im British Museum.
Bamberg. H. Uhlenhuth. 1894.   KPB Zc 3209.

167. EMIL KOEPPEL. Quellen-Studien zu den Dramen George Chapman's, Philip Massinger's und John Ford's.
Strassburg. Karl J. Trübner. (Quellen und Forschungen,
LXXXII.) 1897.   KPB Yc 7586.

168. B. HOENIG. Memoiren englischer Offiziere im Heere Gustav Adolfs und ihr Fortleben in der Literatur.
In "Beitr. z. n. Phil." pp. 324–350.
Vienna. Braumüller. 1902.   UBB.

169. THOMAS MARC PARROTT. The Tragedies of George Chapman.
London. Routledge. 1910.   UBB Zc 33546.

CHAPTER VII. *The English Philosophers.*

170. FRANCIS BACON. Opera Francisci Baronis de Verulamio, Vice-Comitis Sancti Albani Tomus primus Qui continet De Dignitate & Augmentis Scientiarum Libros IX. Ad regem Suum.
London. John Haviland. 1623.   KPB Ak 5461.

171. —— Francisci Baconi, Baronis de Verulamio, Vice-comitis Sancti Albani, operum moralium et civilium Tomus. Qui continet Historiam Regni Henrici Septimi, Regis Angliae. Sermones Fideles sive Interiora Rerum. Tractatum de Sapientia Veterum. Dialogum de Bello Sacro. Et Novam Atlantidem. Ab ipso Honoratissimo Auctore, praeterquam in paucis, Latinitate donatus. Cura & Fide Guilelmi Rawley, Sacrae Theologiae Doctoris, olim Dominationi suae, nunc Serenissimae Majestati Regiae, a Sacris. In hoc volumine, iterum excusi, includuntur Tractatus de Augmentiis Scientiarum. Historia Ventorum. Historia Vitae & Mortis.
London. Richard Whitaker. 1638.   KPB Ak 5467.

172. (JOHANN WILHELM VON STUBENBERG.) Francisci Baconi, Grafens von Verulamio, Fürtrefflicher Staats-Vernunfft- und Sitten-Lehr-Schrifften. I. Von der Alten Weissheit. II. Etliche Einrahtungen / aus den Sprüchen Salomonis. III. Die Farben (oder Kennzeichen) des Guten und Bösen. Übersetzet durch Ein Mitglied der Hochlöblichen Fruchtbringenden Gesellschafft den Unglückseligen.
Nürnberg. Michael Endter. 1654.   BM 12355 a 33.

W. L. R.   11

No.

173. —— Francisci Baconis Grafens von Verulamio, weiland Englischen Reichscantzlers Getreue Reden: die Sitten-Regiments- und Hausslehre betreffend / Aus dem Lateinischen gedolmetschet / durch ein Mitglied der Hochlöblichen Fruchtbringenden Gesellschafft den Unglückseligen.
Nürnberg. Michael Endter. 1654.   KPB Nh 2906.

174. FRANCISCI BACONI, Baronis de Verulamio, Vice-Comitis S. Albani, Summi Angliae Cancellarii, Opera Omnia, Quae extant: Philosophica, Moralia, Politica, Historica...Hactenus nunquam conjunctim edita, Iam vero Summo studio collecta, uno volumine comprehensa: & ab innumeris Mendis repurgata: Cum Indice Rerum ac Verborum Universali absolutissimo. His praefixa est Auctoris vita.
Frankfort o/M. Joh. Bapt. Schönwetter. 1665.
UBB 3411 ab. KPB 5485.

175. FRANCISCI BACONI, Baronis de Verulamio, Vice-Comitis S. Albani, summi Angliae cancellarii, Opera Omnia, cum Novo eoque insigni Augmento Tractatuum hactenus ineditorum, & ex idiomate anglicano in latinum sermonem translatorum, Opera Simonis Johannis Arnoldi, Ecclesiae Sonnenburgensis Inspectoris. Leipzig. Johann Justus Erythropilus. 1694.
UBB 3011 KPB Ak 5490.

176. JOHANN BALTHASAR SCHUPP. De Arte Ditescendi Dissertatio Prior ex Avellino ad Philosophos in Germania.
(Marburg.) 1648.   KPB Xh 11188.

177. —— Salomo, oder Regenten-Spiegel / Vorgestellet Aus denen eilff ersten Capitulen des ersten Buchs der Königen. Andern Gottsfürchtigen und Sinnreichen Politicis auszuführen und genauer zu elaboriren überlassen: Von Antenore, Einem Liebhaber der H. Schrifft.
1658.   KPB Bm 8530.

178. —— Doct: Ioh: Balth: Schuppii Schrifften.
(Hanau.) (1663.)   KPB Yy 2051.

179. (GEORGE PHILIPP HARSDOERFER.) Prob und Lob der Teutschen Wolredenheit. Das ist: dess Poetischen Trichters Dritter Theil / ...Zu nachrichtlichem Behuff Aller Redner / Poeten / Mahler / Bildhauer und Liebhaber unsrer löblichen Helden Sprache angewiesen / durch Ein Mitglied der Hochlöblichen Fruchtbringenden Gesellschafft.
Nürnberg. Wolfgang Endter, Sen. 1653.   UBB Yb 11031.

180. JULIUS WILHELM ZINCGREF. Teutsche Apothegmata das ist Der Teutschen Scharfsinnige Kluge Sprüche In Fünff Theil Zusamen Getragen durch Julius Wilhelm Zinkgräfen Der Rechten Doctoren, Nebst einer Vorrede von Christian Weisen, Rect. Gymn. Zitt. Leipzig. Moritz Georg Weidmann. 1693.
KPB Bibl. Diez. 9747–9.

181. MAX, FREIHERR VON WALDBERG. Die Renaissance Lyrik.
Berlin. W. Hertz. 1888.   UBB Ye 20579.

182. FRIEDRICH UEBERWEG. Grundriss der Geschichte der Philosophie der Neuzeit bis zum Ende des achtzehnten Jahrhunderts.
Berlin. Mittler. 1901^9.   UBB (LS) 10. 160. 700.

No.

183. KUNO FISCHER. Francis Bacon und seine Schule.
Heidelberg. Carl Winter. 1904³.   UBB (LS) 10. 194.

184. WALTHER WOLFGANG ZSCHAU. Quellen und Vorbilder in den
"Lehrreichen Schrifften" Johann Balthasar Schupps.
Halle. Ehrhardt Karras. 1906. UBB Phil. Diss. Halle. 1906.

185. CARL VOGT. Johann Balthasar Schupp. Neue Beiträge zu seiner
Würdigung.
In "Euph."   XVI. 6 ff., 245 ff., 673 ff. 1909.
           XVII. 1 ff., 251 ff., 473 ff. 1910. KPB (LS) 3. 54.

186. JAMES I. Serenissimi et Potentissimi Principis Jacobi Magnae
Britanniae, Franciae, et Hiberniae, Regis, Fidei Defensoris, Opera
edita a Jacobo Montacuto Winthoniensi episcopo et sacelli Regii
Decano.
Frankfort o/M & Leipzig. Christian Gensch. 1689. KPB 907.

187. SIR THOMAS BROWNE. Religio Medici. The fourth edition, Corrected and amended. With Annotations Never before published,
upon all the obscure passages therein.
London. Andrew Crook. 1656.   BM 852. q. 3.

188. —— Religio Medici cum Annotationibus.
Strassburg. Friedrich Spoor. 1665.   BM 1019. c. 15.

189. —— Thomae Brownes Medici Angli, ac Patroni Syncretismi universalis, imo crassioris, (Hominem in quavis Religione salvari
posse) Libellus de Religione Medici Ab ipso primum Anglico
idiomate conscriptus, post a conterraneo Iohan. Merryweather
in latinum versus nunc vero Annotationibus Eruditissimis, ac
Satis Lutheranis illustratus a Politico Juvene, frequentibus migra-
tionibus ac Principum Servitiis claro L. N. M. E. M.
Frankfort & Leipzig. Friedrich Groschuff. 1692.

KPB Dd 5425.

190. CHRISTIAN RAUTNER. Des vortrefflichen Engelländers Thomas
Brown, der Artzney Dr. Psevdodoxia Epidemica, Das ist Untersuchung derer Irrthümer / so bey dem gemeinen Mann / und
sonst hin und wieder im Schwange gehen. In Sieben Büchern
also und dergestalt abgefasset / dass darinn anfangs von den
Irrthümern ins Gemein / mit Beyfügung unterschiedlicher Curiöser
Tractätlein / als eines Handbuchs der wieder zu recht gebrachten
Naturkunst / darinn der Grund der gantzen Chymischen Wissen-
schaft enthalten ; Item eines Werkes wider die gemeinen Irrthümer
von der Bewegung natürlicher dinge ; Ingleichen Herrn D. Henrici
Mori von unkörperlichen Dingen in der Welt / wider Cartesium ;
Und dann ferner in denen übrigen Sechs Büchern von den Irrthümern / die Mineralien / Gewächse / Thiere / Menschen / Bilder
und Gemählde / Welt- und Geschicht-Beschreibungen betreffend /
gehandelt wird. Alles mit sonderbarem Fleiss / aus dem Englischen
und Lateinischen / mit Beyfügung der Lateinischen Kunstwörter /
in die reine Hochteutsche Sprach übersetzet / mit ungemeinen
Anmerkungen erläutert / und unterschiedlichen Kupferfiguren
versehen durch Christian Peganium in Teutsch Rautner genannt...
Frankfort und Leipzig. Christoff Riegel. 1680. KPB Ah 144.

No.

191. The Works of SIR THOMAS BROWNE. Edited by Charles Sayle.
London. (I & II.) Grant Richards. 1904.
Edinburgh. III. John Grant. 1907.   KPB Ak 5977.

CHAPTER VIII. *The Theologians.*

192. MARTIN LUTHER. Tischreden Oder Colloquia Doct. Mart: Luthers /
So er in vielen Jaren / genen gelarten Leuten / auch frembden
Gesten / vnd seinen Tischgesellen gefüret / nach den Haubtstücken
vnserer Christlichen Lere / zusammen getragen. Johan. 6. Cap.
Samlet die vbrigen brocken / Auff das nichts vmbkome.
Eisleben.   Urban Gaubisch.   1566.   KPB 8511. Luth.

193. Dris MARTINI LUTHERI Colloquia Mensalia : or, Dr. Martin
Luther's Divine Discourses at his Table, &c. Which in his life
Time hee held with divers Learned men (such as were Philip
Melancthon, Casparus Cruciger, Justus Jonas, Paulus Eberus,
Vitus Dietericus, Joannes Bugenhagen, Joannes Forsterus, and
others) conteining Questions and Answers touching Religion, and
other main Points of Doctrine, as also many notable Histories,
and all sorts of Learning, Comforts, Advises, Prophecies, Admoni-
tions, Directions and Instructions. Collected first together by
Dr. Antonius Lauterbach, and afterward disposed into certain
Common-places by John Aurifaber Dr in Divinitie. Translated
out of the high Germane into the English Tongue By Capt.
Henrie Bell. John 6. 12. Gather up the fragments, that nothing
bee lost......
London.   William Du-Gard.   1652.   KPB Luth 8681.

194. JACOB BOEHME. Two Theosophicall Epistles : Wherein the Life of
a true Christian is described, Viz What a Christian is; And, How
he cometh to be a Christian. Together, with a Description, what
a titular Christian is; and what the Faith and Life of both of
them is. Whereunto is added, A Dialogue between an Enlightened
and a Distressed Soule. By Jacob Bohmen. Written to a good
Friend of his, in a Christian Brother-like and Member-like ad-
monition and good intention. Lately Englished out of the German
Language.
London.   B. Allen.   1645.   BM E 1170.

195. —— The Epistles of Jacob Behmen aliter, Tevtonicvs Philosophvs.
Very usefull and necessary for those that read his Writings, and
are very full of excellent and plaine Instructions how to Attaine
to The Life of Christ. Translated out of the German Language.
London.   Pr. Matthew Simmons.   1649.   UBG.

196. —— Several Treatises of Jacob Behme Not printed in English
before, according to the Catalogue here following, viz. I. A Book
of the Great Six Points : As also A Small Book of the other Six
Points. II. The, 177, Theosophick Questions: the first Thirteen
Answered. III. Of the Earthly and of the Heavenly Mystery.
IV. The Holy-Week, or a Prayer-Book. V. Of Divine Vision.
To which are annexed the Exposition Of the Table of the Three
Principles ; Also an Epistle Of the Knowledge of God, and of All
Things. And of the True and False Light. With a Table of the
Revelation of the Divine secret Mystery. Englished by John
Sparrow.
London.   L. Lloyd.   1661.   BM 3716. bb.

No.

197. (JOHN SPARROW ?) Mercurius Teutonicus ; or A Christian Informa-
tion concerning the last Times. Being Divers Propheticall
Passages of the Fall of Babel, and the New Building in Zion.
Gathered out of the Mysticall Writings of that famous Germane
Author, Jacob Behmen, alias, Teutonicus Phylosophus. Despise
not Prophesyings. Prove all things ; hold fast that which is good,
1 Thes. 5. 20, 21.
London. H. Blunden. 1649.   UBG.

198. DURAND HOTHAM. The Life of Jacob Behmen. Written by Durand
Hotham, Esquire, Novemb. 7. 1653.
London. H. Blunden. 1654.   BM E. 1068.

199. HENRICI MORI, Cantabrigiensis Opera Theologica, Anglice quidem
primitus scripta, Nunc vero Per Autorem Latine reddita. Hisce
novus praefixus est de Synchronismis Apocalypticis Tractatulus,
cum Luculenta demonstratione necessariae & inevitabilis Intelli-
gibilitatis Visionum Apocalypticarum calci ejusdem Tractatus
adjecta...
London. John Martyn & Walter Kettilby. I. 1675. II &
III. 1679.   BM 830 m 12.

200. EDWARD TAYLOR. Jacob Behmen's Theosophick Philosophy un-
folded; in divers Considerations and Demonstrations, shewing
The Verity and Utility of the several Doctrines or Propositions
contained in the writings of that Divinely Instructed Author,
Also, The Principal Treatises of the said Author Abridged.
And Answers given to the Remainder of the 177 Theosophick
Questions, Propounded by the said Jacob Behmen, which were
left unanswered by him at the time of his Death. As a help
towards the better Understanding the Old & New Testament.
Also what Man is with respect to Time & Eternity. Being an
Open Gate to the Greatest Mysteries. By Edward Taylor. With
a short Account of the Life of Jacob Behmen.
London. Thomas Salusbury. 1691.   BM 853 h 14.

201. JACOB BOEHME. The High and Deep Searching Out of The Three-
fold Life of Man through (or according to) The Three Principles.
By Jacob Boehme *alias* Teutonicus Philosophus. Written in
the German Language Anno 1620. Englished by J. Sparrow,
Barrister of the Inner Temple, London....Reissued by C. J.
B(arker), with an introduction by the Rev. G. W. Allen.
London. John M. Watkins. 1909. (First ed. 1650.)
    BM 3558 e 19.

202. WILLIAM PERKINS. Der Catholische Reformierte Christ: Das ist /
Richtige Erklerung vnd bericht / wie nahe oder ferne die Kirchen /
so auss vnd nach Gottes Wort reformiert oder verbessert sind / in
vilen vnd vnterschiedlichen Religionspuncten / mit der Römischen
Kirchen / wie sie heut zu tage beschaffen / vbereinstimmen; auch
in welchen stücken / vnd wie fern sie es nicht mit derselbigen
halten / ja auch nimmermehr mit jro einig werden können. Neben
einer kurtzen Vermahnung an die jenigen / so der Römischen
Kirchen zugethan sind / darin erwisen wird / dass die Römische
Lehr den grundvesten vnd Artickeln des Glaubens / so von allen
Christen bekant vnd für vnbeweglich gehalten werden / streite /

No.

vnd denselbigen zu wider sey. Alles erstlich beschrieben / vnd
an tag gegeben in Englischer sprache / durch den Hochgelehrten
Herrn Guilielmum Perkinsum Cantabrigiensem, der H. Schrift
Licentiaten : darnach aber in die Spanische / folgends in die La-
teinische / vnd nun endlich in die Teutsche sprache gebracht :
welches von allen liebhabern der götlichen warheit / dem weit-
läuftigen mehrtheils vnwarhaftem geschwetz des Jesuiten Roberti
Bellarmini, vnd dem irrigen Wegweiser Iohannis Pistorii mit
gutem fug vnd grund kan entgegen gesetzt werden.

Herborn. 1602.   KPB Dg 9756.

203.   —— Christliche Vnd Gründliche Erklärunge / der zehen Gebott /
Vnd Gebets dess Herren. Auss Gottes Wort / durch den tref-
flichen Vnd trewen Diener Christi in Engelland / M. Wilhelmum
Perkinsum, Christlicher Gedächtnus. Itzt auss dem Niderländi-
schen ins Hochteutsch bracht / durch Iohannem Heupelium,
Diener dess Worts Gottes / in der löblichen Graffschafft Hanaw.

Hanau. Guilielmus Antonius. 1604.   KPB Eo 7010.

204.   —— Tractätlein Von des Menschen natürlichen Gedancken /
Darinnen fürgestellet werden Seine natürliche böse Gedancken /
Sein Mangel guter Gedancken / Weg und Mittel die bösen
Gedancken zu ändern und zubessern. In Englischer Sprach
beschrieben Durch Hn. Wilhelmum Perkinsum Seel. gewesenen
geistreichen Theolog. und berühmten Professorem der H. Schrifft
zu Cambridg in Engelland. Nebst einem kurtzen Anhang von
gottslästerlichen Gedancken die der Sathan dem Menschen eingibt
auss Hn. Johann Dounams s. Christen-Kampf Ins Teutsche
übersetzet und auff Begehren zum Druck gegeben durch Georgium
Heinium.

Cassel. Johann Ingebrandt. 1674². (First ed. 1667?)
                                          KPB 5889.

205.   —— The Fundation of Christian Religion, Gathered into sixe
Principles, of that famous and worthy Minister of Christ in the
Universitie of Cambridge, M. William Perkins...

(Hamburg.) Gotfried Schultz' Widow. 1688.   KPB 8650.

206.   —— Guilielmi Perkinsi, weitberühmten Theologi in Engelland /
Gewissens-Spiegel / Darinn zuersehen allerley Zufälle des Menschlichen Gewissens durch welche dasselbe mag angefochten werden /
Samt Beygefügter gründlicher Lehre / wie mann sich in alle
dieselbige zurichten habe / Übersetzet / Und mit nötigen und
nützlichen Registern versehen Durch T. D.

Frankfort & Leipzig. Paul Zeising. 1690.   KPB D 2352.

207.   JOSEPH HALL. Vorbildung der Tugenden uñ Vntugenden. Das
ist : Kurtze / aber deutliche und anmutige Beschreibung der vor-
nembsten Tugenden / deren sich ein frommer Mensch befleissen
soll / Vnd auch der meisten Vntugenden oder Laster / dafür man
sich hüten solle. Zuvor niemals in unser Deutschen Sprach
aussgegangen / Anitzo Aus dem Englischen uñ Frantzösischen
verteutscht / Durch den W. H. N. N.

Emden. Helwig Kallenbach. 1628.   KPB Df 9030.

208.   —— Joseph Hallens Weiland Engelländischen Bischoffs Merckzeichen Der Tugenden und Laster / ins Teutsche übersetzet Durch
Balthasar Gerhard Koch Helmst. S. Theol. St.

Helmstädt. Heinrich Hesse. 1685.   KPB Bg 125.

No.

209. —— Joseph Hall Bischoff zu Excester in Engeland Kenn-Zeichen Der Tugend und Laster auss dem Englischen übersetzet Durch G. P. Harsdorffer.
Bremen. Johann Wessel. 1696. (First ed. 1652.)
KPB D 2578.

210. —— Joseph Hallens Himmel auf Erden. Auss dem Engelländischen Lateinisch, vnd auss disem Deütsch gegeben.
(Breslau.) David Müller. 1632. KPB Es 10712.

211. —— Die Alte Religion / Das ist: Ein Tractat / darin gantz Herzlich / kurz und Sinnreich auss der H. Schrifft / auss der Antiquität / und auss der Vernunfft erwiesen wird / dass die Religion der Evangelischen Kirchen / die uhralte Religion / und hingegen die Religion der Römischen Kirchen / eine Newe und von Menschen erfundene Religion sey / Vormahls in Englisch Durch Den Fürtrefflichen Josephum Hall Bischoff von Exon beschrieben / Jetzt aber / wegen seiner sondern Nutzbarkeit und Anmuth / auss dem Englischen gedeutschet Durch Theophilum Grossgebauer Predigern in Rostock.
Frankfort. Matthaeus Kempffer. 1662. KPB D 2578.

212. —— Balsaam aus Gilead Oder Tröster In Kranckheit / Noth / Tod und für dem Jüngsten Gericht. Sehr bequeme / Für Diese elende Zeiten / Anfänglich in Englischen Sprache beschrieben / Durch Joseph Hall SS. Th. D. und Bischoff zu Norvvic, &c. Anietzo aber in unsere Hoch-Deutsche übergesetzet / Durch H(einrich) S(chmettau).
Breslau. Veit Jacob Drescher. 1663. KPB Es 10720.

213. —— Balsam auss Gilead: oder Kräfftige Hertzstärckungen wider Allerley Geistliche vnd Leibliche Trübsalen / bey diesen jamerhafften Zeiten / sehr nutzlich vnd dienstlich zu gebrauchen. Anfangs in englischer Sprach beschrieben / Durch Herrn Joseph Hall / der H. Schrifft D. vnd Weiland Bischoff zu Norvvich. Nun aber zu vielfaltigen Trost mit allem fleiss auss dem Englischen übergesetzt Durch Johann-Jacob Schädlern. V. D. M.
Zürich. Michael Schaufelberger. 1663. KPB Es $\frac{10720}{8}$.

214. —— Joseph Halls / Bischoffs zu Norvvich, Drey Tractätlein I. Soliloquia oder heimliche Gespräche der gläubigen Seelen mit ihrem Gott vnd Ihr selbsten. II. Der gläubigen Seelen Irdisches Valet vnd himlischer Wilkommen. III. Der Rechte Christ. So von dem Authore selbsten in Englischer Sprache beschrieben; Anjetzo aber in vnsere hochdeutsche übersetzet / von Heinrich Schmettaw / Fürstlichen Lignitzischen Hoffprediger &c.
Basel. Johann Buxtorff. 1663. KPB Es 10722.

215. —— Joseph Halls Biblische Gesichter / Oder Betrachtungen der Biblischen Historien / Aus dem Englischen ins Hochdeutsche übergesetzet von H(einrich) S(chmettau).
Breslau. Veit Jacob Trescher. 1666. KPB Bh 1680.

216. —— Andrer Theil Joseph Halls Biblischer Gesichter / Oder Betrachtungen der Biblischen Historien / Von dem Authore in Englisch beschrieben / Anitzo aber in unsere Hochdeutsche über gesetzet / von H(einrich) S(chmettau).
Breslau. Veit Jacob Trescher. 1665. KPB Bh 1680.

No.

217.   —— Joseph Halls Biblische Geschichte / Oder Betractungen der Biblischen Historien; Aus dem Englischen in das Hoch-Teutsche übersetzet / an vielen dunckelen Orten verbessert / und mit den Schrifft-Oertern vermehret / Zum andernmahl herausgegeben von Heinrich Schmettauen / Churfl. Brandenb. Hof-Prediger.
Breslau.   Veit Jacob Trescher.   I. 1672.   II. 1674.   III. 1679.
KPB Bh 1681.

219.   —— Joseph Halls Biblische Geschichte / Oder Betrachtung der Biblischen Historien des Alten und Neuen Testaments in drey Theilen / Aus dem Englischen ins Hochteutsche übersetzet / an vielen dunckelen Orten verbessert und mit denen Schrifft-Örtern / auch vollständigen Registern derer Rahmen und Realien / ingleichen der angeführten und erklärten Sprüchen vermehret Nunmehro zum drittenmahl heraus gegeben Von Heinrich Schmettawen / anitzo Churfürstl. Brandenb. Consistorial-Rath und ältesten Hoff-Prediger.
Leipzig.   Johann Herbord Kloss.   1699.   KPB Bh 1682.

220.   —— Joseph Hallens Weiland Engelländischen Bischoffs / I. Nacht-Lieder Oder Freude im Creutz / II. Der heilige Orden Oder Die Brüderschafft der Klagenden in Sion / III. Die Klage und Thränen Sion / Ins Teutsche übersetzet von M. Henningus Koch. Eccl. Helmst. Past.
Helmstadt.   Friedrich Lüderwaldt.   1683.   KPB Bg 125.

221.   —— Des fürtrefflichen und seiner Schrifften halber weitberühmten Theologi Joseph Halls / Bischoffs zu Cron-Engelland Nützlicher Gebrauch Der Heil. Schrifft / Oder der Christen angebohrnes Recht / in Verwahr- und Nützung derselben / Anfangs in Englischer Sprache beschrieben / nunmehro aber wegen seiner Vortrefflichkeit halber in unser Teutsche Mutter-Sprache übersetzet Von Einem berühmten Liebhaber Göttlicher Schrifft.   In Hannover.
Frankfort and Leipzig.   Thomas Heinrich Hauenstein.   1684.
KPB Bg 125.

222.   (GEORG PHILIPP HARSDOERFER.)   Die Hohe Schul Geist- und Sinn-reicher Gedancken / in C C C C Anmuthungen / aus dem Buch Gottes und der Natur vorgestellet / durch Dorotheum Elevtherum Meletephilum.   Mit Anfügung Salomonis Tugend- Regiments- und Hauslehre.
Nürnberg.   Wolffgang Endter, Jnr. and Johann Andreas Endter.
(No year.)   UBG Scr. var. arg. VIII. 260.

223.   JOSEPH HALL.   Salomons Regir- Haushaltungs- und Sitten-Kunst / Von Joseph Hall / Erstlich in Engeländischer / Nunmehr aber in Hochteutscher Sprache Regenten und Unterthanen / Eltern und Kindern / Herren und Knechten / Frauen und Mägden / Jungen und Alten Zum besten und nothwendigen Unterricht beschrieben / und weitläufftig vermehrt heraus gegeben Von M. Andreas Beyern / Predigern in Freybergk.
Frankfort and Leipzig.   David Fleischer.   1684.
KPB Bn 7345.

224.   DANIEL DYKE.   Nosce Teipsum: Das grosse Geheimnis dess Selb-betrugs / oder Reiche / vnd in Gottes Wort gegründete Betrachtung / vnd Entdeckung der grossen Betrüglichkeit vnd Tücke dess Menschlichen Hertzens / dardurch nicht allein einer den andern /

No.

sondern / ein jeder allermeist sich selbsten / zu betriegen vnd zu verführen pfleget : Anfänglich Durch H. Jeremiam[1] Dyke, Fürnehmen Theologum vnd Predigern / in Englischer Sprach beschrieben / Nun aber / Männiglich / zu mehrer Erkandnuss vnd Bespieglung seiner selbsten / in die Teutsche-sprach vbersetzet / nach nothdurfft erläutert / vnd zu gemeiner Erbawung vnd Besserung vnser aller / zu betrachten vnd zu behertzigen fürgestellet vnd mitgetheilet / Durch D.H.P. Göttlichen Worts innbrünstigen Liebhaber.

Basel. Georg Decker. 1638. KPB 5796.

225. —— Nosce Teipsum...
Frankfort. Christian Klein & Heirs of Clement Schleich. 1643. KPB Da 4220.

226. —— Nosce Te Ipsum Oder Selb Betrug Sambt der Wahren Buss. Als Das Furnembste Stück der Gottseligkeit / welches folgen soll / vff den Selb-betrug / oder wahren Erkandnuss seiner selbsten. Erstlich Uff Englisch geschrieben Durch H. Jeremiam Dyke, In Teutsch vorlängst vbersetzt, vnd zum Dritten mahl vffgelegt / vbersehen / vnd mit den Sprüchen am Rande sehr verbessert. Durch D.H.P.

Frankfort. Johann Jacob & Philipp Weiss. 1643. (Wrongly dated 1663; correction in pencil in Berlin copy. Cf. also No. 228.) KPB Da 4223.

227. —— Nosce Teipsum: Das grosse Geheimnuss dess Selb-Betrugs / Oder Reiche / vnd in Gottes Wort gegründete Betrachtung / vñ Entdeckung der Grossen Betrüglichkeit vnd Tücke des Menschlichen Hertzens / dadurch nicht allein einer den andern / sondern / ein jeder allermeist sich selbsten / zu betriegen vnd zu verführen pfleget: Anfänglich Durch H. Daniel Dyke, Fürnehmen Theologum vnd Predigern / in Englischer Spraach beschrieben / vnd nach seinem Todt durch seinen Bruder Jeremiam an Tag gegeben / Nun aber / Männiglich / zu mehrer Erkandnuss vnd Bespiegelung Seiner Selbsten / in die Teutsche-Sprach übersetzet / nach Nothdurfft erläutert...(See 224.)

Danzig. Andreas Hünefeld. 1643. KPB Da 4222.

228. —— Weltlicher Selbstbetrieger welcher das Nosce Te Ipsum Oder den Selb-Betrug / die Erkandnuss seiner Selbsten / Sambt der Wahren Buss. Als Das Fürnembste Stück der Gottseligkeit / welches vff den Selb-betrug / oder wahre Erkändnuss seiner selbsten / folgen soll / hindansetzet Erstlich Vff Englisch beschrieben. Durch H. Danielem Dyke. In Teutsch vorlängst vbersetzt vnd zum Funfftenmahl vffgelegt / vbersehen / vnd mit den Sprüchen am Rande mehr als jemahlen / beneben einem vollkömlichen Register vermehret. Durch D.P.H. (sic.)

Frankfort. Johann Philipp Weiss. 1652. KPB Da 4225.

229. —— Nosce Te Ipsum, Oder Selbs-Betrug / Sampt der Wahren Buss / Welche das fürnehmste Stück der Gottseligkeit ist / und auff den Selbs-Betrug oder sein Selbs-Erkantnuss nothwendig folget. Erstmahlen von Hn. Daniel Dyke, in Englischer Sprach geschrieben. Hernach Von H.D.H.P. ins Teutsche übersetzet / bissher zum öfftern gedruckt / anjetzo wiederumb zum fleissigsten

[1] This mistake is first corrected in the fourth edition, Bibl. 227.

No.

übersehen / und nicht nur mit Sprüchen am Rand und schönen Gebetlein uber jegliches Capitel ; sondern auch mit einem herrlichen Tractätlein von der Selbs-Prüfung / und einem vollkommenen Register vermehret.

Frankfort.   Martin Hermsdorff.   1691.   KPB Da 4228.

230.   —— Eine Sehr nothwendige vnd vberauss nützliche Betrachtung vnd Beschreibung Der Wahren Busse / Als Dess ersten vnd fürnembsten Grundwercks zum wahren Christenthumb / dess ersten vnd nothwendigsten Alphabets zur rechten vnd seeligen Erkantnuss Christi / vnd dess einigen vnd richtigsten Weg zum Himmelreich. Anfänglich Durch H. Jeremiam Dyke, Fürnehmen Theologum vnd Predigern / in Englischer Spraach beschrieben / Nun aber / Männiglich / zu mehrer Erkantnuss vnd Bespiegelung seiner selbsten / Correct in die Teutsche Spraach vbersetzet / Durch D. H. P. Göttlichen Worts inbrünstigen Liebhaber.   Matth. 3. Thut Buss / dann das Himmelreich ist nah herbey kommen.

Frankfort.   Clement Schleich's Heirs & Christian Klein.   1643.
KPB Da 4220.

231.   JOHN BARCLAY.   Johan Barclai Ermahnung an Die Vncatholische dieser Zeit / von der wahren Kirchen dem Glauben vnd Gottes Dienst Vor 45. Jahren Lateinisch geschrieben / aber noch nie widerleget : Jetzo auss Liebe zur Catholischen Warheit vnd zu Fortpflanzung derselbigen verteutscht / Sambt dess Barclaij Leben Von H. E. V. R.

Frankfort.   Johann Arnold Cholin.   1663.   KPB Dh 1752.

232.   SIR RICHARD BAKER.   Richard Bakers Engelländischen Ritters Frag-Stück und Betrachtungen über Das Gebett des Herren. Verdolmetschet durch Andream Gryphium.

Leipzig.   Veit Jacob Trescher.   1663.   UBG Theo. Past. 403a.

233.   —— Richard Bakers Engländischen Ritters / Betrachtungen der 1. Sieben Buss-Psalm. 2. Sieben Trost-Psalm. 3. Glückseligkeit des Gerechten. 4. Von Unsterblichkeit der Seelen. 5. Auf ieden Tag der Wochen. übersetzt durch Andream Gryphium.

Frankfort & Leipzig.   Veit Jacob Trescher.   1688.
KPB Es 12830.

234.   VICTOR MANHEIMER.   Eine Gryphius-Bibliographie.
In "Euphorion," XI.   1904.   KPB(LS) 3. 54.

235.   RICHARD BAXTER.   Der Quacker Catechismus Oder Die Quacker untersuchet / Ihre Fragen beantwortet / und ans Liecht gegeben. Denen zu gut / die unter ihnen noch nicht zum Tode gesündiget ; Als auch den ungegründeten Neulingen / die wegen ihrer Verführung in höchster Gefahr stehen.   Zu erst in Englischer Sprache aussgegeben durch Richard Baxter, und zu Londen gedruckt Anno MDCLVII.

? (1663 ?)   BM 4139 bb 63.

236.   —— Die nothwendige Lehre von der Verläugnung Unser Selbst. Aus Gottes Wort ausgeführet durch Richard Baxter. welche von dem Authore in Englischer Sprache beschrieben : Nun aber in Deutsch übergesetzet und heraus gegeben durch J. F. L.   Phil. 2, 20, 21.   Ich habe keinen / der so gar meines Sinnes ist / der so hertzlich für euch sorge : Sie suchen alle (Geistliche und Weltliche / Obrigkeit und Prediger) das Ihre / nicht das Christi Jesu ist.

Hamburg.   Zacharias Hertel.   1665.   KPB Es 14166.

No.

237. —— ——
        Frankfort.   Zacharias Hertel.   1675.   KPB Es 14168.

238. —— ——
        Hamburg.   Gottfried Liebernickel.   1697.   KPB Es 14169.

239. —— Die Wahre Bekehrung / kräfftig geprediget und herauss-
        gegeben / Durch Richard Baxter / Predigern zu Kidemünster in
        Engeland / Nunmehr aber Ins Hochteutsche übersetzet / Durch
        J.D.B. 2 Cor: 5. 17.   Darumb ist Jemand in Christo / so ist Er
        eine neue Creatur. Das alte ist vergangen / siehe / es ist alles neu
        worden.
        Cassel.   J.D.B.   1673.   KPB Es 14116.

240. —— Richard Baxters Nun oder Niemahls.   Aus dem Englischen
        ins Teutsche übersetzt.
        Hamburg.   Christian Guth.   1678.   KPB 5889.

241. —— Richard Baxters Christliches Hauss-Buch / Woraus Auch ein
        einfältiger gemeiner Mann lernen kan I. Wie Er ein rechter
        Christ werden möge. II. Wie Er gegen Gott / gegen sich selbst /
        gegen Andere in allen seinen Verwandtnissen / sonderlich in
        seinem Hause / als ein Gott gefälliger Christ leben müsse.
        III. Wie Er endlich in Hoffnung und Trost / als ein seliger
        Christ / sterben / und also mit Christo in der ewigen Herrlichkeit
        leben könne. Abgefasset Als eine freundliche deutliche Unter-
        redung eines Lehrers und Lernenden / Sampt einem Zusatz
        gottseliger Gebäte / und was sonst zur Hauss-Andacht nöthig ist /
        Nebst einer Bitte an grosse Herren und reiche Leute / dass
        sie ihren Unterthanen und armen Nachbarn dieses oder der-
        gleichen Bücher geben wollen ; Ins Teutsche übersetzet Aus dem
        Englischen / so Anno 1677. zum drittenmahl gedrucket / Von
        Antonio Brunsenio, Churfl. Brand. Hof-Prediger.
        Berlin.   Christoff Runge's Widow.   1685.
                                                UBG Theo. Past. 399.

242. —— Ein Heiliger oder Ein Vieh.   Das ist : Eine Verhandlung
        des elendigen Standes derer ohne Gott und Heiligkeit lebenden
        Menschen. Worin sowol durch vernünfftige als Schrifftmässige
        Beweiss-Gründe die hohe Nothwendigkeit und Fürtreflflichkeit
        der Heiligung / zur Uberzeugung der Unbussfertigen und Gottlosen
        Menschen / vnd zur Erhaltung ihrer Seelen deutlich und kräfftig
        angewiesen wird. Anfangs in der Engeländischen Sprache ge-
        prediget und beschrieben Durch Herrn Richard Baxter. Nunmehr
        aber der ungemeinen Fürtreflflichkeit halber verteutscht Von J. D.
        Frankfort.   Johann David Zunner.   1685.   KPB Es 14156.

243. —— Theologische Politick / Oder Christliche Bürger-Lehre / ...
        Auss Des Hochgelehrten und Berühmten Engelländischen Theologi
        und Predigers / Herren Richard Baxters / Theologischen Wercken
        zusammen gezogen / verteutschet / und in bequeme Ordnung ge-
        bracht / Durch Johañ Heinrich Ringier / Diener am Wort Gottes
        zu Madisweil / Berner-Gebiets: Erst nach dessen Tod / von den
        Seinen heraussgegeben. Prov. 10. v. 7.   Die Gedächtnuss des
        Gerechten bleibt im Segen.
        Basel.   Emanuel & Johann Georg König.   1697.   UBB 930 a.

No.

244. —— Richard Baxters Ausgesonderte Schrifften Als : I. Die rechte
Arth und Weise / wodurch man zum beständigen und wolge-
gründeten Frieden und Ruhe des Gewissens / wie auch zum
geistlichen Trost gelangen konne. II. Das Leben des Glaubens /
oder ein Beweiss der unsichtbaren Dinge. III. Ein Heiliger oder
ein Heuchler. IV. Der Narren Glückseligkeit / und die Gelegen-
heit ihres Verderbens. V. Die Ausskauffung der Zeit. Sämtlich
in Engelländischer Sprache geschrieben / und nun aus dem vierten
verbesserten und vermehrten Druck ins Teutsche übersetzet
von J. D.
    Bremen. Philipp Gottfried Saurmann. 1697.   KPB 5772.

245. WILLIAM BATES. Des Ehrwürdigen und Berühmten Englischen
Lehrers Herrn Richard Baxters / Vormals zu Kedemünster und
hernach zu Londen Predigers des Worts / Ehren-Gedächtniss /
Welche Ihm Nach seinem tödtlichen Hintritt so wohl in einer
Leichen-Rede als beygefügtem Lobsprüche auffgerichtet worden
von William Bates. Aus der Englischen Sprache ins Deutsche
gebracht Von Joh. Georgio Pritio. Darbey zufinden Ein Ver-
zeichniss der Baxterischen Wercke / und welche von denselben ins
Deutsche übersetzet worden.
    Leipzig. Johann Heinichen's Widow. 1701. KPB Aw 4128.

246. (JAMES USSHER ?) Harmonica Evangeliorum, Oder Zusammenfügung
der vier H. Evangelisten. Worinnen alle und jede deroselben
Wort beydes nach Lutheri und der Englischen version in Ordnung
gebracht / Doch mit sonderlichen Buchstaben unterschieden / und
durch kurtze Vornemlich zu Erbauung dess Christlichen Lebens
zielende Anmerckungen erkläret sind. Dem ist beygefüget eine
Chronologische Vorbereitung Uber das Neue Testament / zu
dessen richtigem Verstand nutzlich zu gebrauchen. Welche beyde
Schrifften in Jacobi Usserii, Ertzbischoffen zu Armach und
Primaten in Irland / hinterlassener Bibliothec gefunden worden.
Auss dem Englischen ins Teutsche übersetzt.
    Frankfort. Johann David Zunner. 1672.   KPB Br 8563.

247. —— Harmonica Evangeliorum, Oder Zusammenfügung der vier
Heil. Evangelisten / Nach Lutheri und der Englischen Version,
mit sonderlichen Buchstaben ordentlich unterschieden / Und mit
erbaulichen Anmerckungen erkläret ; Nebenst einer sehr nützlichen
Chronologischen Vorbereitung über das Neue Testament : Wie
solche beyde Schrifften sind gefunden In Jacobi Usserii, Ertz-
Bischoffen zu Armach und Primaten in Irrland / Bibliothec / Aus
dem Englischen ins Teutsche übersetzet / Nunmehr nach dem
Original zum andernmal gedruckt / Mit einer Vorrede Hrn. M.
Aug. Herm. Francken / SS. Th. Gr. & OO. LL. P. P. & P. Gl.
    Halle. "Waisenhaus." 1699.   KPB Br 8565.

248. ISAAC BARROW. Nutz der Gottesfurcht / Von dem Weyland Hoch-
gelehrten Herrn Isaaco Barrow, SS. Theol: Doct. Der Cambridschen
Academie gewesenen Procancellario und Inspect : Colleg : SS.
Trinit : Vor wenig Jahren in Englischer Sprache vorgestellet /
Anjetzo aber aus dem Englischen ins Hochteutsche übersetzt /
Durch M. David Rupertum Erythropel : Hannov :
    Hannover. Pr. Georg Friedrich Grimm. 1678.
                                KPB Da 424.

No.

249. JOHANN BURCHARD MENKE. Philanders von der Linde Ernsthaffte Gedichte, Darinnen So wol andächtige Gedancken, als unterschiedene Trauer-Gedichte, wie auch insonderheit des geistreichen Engelländers Samuel Slaters Ausführliches Gespräch zwischen dem Glauben und der Seele enthalten. Andere und verbesserte Auflage.
Leipzig. Johann Friedrich Gleditsch & Son. 1713. (First ed. 1706.) UBB Yp 37302.

250. JOHN JULIAN. Dictionary of Hymnology.
London. J. Murray. 1892. KPB Ef 460

CHAPTER X.

The Awakening of Germany and the Growth of English Influence.

251. RENE RAPIN. Reflections on Aristoteles Treatise of Poesie. Containing the Necessary, Rational, and Universal Rules for Epick, Dramatick, and the other sorts of Poetry. With Reflections on the Works of the Ancient and Modern Poets, And their Faults Noted. By R. Rapin. (Tr. T. Rymer.)
London. H. Heringmann. 1674. BM 11825 bbb 17.

252. CHRISTIAN HOFMANN VON HOFMANNSWALDAU. C. H. V. H. Deutsche Ubersetzungen Und Getichte. Mit Bewilligung dess Autoris.
Bresslau. Esaias Fellgibel. 1679. UBB Yo 69011.

254. DANIELIS GEORGI MORHOFI, Polyhistor. Sive de Notitia Auctorum et rerum commentarii. Quibus praeterea varia ad omnes disciplinas consilia et subsidia proponuntur. Editio secunda auctior.
Lübeck. Peter Böckmann. 1695 (First ed. 1688–92.) KPB 5342.

255. DANIEL GEORG MORHOFENS Unterricht von der Teutschen Sprache und Poesie / Deren Ursprung / Fortgang und Lehr-Sätzen / Samt dessen Teutschen Gedichten / Jetzo von neuem vermehret und verbessert / und nach des Seel. Autoris eignem Exemplare übersehen / Zum andern mahle von den Erben herausgegeben.
Lübeck & Frankfort. Johann Wiedemeyer. 1702. (First ed. 1682.) KPB Yc 4560.

256. HERMANNI DIETERICI MEIBOMII Programma publicis In notitiam Regnorum & Rerumpublicarum Europae praelectionibus praemissum in qua simul De Anglicanae Historiae periodis & praecipuis Scriptoribus disseretur.
Helmstadt. Georg-Wolffgang Hamm. 1702. KPB Tq 30.

CHAPTER XII. *Later Satire.*

257. JOHN HALL. Poems...
Cambridge. R. Daniel (pr.). 1646. BM E 1166*.

258. RICHARD FLECKNOE. A Collection of the choicest Epigrams and Characters of Richard Flecknoe. Being rather a New Work, then a New Impression of the Old.
? 1673. BM 11623 aa 12.

No.

259. JOHANN BURCHARD MENKE. Philanders von der Linde Vermischte Gedichte Darinnen So wol allerhand Ehrengedichte, bey Beförderungen, Hochzeiten und Begräbnissen, als auch einige Adoptirte Gedichte, nebst einer ausführlichen Unterredung Von der Deutschen Poesie und ihren unterschiedenen Arten enthalten.
Leipzig. Joh. Friedrich Gleditsch & Son. 1710.
UBB Yp 37302.

260. ——— Philanders von der Linde Scherzhaffte Gedichte Darinnen So wol einige Satyren, als auch Hochzeit- und Schertz-Gedichte, Nebst einer Ausführlichen Vertheidigung Satyrischer Schrifften enthalten. Andere und vermehrte Auflage.
Leipzig. Joh. Friedrich Gleditsch & Son. 1713. (First ed. 1706.)   UBB Yp 37302.

261. JOHN DRYDEN. The Dramatic Works of John Dryden with a Life of the Author by Sir Walter Scott, Bart. Edited by George Saintsbury.
Edinburgh. William Paterson. 1882.   KPB Zc 10244.

262. K. KUCHENBÄCKER. Dryden as a Satirist. In "Jahresbericht über das Königl. Dom-Gymnasium zu Magdeburg."
Magdeburg. Carl Friese. 1899.   UBG.

263. ALBERT EICHLER. Christian Wernicke's Hans Sachs und Sein Drydensches Vorbild Mac Flecknoe. Zur Geschichte deutscher Kritik.
In Z. vgl. LG. (N.F.) XVII. 1909.   KPB(LS) G. 3. 150.

264. RUDOLF PECHEL. Christian Wernicke's Epigramme.
Berlin. Mayer und Müller. 1909.   KPB X 8426.

CHAPTER XIII. *Milton in Germany.*

265. T(HEODOR) H(AAKE). Das Ver-Lustigte Paradeiss aus und nach dem Englischen I. Ms. durch T. H. Zu übersetzen angefangen —voluisse sat—
c. 1680.   LBC MS. Poet. 4°. 2.

266. (ERNST GOTTLIEB VON BERGE.) Das Verlustigte Paradeis / Auss Johann Miltons Zeit seiner Blindheit In Englischer Sprache abgefassten unvergleichlichen Gedicht In Unser gemein Teutsch übergetragen und verlegt Durch E. G. V. B.
Zerbst. Johann Ernst Bezel. 1682.   KPB Za 7448.

267. JOHN MILTON. Literae nomine Senatus anglicani, Cromwellii Richardique Ad diversos in Europa Principes & Respublicas exaratae a Joanne Miltono, quas nunc primum in Germania recudi fecit M. Jo. Georg. Pritius.
Leipzig and Frankfort. Johann Caspar Mayer. 1690.
KPB 4936.

268. JOHANN ULRICH VON KÖNIG. Untersuchung Von der Beschaffenheit Der einsylbigen Wörter in der Teutschen Dicht-Kunst / Nach den Grund-Sätzen des Poetischen Zahlmasses Und der daraus entspringenden Übereinstimmung / ausgefertiget von Johann Ulrich König. (In "Des Herrn von Besser Schrifften.")
Leipzig. Johann Friedrich Gleditsch's son. 1732.
UBB Yp 17008.

No.

269. ALFRED STERN. Milton und seine Zeit.
Leipzig. I. 1877. II. 1879.   KPB Aw 11432.

270. ALOÏS BRANDL. Zur ersten Verdeutschung von Miltons Verlorenem
Paradies.
In "Anglia." I. 1878.   UBB(LS) 4. 1210.

271. JOHANNES BOLTE. Die beiden ältesten Verdeutschungen von Miltons
Verlorenem Paradies.
In "Z. vgl. LG." NF 1. 1888.
Berlin. A. Haack.   KPB(LS) 3. 150.

272. WILHELM MÜNCH. Versuche der Verdeutschung von Miltons
"Paradise Lost."
In "Deutsche Litteraturzeitung," 19. Nov. 1910.

CHAPTER XIV. *Conclusion.*

273. JOHN LOCKE. Unterricht von Erziehung der Kinder / aus dem
Englischen ; Nebst Herrn von Fenelon Erts-Bischoffs von Cam-
merich Gedancken von Erziehung der Töchter / aus dem Frantzösischen übersetzet. Mit einigen anmerckungen und einer vorrede.
Leipzig. Thomas Fritsch. 1708.   KPB Nd 524.

274. —— Des berühmten Engelländers / Herrn Johann Locks Neuer-
fundene Manier / Excerpta und Locos Communes einzurichten.
Nebst allerhand curiösen Anmerckungen. Aus dem Frantzösischen übersetzet.
Frankfort & Leipzig. Johann von Wiering. 1711. KPB 7742.

275. THOMAS STANLEY. Historia Philosophiae, Vitas opiniones, resque
gestas et dicta Philosophorum sectae cuiusvis complexa autore
Thoma Stanleio ex Anglico sermone in Latinum translata, emen-
data, & variis dissertationibus atque observationibus passim aucta.
accessit Vita Autoris.
Leipzig. Thomas Fritsch. 1711.   KPB Nk 670.

276. GUSTAV ZART. Der Einfluss der englischen Philosophie seit Bacon
auf die deutsche Philosophie des XVIII. Jahrhunderts.
Berlin. 1881.   KPB Nk 17120.

277. MAX KOCH. Über die Beziehungen der englischen Literatur zur
deutschen im 18 Jahrhundert.
Leipzig. Teubner. 1883.   UBB X 7728.

278. FRANZ MUNCKER. F. G. Klopstock. Geschichte seines Lebens und
seiner Schriften.
Stuttgart. 1888.   KPB Au 14176.

279. JOHN TOLAND'S Christianity not mysterious (Christentum ohne
Geheimnis) 1696 Übersetzt von W. Lunde Eingeleitet und unter
Beifügung von Leibnizens Annotatiunculae 1701 herausgegeben
von Lic. Leopold Zscharnack Privatdozent an der Universität
Berlin. In "Studien zur Geschichte des neueren Protestantismus."
Giessen. A. Töpelmann. 1908.

APPENDIX B

The following books and articles, in spite of their occasionally promising titles, throw no light on the literary relations of England and Germany in the seventeenth century.

For abbreviations see p. 145.

N.B. The names of many English and German authors of the period, whose actual works I consulted to no purpose, are not included in this list.

ANON. "Übersetzungen deutscher Lieder ins Englische." *Grenzb.* XIII. 1854.
> (Review of Baskerville: *Poetry of Germany.* 1854.)

ANON. "Influence of the English Literature on the German." *N. Am. R.* Aug. 1857.
> (Deals with Milton, Bodmer, Thomson, Young, Haller, Klopstock, Ossian, Sterne, etc.)

GEORGE M. BAKER. "Some references to German Literature in English Magazines of the early eighteenth century." *M. L. N.* XXIV. No. 4. April, 1909. Baltimore.

SIEGMUND JACOB BAUMGARTEN. Nachrichten von einer Halleschen Bibliothek. 1748–1751. 8 vols. Halle. Joh. Justinus Gebauer.
> (Appeared monthly.)

FELIX BOBERTAG. Die Zweite Schlesische Schule. Berlin and Stuttgart. No year.
> (Nos. 36–7 of Kürschner's "Deutsche National-Literatur." No reference to England.)

MARTIN BRESLAUER. Katalog III, Das deutsche Lied, geistlich und weltlich bis zum achtzehnten Jahrhundert. Berlin. M. Breslauer. 1908.

RUDOLF BROTANEK. "State Poems (Seventeenth century)." In *Beiträge zur neueren Philologie, Jacob Schipper dargebracht.* Vienna. Braumüller. 1902.
> (Deals solely with English political poems.)

FANNY BYSE. "Milton on the Continent." In *M. L. Q.* III. 1900.
> (Deals with Milton's travels.)

JULIUS DUBOC. "Über Staatsromane." In *Streiflichter.* Leipzig. O. Wigand. 1902.
> (Mentions More's *Utopia.*)

EDUARD ENGEL. "Deutsche Kindermärchen in englischer Dramatisierung." In *Mag.* XLVIII. No. 47. 1879.
> (Review of Käthe Freiligrath Kroeker: *Alice and other Fairy Plays for children.* 1880.)

THOMAS A. FISCHER. Drei Studien zur englischen Literaturgeschichte. Gotha. Fr. Andr. Perthes. 1892.
(Contains an article on Roger Ascham.)
OTTO GRUPPE. Deutsche Übersetzungskunst. Hannover. 1866.
(Begins with Bodmer and Klopstock.)
WILLIAM HENKEL. "Alte und neue Stimmen aus England über Deutschland." *Grenzb.* No. 31. 1901.
(Review of Sidney Whitman : *Imperial Germany.* 1895.)
G. HERZFELD. William Taylor of Norwich. Halle. 1897.
(Mentions English translations of Jacob Böhme, without giving details.)
W. HÜTTEMANN. "Eignes und Fremdes im deutschen Volksmärchen." *Z. vgl. LG.* xv. 1904.
C. F. L. "Deutsche Dichtungen in englischen Übersetzungen." *Grenzb.* XXVIII. 1869.
(Deals with the eighteenth century and after.)
TYCHO MOMMSEN. Die Kunst des deutschen Übersetzers aus neueren Sprachen. Leipzig. Adolf Gumprecht. 1858.
—— Die Kunst des Übersetzers fremdsprachlicher Dichtungen ins Deutsche. Frankfort o/M. Carl Jügel. 1886.
THOS. SERGEANT PARRY. "German Influence on English Literature." *Atl. M.* 1877.
(Discusses Wordsworth, Coleridge, Byron, Carlyle.)
A. PASSOW. "Deutschlands Einfluss auf die englische Literatur." *Mag.* pp. 437-52. 1878.
(Based on the preceding.)
VALENTIN ROSE. Verzeichnis der lateinischen Handschriften der Königlichen Bibliothek zu Berlin. 4 vols. Berlin. Asher. 1893-1905.
AUG. SAUER. Bibliothek älterer deutscher Übersetzungen. 1894-9.
LESLIE STEPHEN. "The Importation of German." *Nat. R.* Dec. 1897.
O. WEDDIGEN. "Vermittler des deutschen Geistes in England und Nordamerika." *Archiv*, LIX. 1878.
(Deals with the eighteenth and nineteenth centuries.)
SPIRIDION WUKADINOVIĆ. Prior in Deutschland. Graz. 1895.
(Deals with early eighteenth century.)

APPENDIX C

I was for various reasons unable to consult the following books and articles. They may afford further information on the literary relations of England and Germany in the seventeenth century.
For abbreviations see p. 145.

G. A. ANDREAS. Studies in the idyl in German Literature. Rock Island. III. Lutheran Augustana Book Concern. 1902.
>(Review by R. M. Meyer in *Archiv*, p. 432. 1902.)

ANON. "Die Englische Litteratur in Deutschland." *Europa*, No. 42. 1855.

ANON. "Shakespeares Sonette und die deutschen Übersetzer." *Mag.* No. 73 (?). 1871 (?).
>(The reference, given by Betz, is apparently incorrect. I could not discover the article.)

ANON. "Die Engländer im Urteil deutscher Dichter und Denker." *Freiburger Z.* 54, 55. 1901.

L. ANTHEUNIS. "Quelques mots sur la littérature pastorale en Angleterre." In *Revue générale* for June, 1902. Brussels. O. Schepens & Cie.

P. BAILLIÈSE. Poètes allemands et Poètes anglais.
>(Quoted in *Euph.* xv. 1908.)

JOHN BARCLAY. Argenis. (German translation by A. Bohse, 1701.)

G. BINZ. "Deutsche Besucher im Shakespeare'schen London." *Beil. zur Allg. Zg.* Munich, 23/5 Aug. 1902.

FELIX BOBERTAG. Über einige den Robinsonaden verwandte Erscheinungen in der deutschen Litteratur des XVII Jahrhunderts. 1873.

—— Geschichte des Romans und der ihm verwandten Dichtungsgatten in Deutschland. I. 1876. II. 1879.

W. BRANDIS. "Die Dichter des 'Verlorenen Paradieses.'" *Daheim*, XLV. No. 10. 1908.

G. FUCHS. "Miltons Verlorenes Paradies." *Beil. zur Leipz. Zg.* No. 49. 1908.

M. MARTINII KEMPII Bibliotheca Anglorum Theologica. Königsberg. 1677.

V. LOEWE. J. Johnston, ein Polyhistor des 17. Jahrhunderts. Posen. Jolowicz. 1909.

MAX MEYERFELD. "Die historischen Lehn- und geflügelten Worte aus dem Englischen." *Nat. Zg.* No. 90. 1903.

—— PRUTZ. "Zur Geschichte der deutschen Übersetzungslitteratur." *Hall. Jahrb.* 1840.

L. ROLL. "Milton als Erzieher." *Allg. d. Lehrerzg.* No. 50. 1908.

H. SCHAPER. Der 30-jährige Krieg im Drama und im Roman Englands. 1910 (?).

SIEGMAR SCHULTZE. "Englisch-Deutsche Übersetzungsliteratur." *Intern. Litteratur-Ber.* 13 (?). 1898.

MAX SPIRGATIS. "Englische Literatur auf der Frankfurter Messe von 1561–1620." In *Samml. bibliothekswiss. Arbeiten, hrsg. von Karl Dziatzko.* Leipzig. 1902.
(KPB Ao 58. Nicht verleihbar! For official use only.)

WILL VESPER. Deutsche Gedichte des XVII Jahrhunderts. Eine Ehrenrettung dieser vielverschmähten Zeit, namentlich Hoffmannswaldaus. Munich. C. H. Beck. 1907.

MAX VON WALDBERG. "Die Galante Lyrik." *Quellen und Forschungen,* Heft 46 (?).

D. BURCKHARD-WERTHEMANN. "M. Merians Frankfurter Aufenthalt 1625–50." In *Ber. des Baseler Kunstvereins,* Beil. SS. 81–150. 1907.

KATHARINA WINSCHEID. Die englische Hirtendichtung von 1597–1625. Halle. 1895.

H. ZSCHALIG. Englische Gedichte im deutschen Gewande. Dresden. 1896. (Prog.)

INDEX

Abercromby, David (?–1701?), 125
Absalom and Achitophel, 134
Acta eruditorum, 124 ff., 141, 143
Acton, William, 126
Aedler's *High Dutch Minerva*, 117
Aegidius (Gillis, Giles), Petrus (?–1555), 38, 39
Ælianus, 69
Æthiopica, 18
Aleander, Hieronymus (?–1631), 49
Alexander, Sir William (1567?–1640), 19, 25, 26
Alfred, King (849–901), 120
All for Love, 127
Alphonso X (1252–84), 70
Alphonsus, 69, 70
Amadis, 6, 18, 25
Aminta, 18
Amiraut, Paul, 97
Ancumanus, Bernhardus Nicaeus, 61, 63
Anjou, Henri, Duke of (1551–89), 18
Anne (Boleyn), Queen (1507–36), 75, 76
Anthology, Greek, 59
Antonius, Gulielmus, 45
Apollonius, 122
Apologie for Poetrie, 21
Aranea, 51
Arcadia, (Sannazaro's) 18, (Sidney's) 18 ff., 55 ff., 118
Argenis, 34, 38, 47 ff.
Ariana, 36, 55
Ariosto, Lodovico (1474–1533), 20
Aristarchus, 20
Aristotle, 78, 90
Arnold, Christoph (1627–85), 115, 122
—, Simon Johann, 86
Arragon, Queen Catherine of (1485–1536), 74 ff.
Arundel, Thomas Howard, Earl of (1586–1646), 114
Ascham, Roger (1515–68), 123
Ash, George, 125
Ashmole, Elias (1617–92), 115
Astrea, 36
Augspurger, August (fl. 1644), 61

Aureng-Zebe, 132
Aurifaber, Johann (1519–75), 97
Aytoun, Sir Robert (1570–1638), 91

Bacon, Francis, Lord Verulam (1561–1626), 38, 41, 55, 85 ff., 123, 126, 127
—, Roger (1214?–94), 124
Baden, 5
Badenfahrt, Beschreibung der, 2
Baker, E. A., 26
—, Sir Richard (1568–1645), 107
—, Thomas (1625?–89), 126
Bale, John (1495–1563), 123
Ballets to five voices, Morley's, 10
Balzac, J. L. G. de (1594–1655), 124
Barclay, John (1582–1621), 5, 34, 38, 47 ff., 89, 91, 107
—, William (1546?–1608), 47
Barker, C. J., 99
Barlow, Thomas (1607–91), 116, 125
Barnes, Joshua (1654–1712), 127
Barrow, Isaac (1630–77), 110, 126
Bashful Lover, Massinger's, 73
Bates, William (1625–99), 110
Baudouin, 19
Baumgarten, Siegmund Jakob (1706–57), 40, 44
Bavaria, 46
—, Maximilian, Duke of (1573–1651), 114
Baxter, Richard (1615–91), 101, 108 ff.
B.D.B.V.B., 81
Beaumont, Francis (1584–1616), 120
Becker, P. A., 49
Behn, Afra (1640–89), 130, 131
Beling, Richard, 19, 26
Bell, Henry, 95 ff.
Benjamin, tribe of, 3
Bentley, Richard (1662–1742), 115, 125, 126
Berge, Ernst Gottlieb von (1649–c. 1712), 114, 115, 136 ff., 143
Berlin University Library, 30
Bernegger, Matthias (1582–1640), 48, 51
Besser, Johann von (1654–1729), 137
Beyer, Andreas (1635–1716), 106

Bibeus (Bibby?), Simon, 2
Bibran, Abraham (?) von, 79
Biondi, 55
Birken (Betulius), Sigmund von (1626–61), 35, 36, 55, 68, 116
Blackmore, Richard (?–1729), 125, 126, 127
Black Prince, 69
Bloedau, C. A. von, 37, 56
Blome, Richard (?–1705), 126
Blount, Thomas Pope (1649–97), 127
Blumenorden, Pegnesischer, 35, 115, 116
Blunden, Humphrey, 99
Bodinus, Johannes, 39
Bodleian Library, 5, 47, 122, 123
Bodley, Sir Thomas (1545–1613), 122
Bodmer, Johann Jakob (1698–1783), 138, 143
Boeclerus, Johann Heinrich (1611–92), 79
Boehme (Behme, Behmen), Jakob (1575–1624), 98 ff.
Boeotia, 5
Boethius, Hector (1465?–1536), 77
Bohm, W., 13 ff.
Bohse, August (1661–1730), 50
Bolle, W., 10
Bolte, J., 3, 71, 74, 137
Bongarsius, Jacobus (1571–1612), 91
Borinski, K., 21, 30, 53
Bostel, Nicolai von (1670–1704), 128, 129
Boyle, Charles (1676–1731), 127
—, Robert (1627–91), 116, 123, 125, 126
—, Roger (1617?–87), 125
Brandenburg, Karl Philipp, Margrave of, 86
Brederodius, P., 79, 91
Bressand, F. C., 37
Brie, F., 30, 37
Briggs, William (1642–1704), 125
Britannicus, Mercurius (Joseph Hall?), 42, 44, 45
British Museum, 30, 41, 108
Brown, John (?–1736), 126
Browne, Edward (1644–1708), 113, 125
—, Sir Thomas (1605–82), 91 ff., 113, 124
Brunhuber, K., 18 n., 30 n., 37
Brunsen, Anton, 109
Brunswick, Heinrich Julius, Duke of (1564–1613), 70
—, Ulrich, Duke of, 37
Brutus, Cowley's, 119
Buchanan, George (1506–82), 60, 112
Buchner, August (1591–1661), 20 n., 36, 52, 55, 56, 81

Buch von der deutschen Poeterey, 20, 34
Buckingham, George Villiers, 1st Duke of (1592–1628), 80
—, —, 2nd Duke of (1628–87), 132
Budaeus (Budé), Guillaume (1497–1540), 38
Buelerus, Marcus, 4
Bugnot, 54
Bullinger, Heinrich, 4
Buon, Nicholas, 48
Burnet, Gilbert (1643–1715), 115, 125, 126, 127
—, Thomas (1635?–1715), 125, 127
Burridge, Ezekiel, 126
Burscough, Robert (1651–1709), 125
Burton, Robert (1577–1640), 123
Bury, Richard de (1281–1345), 122, 123
Buslidius (Busleiden), Hieronymus (?–1517), 38
Butler, Samuel (1612–80), 132, 134
Buwinckhausen, Benjamin von (1571–1635), 2, 11

Calpurnius, 20
Cambridge, 2, 83, 115, 122
Camden, William (1551–1623), 123, 126, 127
Cantiuncula, Claudius (fl. 1535), 38, 39
Canzonets, Morley's, 9
Carew, Thomas (1598?–1639?), 15
Carlyle, Thomas (1795–1881), 144
Carolus Stuardus, 79, 81 ff.
Carr, Richard (1651–1706), 126
Carve (Carue, Carew), Thomas (1590–1672?), 72
"Casta Vidua," 3
Castile, Alphonso X of (1252–84), 70
Castilion, Balthasar (Castiglione, Baldassare, 1478–1529), 20
Catherine of Arragon, Queen (1485–1536), 74 ff.
Catholic princes, 1
Cato, 66
Cave, William (1637–1713), 125
C.E., 128
C.H.A.H.S., 82
Chaireas and Calirrhoë, 18
Chamberlain, Edward (1616–1703), 127
Chapelain, Jean (1595–1674), 122
Chapman, George (1559?–1634?), 70
Chappelain, Geneviefve, 19, 34
Characters of Virtues and Vices, 88 n., 102 ff.
Chariton, 18
Charles I (1600–49), 74, 76, 77, 80 ff.
— II (1630–85), 77, 84
Charleton, Walter (1619–1707), 125

Chaucer, Geoffrey (1340?-1400), 119, 120

Chettle, Henry (?-1607?), 69

Chilmead, Edmund (1610-54), 126

Chinese language, 119

Christian IV, King of Denmark (1577-1648), 9

Claius, 26 ff., 35, 36

Clark (Clerke), Gilbert (1626-97), 126

Clarke, Francis (fl. 1594), 125

—, Samuel (1599-1683), 126

Cleveland, John (1613-58), 120

Clifford, Martin (?-1677), 132

Cocastello, C. A., 50

Cockburn, William (1669-1739), 126

Coëffeteau, N., 49, 50, 54

Coggeshall, Henry (1623-90), 126

Coke, Sir Edward (1552-1634), 16

Colbatch, John (?-1729), 126

Cole, William (1635-1716), 125, 126

Colerus (Koeler), Kristof (1602-58), 51, 52

Colli, Hippolytus von (1561-1612), 2

Colloquia Mensalia, 95 ff.

Comber, Thomas (1645-99), 125

Comedians, English, 1, 7, 113

Commerce, 1

Commons, House of, 97

Commonwealth, The, 99

Connor, Bernard (1666?-98), 126, 127

Corbet, Edward (?-1658), 97

Corkine, William, 9

Corneille, Pierre (1606-84), 127

Cornwall, Richard, Duke of (1209-72), 70

Corral, Gabriel de, 50

Coryat, Thomas (1577-1617), 3, 4, 6

Costlie Whore, 69

Coverdale, Miles (1488-1568), 117

Cowley, Abraham (1618-67), 119, 120, 121, 123

Cowper, William (1666-1709), 126

Cozen garmombles, 1

Craig, John (?-1731), 126

Cranmer, Thomas (1489-1556), 112

Creech, Thomas (1659-1700), 126

Cromwell, Oliver (1599-1658), 81 ff., 115

—, Thomas (1485-1540), 75

Crudities, 3

Czepko, Daniel, von Reigersfeld (1605-60), 62

D.A., 71

Dach, Simon (1605-59), 36

Dale, Samuel (1659?-1739), 126

Dampier, George, 126

Daniel, Samuel (1562-1619), 15

Darnley, Henry, Lord (1545-67), 77

D'Avenant, Sir William (1606-68), 120

Dawson, George (1637-1700), 126

Dearing, Sir Edward, 97

Defiance to Fortune, A, 69

Dempster, Thomas (1579?-1625), 123

Denaisius, Petrus (1560-1610), 91

Denham, Sir John (1615-69), 119, 120, 121

Derham, Samuel (1655-89), 125

Descartes, Réné (1596-1650), 94

D.H.P. (Dietrich Haake?), 106, 107

Diana, 18 *n.*, 36, 55

Digby, Sir Kenelm (1603-65), 92

Dodwell, Henry (1641-1711), 125, 126

Doncaster, James Hay, Viscount (?-1636), 3, 16

Donne, John (1573?-1631), 3, 17, 119 ff., 123, 124

Donneau, 47

Dorchester, Dudley Carleton, Viscount (1573-1632), 16

Dorn, W., 128

Doughty, John (1598-1672), 125

Dounam, John (?-1644), 102

Dowland, John (1563-1626), 9

Drayton, Michael (1563?-1631), 119

Drogius, 45

Drummond, William (1585-1649), 15

Dryden, John (1631-1700), 120, 121, 127, 132 ff.

—, William, 127

du Bartas, Guillaume de Salluste (1544-90?), 19 *n.*, 20

Dudley, Edmund (1462?-1510), 89

Dugdale, Sir William (1605-86), 126, 127

Duisburg, English Protestants in, 1

Duncan, Daniel (1649-1735), 125

Dyke, Daniel (?-1614), 106, 107

—, Jeremiah (?-1620), 106, 107

Eclogues, 18

Edwards, John (1637-1716), 125

—, Jonathan (1629-1712), 125

Ehrenström, J., 50

Eichler, A., 134

Einarsson, J., 50

Eisenmenger, Johann Andreas (1654-1704), 114

Ejectment Act, 108

Elizabeth, Queen (1533-1603), 2, 11, 18, 19, 22, 79, 80

—, Princess and Electress (1596-1662), 3, 11, 12, 14, 15, 79

—, Amalia Magdalena, Electress, 107

Ellistone, John, 99, 100

Eltester, Christian (1671-1700), 128

Elze, K., 1, 70, 73

Emmanuel College, Cambridge, 43

Empson, Sir Richard (?-1510), 89

Ender, Karl von, 98

England
    commerce, 1
    German Protestants in, 1, 2
    language, 118, 119, 120
    libraries, 5, 115, 116, 122, 123
    religious persecution in, 1
    theatres, 2
    universities, 2
English comedians, 1, 7
Epigrams, 17, 59 ff.
Erasmus (1466–1536), 6, 38, 39, 55
Eromena, 55
Erythropel, David Rupert (1556–1626), 110
Essays, Bacon's, 85 ff.
Etheredge, Sir George (1635?–91), 113
Evelyn, John (1620–1706), 117, 127
Everard, Thomas (1560–1633), 126
Evordanus, 69
Example, Shirley's, 73

Fabricius, Johann Sebald (1622–?), 137
Faery Queene, 119
Fairfax, Thomas, Baron (1612–71), 81 ff.
Faust, Doctor (fl. 1500?), 6
Feinler, Gottfried (*c.* 1650–after 1704), 62, 67, 68
Fejér, A., 50
Fellgibel, 21
Ferdinand II, Emperor (1578–1637), 34, 96
Fischer, H., 13
—, Kuno, 86
—, Kurt, 9 *n.*
Fisher, John, Bishop of Rochester (1459–1535), 76
Five Mile Act, 108
Flamsteed, John (1646–1719), 126
Flecknoe, Richard (?–1678?), 112, 130 ff.
Fleetwood, William (1656–1723), 127
Fleming, Paul (1606–40), 19 *n.*, 35, 36, 56, 61
Fletcher, John (1579–1625), 121
Flögel, Carl Friedrich (1729–88), 40, 44
Fludd, Robert (1574–1637), 124
Fordun, John (?–1384?), 126
Francke, August Hermann (1663–1727), 110
—, Johann (1618–77), 61
Frankfort-on-Main, 1, 5 ff., 19, 21, 22, 25, 38, 85, 106, 117
Fremonville, Count de, 116
Friderici, A., 50, 54
—, Daniel, 10
Friedrich, Duke of Würtemberg (1557–1608), 1
— IV, Elector of the Palatinate (1574–1610), 5

Friedrich V, Elector of the Palatinate (1596–1632), 12, 79
Frobenius, Johann (1460–1527), 39
Fruchtbringende Gesellschaft, 20 *n.*, 30, 116
Fürer, Christoph (1663–1732), 115
Fürst, Johann Georg, Freiherr von, 75

Gaistliche und weltliche Gedichte, Weckherlin's, 16, 17
Galathe, Rist's, 9
Gale, Thomas (1635?–1702), 126, 127
Gambara, Lorenzo, 20
Gardiner, S. R., 125
Garmombles, 1
Gärtener, Eduard, 62
Garter, Order of, 2
Gee, Edward (1657–1730), 125
"Gentilhomme François," 19, 32
Gentili, Alberico (1552–1608), 42 ff.
Gentleman's Journal, 129
Gerber, Ernst Ludwig (1746–1819), 10
Germany
    book-trade in, 5
    commerce, 1
    English Protestants in, 1
    language, 8, 113, 117
    Protestant party, 117
    religious persecution, 98, 114
    universities, 5 ff., 113
Gerschow, Friedrich, 2
G.G.L.L., 94
Gibbon, John (1629–1718), 127
Gibson, Edmund (1669–1748), 126
—, Thomas (1647–1722), 126
Gildon, Charles (1665–1724), 127
Gill, Alexander (1597–1642), 73
Giphanius (von Giffen), Obertus (?–1604), 91
Glanvill, Joseph (1636–80), 125
Glapthorne, Henry (fl. 1639), 73, 74
Glazemaker, ?, 50
Globe Theatre, 2
Gloucester, Robert of (fl. 1260–1300), 119
Goad, John (1616–89), 126
Godwin, Thomas (?) (1517–90), 125
Goedeke, K., 20, 30
Golaw, Salomon von, pseud., see Logau
Görlitz, 98
Gould, William, 125
Graphaeus, Cornelius Scribonius (?–1558), 38, 39
Greek Anthology, 59
Greene, Robert (1560?–92), 69
Greflinger, Georg (1620–77), 61, 66, 77
Gregory, Francis (1625?–1707), 125
— XIII, Pope (1502–85), 96

Grew, Nehemiah (1641–1712), 125, 126
Grimmelshausen, Hans Jacob Christoffel von (1625?–76), 48, 57
Grindal, Edmund (1519?–83), 117
Grisons, 4
Grob, Johann (1643–97), 62
Grossgebauer, Theophilus (1627–61), 104
Grotius, Hugo (1583–1645), 79, 101
Gruter, Janus (1560–1627), 5, 51, 75, 80.
Gryphius, Andreas (1616–64), 62, 79, 81 ff., 108.
—, Christian (1649–1706), 108
Guarini, Giovanni Battista (1537–1612), 18
Guibert, N., 49
Gustavus Adolphus, King of Sweden (1594–1632), 3, 71, 73

Haake, Theodor (1605–90), 107, 114, 115, 136 ff., 143
Haken, J. C. L., 50
Hall, John (1627–56), 134
—, Joseph (1574–1656), 38 ff., 63, 88 n., 101 ff., 115
Hallam, Henry (1777–1859), 42
Halley, Edmund (1656–1742), 126
Hallmann, Johann Christoph (?–1704), 74
Hamilton, James, Duke of (1606–49), 3
Hammond, Henry (1605–60), 125
Hansa trade centres, 1
Hans Sachs, Wernicke's, 133, 134
Harrington, Sir John (1561–1612), 17
Harris, Walter (1647–1732), 126
Harsdoerfer, Georg Philip (1607–58), 35 ff., 55, 88, 103
Hartlib, Samuel (?–1670?), 115
Harvey, Gideon (1640?–1700?), 126
Hassan, Grand Vizier, 71
Hatley, Griffith, 125
Hatto, Archbp. (850–913), 69
Haugwitz, August Adolf, Count (1645–1706), 79
Haussmann, Valentin (fl. 1605), 10
Hazlitt, W. C., 70
Healey, John (?–1610), 46
Heathcot, ?, 126
Hector of Germany, 69
Heidelberg, 5, 7, 11, 19, 20, 79, 114, 137
Heidfelt, Johann (fl. 1605), 102
Heinius, Georg, 102
Heinsius, Nicolaus (1620–81), 84
Heliodorus, 18
Henisch, Georg (1549–1618), 116
Henri III, King of France (1551–89), 49

Henri IV, King of France (1553–1610), 49
Henrietta Maria, Queen (1609–69), 80
Henry VII, King (1457–1509), 85, 89, 90
— VIII, King (1491–1547), 75, 76
Henslowe, Philip (?–1616), 3
Hepburn, Sir John (1598?–1636), 72
Herbert, Edward, of Cherbury (1583–1648), 126, 127
—, George (1593–1633), 120
—, Bp. of Hereford (?), 127
Herder, Johann Gottfried (1744–1803), 15
Herford, C. H., 69, 70
Herle, Charles (1598–1659), 97
Hermsdorf, Martin, 107
Heupel, Johann, 102
H.E.V.R., 107
Heydon, John (fl. 1667), 68
Higden, Ranulf (?–1364), 126
Hill, Samuel (1648–1716), 125
Hille, K. G. von (fl. 1647), 118
Hirschberg, 21, 25, 30, 34
Hody, Humphrey (1659–1707), 125, 126
Hoenig, B., 71
Hoffman, Chettle's, 69
Hoffmann, Johann Mauritius (1653–1727), 113
Hofmann von Hofmannswaldau, Christian (1617–79), 62, 63, 84, 116, 119, 128, 133
Homburg, Ernst Christoph (1605–81), 61
Homer, 54
Hooper, John, Bp. (?–1555), 112, 117
Horneck, Anton (1641–97), 114
Hospinianus (Wirth), Rodolphus (1547–1626), 4
Hotman, François (1524–90), 6
Howell, James (1594?–1666), 71, 113, 117, 123, 124
Hudemann, Heinrich, 61, 67
Hudibras, 134
Hudson, John (1662–1719), 126
Hughes, C., 7
Huntingdon, George Hastings, 4th Earl of (1540?–1604), 43
—, Henry Hastings, 3rd Earl of (1535–95), 42, 43, 45
—, Henry Hastings, 5th Earl of (1586–1643), 43, 45
Hyde, Thomas (1549–1618), 44, 116, 123, 126
Hyemsmensius, Gregorius, see Wintermonat
Hymns, 95

Icon animorum, 5, 48, 91
Idylls, 18

Infanta Maria of Spain, 80
Intemperance, German, 5, 113
Italian literature, 18
Itinerary, Moryson's, 6, 7

Jablonski, Daniel Ernst (1660–1741), 114
"Jamanie, Duke de," 1
James I (1566–1625), 1, 2, 11, 47, 71, 79, 80, 91, 96
— II (1633–1701), 84
—, the Old Pretender (1688–1766), 84
—, Thomas (1573?–1629), 5, 123
J.B., 99
J.D., 108, 109
J.D.B., 109
J.E., 100
Jeffreys, George, Baron (1648–89), 108
Jessop, Francis, 126
Jesuits, 51, 77, 78
J.F.L., 108
J.G., 109, 129
Job, 66 ff.
Johann Friedrich, Duke of Würtemberg (1582–1628), 12
"John Bayes," 132
Johnson, Thomas (?–1644), 127
Johnston, Robert (1567?–1639), 127
Jones, John (1645–1709)*, 125
Jonson, Ben (1573–1637), 50, 119, 120, 132, 136
Josse, l'abbé, 49
Jubye, Edward, 3
Junius, Franz (1589–1677), 114

Kaldenbach, Christoph (1613–98), 62
Karl Philipp, Margrave of Brandenburg, 86
Käyser, Joannes (1622–1702), 63
Keck, Thomas, 92
Keiser, Reinhard (1673–1739), 37
Kempe, Martin (1637–82), 62, 116
Kidder, Richard (1633–1703), 125
Kindermann, Balthasar (1636–1706), 35 n., 56
King, Sir Edmund (1629–1709), 126
—, John (1652–1732)?, 118
—, William (1663–1712), 46
Kipka, K., 77 ff.
Kirchner, Hermann (?–1620), 3, 4
Klai, Johann (1616–56), 35
Klein, Christian, 106
Klopstock, Friedrich Gottlieb (1724–1803), 136, 143
Knight, William (fl. 1610), 43 ff.
Knittel, Christian, 62
Knox, John (1505–72), 111
Koberstein, A., 30
Koch, Balthasar Gerhard, 103, 106

Koch, Henning, 106
—, M., 30, 144
Koeler (Colerus), Kristof (1602–58), 51, 52, 102, 104
Koeppel, E., 69 n., 73
Kongehl, Michael (1646–1710), 55, 62, 83, 88, 112
König, Johann Ulrich von (1688–1744), 128, 137, 138, 143
Kormart, Christophorus (1665–c.1720), 97
Kuhlmann, Quirinus (1651–89), 62
Kurandors Unglückselige Nisette, 56, 57

Langbaine, Gerard (1656–92), 127
Langston, John (1641?–1704), 123
Languet, Hubert (1518–81), 19
Lassenius, Johannes (1636–92), 108
Laud, William, Archbishop (1573–1645), 82, 97, 114
Lauterbach, Anton (?–1560), 95
Le Grys, Sir Robert (d. 1635), 50
Leibniz, Gottfried Wilhelm von (1646–1716), 144
Leigh, Charles (1662–1701?), 126
—, Edward (1602–71), 123
Leipzig, 3, 6, 7, 71, 86, 115
Lemcke, K., 20
Le Moyne, 122
Leslie, Alexander (1580?–1661), 71
Leucippe and Clitophon, 18
Leybourn, William (1626–1700?), 126
Library
    Berlin University, 30
    Bodleian, 5, 47, 116, 122
    British Museum, 30, 40
    Cambridge University, 115, 122
    Palatine, 5
    Peterhouse, Cambridge, 122
    Queens' College, Cambridge, 122
    St John's College, Cambridge, 122
Liegnitz, Duke of, 104
Lightfoot, John (1602–75), 125
Lilly, William (1468–1522), 123
Lily, George (?–1559), 123
Lindesay, Alexander (?–1646), 71
Lingelsheim (Lingelshemius), Georg Michael, 5, 20 n., 51, 79, 80, 91, 101
Lister, Martin (1638?–1712), 125, 126, 127
Lloyd, Nicholas (1630–80), 116, 127
—, William (1627–1717), 115, 125, 127
L.N.M.E.M., 92
Löber, Valentin (1620–85), 61, 63, 65 ff.
Locke, John (1632–1704), 125, 126, 127, 143, 144

* The reference may be to an earlier John Jones (fl. 1579).

Loewe, V., 72, 74
Logau, Friedrich von (1604–55), 62, 66 ff., 83
Long, Kingsmill, 50
Longue, L. Pierre de, 49
Louis XIII (1601–43), 48, 53, 80
Ludwig, Christian (1660–1728), 118
Lund, Zacharias (1608–67), 61
Luther, Martin (1483–1546), 6, 15 *n.*, 95 ff.

Macbeth, 77
Macclesfield, Charles Gerard, Earl of (1659?–1701), 144
Mac Flecknoe, 132
Mackenzie, Francis, 126
—, George (1630–1714), 126, 127
Magdeburg, 3, 6
Mainwaring, Everard (1628–99?), 125
Malmborg, J., 50
Mandeville, Sir John (14th cent.), 112
Marcassus, P. de, 49
Margenis, 56
Maria Stuarda, 79
Marini (Marino), Giambattista (1569–1625), 133
Marot, Clément (1495–1544), 15, 20
Martial, 59, 64
Martin, E., 30
Martini, Georg, 62
Mary I, Queen (1516–58), 1
— II, Queen (1662–94), 84, 114
— Stuart, Queen of Scots (1542–87), 47, 77 ff.
Mason, Robert (1571–1635), 80
Massinger, Philip (1583–1640), 73
Maximilian II, Emperor (1527–76), 19
—, Duke of Bavaria (1573–1651), 114
May, Thomas (1595–1650), 50
Medal, 132
— *of John Bayes*, 132
Meibohm, Hermann Dietrich, 127
Meletephilus, Dorotheus Eleutherus, 106
Melville, James (1535–1617), 126
Menke, Johann Burchard (1675–1732), 111, 112, 114, 115, 130, 131, 134, 135, 142
—, Otto (1644–1707), 114, 115, 124
Mercurius Britannicus (Joseph Hall?), 42, 44, 45
Mercurius Teutonicus, 99
Merian, Matthaeus (1593–1651), 21 ff.
Merryweather, John, 92
Merry Wives of Windsor, 1
Messias, Klopstock's, 136, 143
Middleton, Thomas (1570?–1627), 73
Milbourne, Luke (1622–68), 125
Milton, John (1608–74), 115, 119 ff., 123, 127, 136 ff., 143
Mocket, Thomas (1602–70?), 125

Moltkenius, Levinus Nicolaus (fl. 1650), 92
Molyneux, William (1656–98), 125, 126
Monk, George, Duke of Albemarle (1608–70), 114
Monmouth, James, Duke of (1649–85), 84
Monro, Robert (?–1680?), 71
Montbéliard (Mümpelgart, Mompelgard), 1, 11
Montemayor, Jorge (1520?–61), 18, 36
Moore, Sir Jonas (1617–79), 126
More de Venise, 2
More, Henry (1614–87), 94, 100, 122, 125
—, Sir Thomas (1478–1535), 17, 38 ff., 55, 59, 76, 91, 112, 127, 131, 135
Morgenröthe im Aufgang, Boehme's, 98
Morhof, Daniel Georg (1639–91), 54, 62, 68, 88, 90, 94, 111, 114, 119 ff., 136, 141
Morland, Sir Samuel (1625–95), 126
Morley, Thomas (1557–1604?), 9, 10
Moronia, 46
Morton, Richard (1637–98), 126
— Thomas (1564–1659), 104
Moryson, Fynes (1566–1630), 6, 7, 117
—, Henry, 6
Moscherosch, Johann Michael (1601–69), 68
Mouchemberg, A. de, 54
Mundus alter et idem, 38 ff.
Müller, Andreas (1630–94), 114
—, David, 53, 54, 104
Muretus, Marc Antoine (1526–85), 68
Musaeum Minervae, 117

Nanton (Naunton), Sir Robert (1563–1635), 126
Negelein, Joachim (1675–?), 115
Nemesianus, Marcus Aurelius Olympianus (3rd cent.), 20
Neukirch, Benjamin (1665–1729), 84, 128
Neumark, Georg (1621–81), 118
New Atlantis, 85, 89
Newton, Sir Isaac (1642–1727), 126
Nichols, William (1655–1716), 125
Nicholson, William (1591–1672), 125, 127
Norris, John (1657–1711), 125
Novel
    Latin, 38 ff.
    Spanish picaresque, 48
Noviomagus (Geldenhauer), Gerhardus (1482?–1542), 38, 39
Nuremberg, 6, 10, 35
Nüsler, ?, 102

Oden und Gesänge, Weckherlin's, 13, 15

Oecolampadius, Johann (1482–1531), 6

Œdipus, Lee's and Dryden's, 127

Offelen, Heinrich, 117, 118

O'Flaherty, Roderick (1629–1718), 126

Opera, German, 37, 133

Opitz, Martin (1597–1639), 19, 25 ff., 35, 48, 50 ff., 60 *n.*, 65, 102, 104, 112

Opportunity, Shirley's, 73

Orator Ineptus, Schupp's, 35

Orgilia, 46

Overall, John (1560–1619), 125

Owen, John (1560?–1622), 17, 57 ff.

Oxford, 2, 83, 114, 115, 137

Palatinate, 12

Palatine Library, 5, 51

Pamphagonia, 46

Paradise Lost, 115, 121, 136 ff., 143

— *Regained*, 141, 142

Paraenesis ad Sectarios, Barclay's, 48

Parker, Samuel (1640–88), 125

Parr, Richard (1617–91), 126

Parrivilia, 46

Parrott, T. M., 70

Pasor, Matthias (1599–1658), 114

Passerat, Jean (1534–1602), 15

Pastoral poetry, 18

Pastor Fido, 18

Patrick, Simon (1626–1707), 125

Pauli, Christianus (1658–96), 108

Paus, ?, 50

Pearson, John (1613–86), 125

—, Robert, 125

Pechel, R., 59, 133 *n.*

Pechey, John (1655–1716), 126

Peganius, see Rautner

Pegnesischer Blumenorden, 35, 115, 116

Peiresc, Nicolas Claude Favre (1580–1637), 48

Pembroke, Mary Herbert, Countess of (1555?–1621), 18, 21 ff.

Perkins, William (1558–1602), 101, 102, 104

Peterhouse, Cambridge, 122

Petherick, E. A., 41, 42, 45

Petrarch (1304–74), 19 *n.*, 20

Petronius, 48

Petty, Sir William (1623–87), 126, 127

Philanders von Sittewald, Gesichte, 68, 72 *n.*

Philosophical Society, 114

Pierce, D., 125

—, Robert (1622–1710), 126

Pitseus (Pits), John (1560–1616), 123

Pitt, Christopher (1699–1748), 126

—, Moses (fl. 1654–96), 115

Plot, Robert (1640–96), 125

Plunket, Leonard, 126

Pocock, Edward, 116, 125

Politianus, Angelus (1454–94), 68

Polyhistor, Morhof's, 90, 91, 94, 122 ff., 141

Polyolbion, Drayton's, 119

Pommern-Stettin, Philipp Julius, Duke of, 2

Pona, Fr., 50

Porter, Francis (?–1702), 125

—, John, 42

Postel, Christian Heinrich (1658–1705), 133

Potocki, ?, 50

Potter, John (1674?–1747), 127

Powell, G. H., 81

Pretender, The Old, 84

Prior, Matthew (1664–1721), 143

Pritius, Johann Georg (1662–1732), 110, 140

Protestants, English, 1; German, 1, 2, 117

Pseudodoxia Epidemica, Browne's, 93, 94

Quarles, Francis (1592–1644), 3, 111, 119

Queens' College Library, Cambridge, 122

Querenghi, Antonio (1546–1633), 49

Quick, John (1636–1706), 125

Rabelais, François (c. 1490–1553), 42

Raleigh, Sir Walter (1552?–1618), 112

Rapin, Renatus (1621–87), 120

Rathgeb, ?, 2

Rautner (Peganius), Christian, 93

Reeve, Clara (1729–1807), 50

Register, Stationers', 42, 46

Rehearsal, 132

Reifferscheid, A., 48, 79, 91

Reigersfeld, Daniel Czepko von (1605–60), 62

Religio Medici, 92

Remus, Georg (1561–1625), 79, 80, 91

Renaissance, 59

Renialme (Rialme?), Ascanius de, 45

Rhythmer, Victorinus, 114

Richard, Duke of Cornwall (1209–72), 70

Richardson, Samuel (1689–1761), 143

Richter, Georg (1658–1737), 122

—, Gregorius (1560–1624), 98, 100

Ridley, Humphrey (1653–1708), 126

—, Nicholas (1500?–55), 113

Riederer, Johann Friedrich (1678–?), 115

Riemer, Johann, 78, 79

Ringier, Johann Heinrich (?–after 1741), 109

Rist, Johann (1607–67), 9, 61

Robert of Gloucester (13th cent.), 119
Robertson, William (?–1686?), 127
Robinson, Ralph (fl. 1551), 38
Rochester, John Wilmot, Earl of (1647–80), 129, 130, 131, 134
Ronsard, Pierre de (1524–85), 20, 21, 35
Rosarium, 63
Rosseter, Philip (1575?–1623), 9
Row, Thomas, 5
Rowley, Samuel (?–1633?), 3
Royal Society, 115, 116, 123
Rudolf II, Emperor (1552–1612), 19, 22, 91, 96
Russworm, Hermann, Count (?–1605), 71
Rye, W. B., 1, 3
Rymer, Thomas (1641–1713), 120, 121

Sachs, Hans (1494–1576), 64, 133
St Bartholomew, Massacre of, 19, 49
St John's College Library, Cambridge, 122
Salas, Pellicer de, 50, 54
Salmasius, Claudius (1596–1653), 141
Samson, 3
Samson Agonistes, 141
Sanders (Saunders), Lawrence (?–1555), 112
Sanderson, Robert (1587–1663), 127
—, William (1586?–1676), 127
Sandford, Francis (1630–94), 126
Sandor, K. Bọér, 50
Sannazaro, Jacopo (1458–1530), 18, 19 n., 20
Savery, Thomas (1650?–1715), 126
Savile, Sir Henry (1549–1622), 91, 127
Savin, M., 49
Scaliger, Julius Caesar (1484–1558), 21
Scarlett, John, 126
Schädler, Johann Jacob, 104
Schaffgotsch, Hans Ulrich (1595–1635), 20
Schaible, K. H., 107, 113, 117, 137
Scherffer, Wencel, von Scherffenstein (?–1674), 61
Schickius, Rodornus, 119
Schirmer, David (c. 1623–after 1682), 36, 61
Schleich, Clement, 106
Schmettau, Heinrich (1629–1704), 104, 105
Schmid, G., 72
—, K. F., 49, 53 ff.
Schoch, Johann Georg (fl. 1660), 62
Schönwetter, J. B., 85
Schottel, Justus Georg (1612–76), 117
Schuldige Unschuld, 79

Schultz, Simon (fl. 1644), 61, 63 ff.
Schupp, Johann Balthasar (1610–61), 30, 35, 41, 54, 55, 67, 83, 88 ff., 93
Schwieger, Jacob (fl. 1654), 62
Scudder, Henry (?–1659?), 107
Scultetus, Abraham (1566–1625), 101
Selden, John (1584–1654), 121, 125, 127
Seneca, 54
Senftleben, ? (fl. 1627), 52
Sesemann, Johann, 10
Shadwell, Thomas (1642?–92), 132, 133
Shaftesbury, Anthony Ashley Cooper, 1st Earl (1621–83), 132
Shakespeare, William (1564–1616), 121, 127
Sheldon, Gilbert (1598–1677), 122
Shephearde's Calendar, 13
Shepherd's Brawl, 31
Sherburne, Sir Edward (1618–1702), 112, 130, 131
Sheringham, Robert (1602–78), 127
Sherlock, William (1641?–1707), 125
Shipton, John, 126
Shirley, James (1596–1666), 73
Sibbald, Sir Robert (1641–1722), 125
Sibbes (Sibs, Sybhes), Richard (1577–1635), 123
Sidenham, George, 5
Sidney, Sir Philip (1554–86), 18 ff., 55, 117, 118
—, Robert, Earl of Leicester (1563–1626), 117
Sieber, Justus (1628–95), 62
Sieg-Prangender Lorbeer-Hayn, 55, 88, 112
Silesia, Christian, Georg, Ludwig, Rudolf, Dukes of, 53
Silvester, Joshua (1563–1618), 15
Simnel, Lambert (fl. 1487–1525), 89
Simplicissimus, 37, 48, 57
Sinolt, Johann Helwig, 85
Slater, Samuel (?–1704), 111
Smith, Thomas (1638–1710), 125, 127
Society, The Philosophical, 114
—, Royal, 115, 116, 123
Sorbière's *Voyage en Angleterre*, 124
Spanheim, Friedrich (1600–49), 114
Spark, Thomas (1655–92), 125
Sparkes, Michael, 114
Sparr, Casparus von, 96
Sparrow, John (1615–55?), 99, 100
Spelman, Sir John (1594–1643), 120, 127
Spencer, John (1630–93), 125
Spener, Jacob Philipp (1635–1705), 110
Spenser, Edmund (1552?–99), 13, 15, 16, 65, 119, 120

Sprat, Thomas (1635–1713), 120, 123, 124, 132
Sprye, Nathaniel, 125
Stanley, Thomas (1625–78), 144
Stapleton, Thomas (1535–98), 38, 39
Stationers' Register, 42, 46
Statius, 47
Steinbach, Johann von, 10
Sterbende Unschuld, 79
Stillingfleet, Edward (1635–99), 125, 127
Strabo, 69
Strassburg, 1, 4, 6, 7, 19, 92
Strephon, 26 ff., 35, 36
Stuarts, The, 77
Stubenberg, Johann Wilhelm von (1631–88), 87, 88
Stuhl-Weissenburg, 2, 70, 71
Sturm, Johann (1507–89), 123, 124
Stuttgart, 11, 12, 16
Suckling, Sir John (1609–42), 3, 121
Sullen Lovers, Shadwell's, 132
Switzerland, 4
Sydenham, Thomas (1624–89), 125, 126

Table Talk, Luther's, 95 ff.
Talander, pseud., see Bohse
Tanner, Thomas (1674–1735), 125
Tasso, Torquato (1544–95), 18, 19 n., 20, 35, 122
Tatius, Achilles, 18
Taylor, Edward, 101
T. D., 102
Teate, Faithful (fl. 1650), 125
Temple, Sir William (1628–99), 126, 127
Tenison, Thomas, Archbp. of Canterbury (1636–1715), 115
Teutsche Poëmata, Opitz', 34
Teutschredender Owenus, 65 ff.
Theatres, 3; Globe, 2
Thebais, 47
Theocritus, 18, 20, 35
—, Valentinus, 21, 24 ff.
Thirty Years' War, 1, 8, 70 ff.
Thomson, James (1700–48), 143
Thorowgood, Thomas, 95
Thwaites, Edward (1667–1711), 125, 126
Tilly, Johann Tserclaes, Count (1559–1632), 73, 114
Tischreden, Luther's, 95 ff.
Titz, Johann Peter (1619–89), 61, 63 ff.
Toland, John (1670–1722), 127, 142, 144
Tonson, Jacob (1656?–1736), 141
Torrington, Christopher, Lord (1653–88), 114
Towerson, Gabriel (1635?–97), 125

Tredjakowskij, ?, 50
Trojan Women, 66
T. S., 132
Tscherning, Andreas (1611–59), 61, 65
Tübingen, 11, 51
Tully, Thomas (1620–76), 116
Turks, 71
Turner, Bryan (fl. 1691), 125
—, Sir James (1615–86?), 72, 125, 127
Tyrconnell, Richard Talbot, Earl (1630–91), 84
Tyrrel, James (1642–1718), 126
Tyson, Edward (1650–1708), 125, 126

Ubaldino, Roberto (?–1632), 49
Universities, English, 2, 122; German, 5, 7, 8, 11, 115
Unterricht von der deutschen Sprache, Morhof's, 119 ff.
Upham, A. H., 118
Urban, E., 60 ff.
Urban VIII, Pope (1568–1644), 49
Urfé, Honoré d' (1568–1625), 20
Ussher, James, Archbp. of Armagh (1581–1656), 104, 110, 125
Utopia, 38 ff., 55
Utopiae Pars II, 39 ff.
Uxbridge, 2

Vega Carpio, Lope Felix de (1562–1635), 35, 36
Venator, Balthasar (1594–1664), 20 n., 51, 52
Vergil, 18, 20, 35, 121
Verville, Béroalde de (1558–?), 45
Vetter, T., 73
Viebing, K. H., 36
Viraginia, 46
Virtuoso, Shadwell's, 132
Vogt, C., 30, 89
Voigtländer, Gabriel (1601?–42?), 9
Vondel, Joost van den (1587–1679), 78
Voss, Isaac (1618–89), 114, 116, 141
—, Johann Gerhard (1577–1649), 114

Wagenseyl, Johann Christoph (1633–1705), 113
Wagner, Gottfried (1652–1725), 125 n.
Wallenstein (Waldstein), Albrecht Wenzel Eusebius von (1583–1634), 72 ff.
Waller, Edmund (1606–87), 119, 120, 121
Wallis, John (1616–1703), 102, 116, 118, 123, 126
Waltz, G., 50
Wansleb, Johann Michael (1635–79), 114

War, Thirty Years', 1, 8, 70 ff.
Ward, Seth (1617–89), 123
Ware, Christopher (fl. 1678), 120
—, James (1594–1666), 127
Warren, Erasmus, 125
Warton, Thomas (1728–90), 42
Warwick, Earls of, 22
Waserus, Caspar (1565–1625), 4
Webbe, John (fl. 1669), 119
Wechel, Andreas (?–1581), 19
Weckherlin, Georg Rudolf (1584–1653), 2, 8, 11 ff., 59, 70
Wegleiter, Christoph (1659–1706), 115
Weg zu Christo, Boehme's, 98
Weidman, Daniel, 84
Weidner, Johann Leonhard (fl. 1650), 111
Weise, Christian (1642–1708), 57
Weiss, Johann Jacob, 107
—, Johann Philipp, 107
—, Philipp, 107
Werder, Dietrich von den (1584–1657), 36, 81
Wernicke, Christian (?–after 1710), 59, 68, 119, 133, 134
Weston, Elizabeth Jane (1582–1612), 36 n., 124
Whalley, Colonel, 108
Wharton, Henry (1664–95), 125, 126
Wheeler, Sir George (1650–1723), 126
—, Maurice (1648?–1727), 126
Wheelocke, Abraham (1593–1653), 122
Whidow's Charm, 3
Whiston, William (1667–1752), 125
Whitby, Daniel (1638–1726), 125
Whitelocke, Bulstrode (1605–75), 126
W.H.N.N., 102
Wilkins, John (1614–72), 123, 124
William III (1650–1702), 84, 114

Willis, Thomas (1621–75), 123
Willoughby, Francis, 126
Wilmot, Henry, Earl of Rochester (1612?–58), 77
Wilton House, 18
Winstanley, William (1628?–98), 126
Wintermonat, Gregor (fl. 1615), 41, 44, 46
Wiseman, Richard (1622?–76), 125
Wither, George (1588–1667), 112
Witkowski, G., 20, 21
Wittenberg, 6, 8
Wood, Anthony (1632–95), 122, 123, 126
Woodward, John (1665–1728), 126
World tost at Tennis, 73
Wotton, Sir Henry (1568–1639), 5, 14, 15
Wren, Sir Christopher (1632–1723), 123
—, Matthew (1629–72), 123
Wurmsser, ?, 2
Würtemberg, Friedrich, Duke of (1557–1608), 1
—, Johann Friedrich, Duke of (1582–1628), 12
—, Ludwig Friedrich, Prince of, 2

Young, Edward (1683–1765), 143
Yuronia, 45, 46

Zart, G., 144
Zesen, Philipp (1619–89), 37, 57, 81, 83
Zincgref, Julius Wilhelm (1591–1635), 11, 20 n., 51, 80, 111
Zinzerling, Justus (fl. 1614), 3
Zouch, Richard (1590–1661), 125
Zschau, W. W., 89, 90
Zürich, 4, 6

For EU product safety concerns, contact us at Calle de José Abascal, 56–1°,
28003 Madrid, Spain or eugpsr@cambridge.org.

www.ingramcontent.com/pod-product-compliance
Ingram Content Group UK Ltd.
Pitfield, Milton Keynes, MK11 3LW, UK
UKHW010046140625
459647UK00012BB/1633